21st CENTURY
U.S. AIR
POWER

NICHOLAS A. VERONICO & JIM DUNN

MBI

This edition first published in 2004 by MBI Publishing Company, Galtier Plaza, Suite 200, 380 Jackson Street, St. Paul, MN 55101-3885 USA

Motorbooks International titles are also available at discounts in bulk quantity for industrial or sales-promotional use. For details write to Special Sales Manager at Motorbooks International Wholesalers & Distributors, Galtier Plaza, Suite 200, 380 Jackson Street, St. Paul, MN 55101-3885 USA.

ISBN 0-7603-2014-4

On the front cover: While Fighting Falcon is the official USAF nickname for the F-16, to its crews it is known as the Viper. This F-16C carries a lethal mix of AMRAAMs and Sidewinders along with its M61A1 20mm cannon. *Greg L. Davis*

On the frontispiece: The U.S. Navy receives a great deal of its aerial refueling support from USAF KC-10s and KC-135s. Photographed off of Hawaii during RIMPAC 2000, this KC-135E from the 116th ARS Washington ANG provides support for the aircraft of Carrier Air Wing Fourteen from the USS *Abraham Lincoln. Richard Vander Muelen*

On the title page: This trio of F-16CJs from the 'Fighting 55th FS at Shaw AFB, South Carolina each carries two AGM-88 HARM air-to-surface missiles for killing enemy radar sites. *Jim Dunn*

On the back cover, top: Over Afghanistan on an Operation Enduring Freedom mission in January 2003, these two AV-8Bs from the Black Sheep of VMA-214 each carry a Northrop Grumman Lightning II Pod under their right wing. This late-model laser designator will be used to guide the 2,000-pound GBU-10 bomb that each Harrier carries under their left wing. *Lou Drummond.* **Middle:** U.S. Navy F-14 Tomcat. *Jim Dunn.* **Bottom:** U.S. Army AH-64 Longbow Apache. *Jim Dunn*

Dedication page: Nose art on F-15E 87-180 of the 412th Operations Group, 445th FLTS, Edwards AFB, California. *Jim Dunn*

Edited by Amy Glaser
Designed by Mandy Iverson

Printed in Hong Kong

For the victims of September 11, 2001, and to those who will avenge them.

ACKNOWLEDGMENTS

The photographs appearing on these pages are the direct result of efforts by U.S. servicemen and women, a number of them reserve and guard personnel who have put their daily lives on hold to serve our country. To them, and every man and woman in uniform, we thank you for serving.

Greg L. Davis and Lou Drummond are due a special note of thanks for providing photographs from the front lines. Also, the authors would like to thank all the crews and public affairs personnel that granted access over the years. In addition, the authors are indebted to the following: David G. Brant, Ed Davies, Rene J. Francillon, Rebecca Frame, Kevin Grantham, Robert Greby, Dave Hunt, Dennis R. Jenkins, Norm Jukes, William T. Larkins, Josh Leventhal, Gerald Liang, Carol McKenzie, Gina Morello, Paul Negri, Joe Sadler, Ron Strong, Scott Thompson, Bernard Thouanel, Richard H. Vander Muelen, and Betty Veronico.

CONTENTS

INTRODUCTION

In the late evening hours of March 19, 2003, President George W. Bush announced to the American public that Operation Iraqi Freedom, the war to liberate Iraq and destroy that nation's weapons of mass destruction, was underway. While under Saddam Hussein's regime, Iraq has been a supporter of terrorism by using chemical weapons against its own people and supporting a government willing to use environmental terrorism as a roadblock against its enemies.

Many believed that the fall of the Soviet Union would bring a safer world, but it only changed the face of the threat against the United States and its allies. Acts of terrorism began to increase in the early 1990s, accomplished by small, fanatical extremist groups supported by various rogue nations. The most horrific act of terrorism occurred on September 11, 2001, when Al Qaeda operatives lead by Osama bin Laden succeeded in destroying New York City's World Trade Centers, downing a civilian airliner, and successfully attacking the Pentagon in Washington, D.C.

In the aftermath of the September 11 attacks, the United States and nations allied to the cause of eliminating the threat of global terrorism began to seek and destroy the infrastructure that supports, trains, and equips terrorists. Afghanistan's Taliban regime, which allowed terrorist groups to build camps and training facilities and assemble weapons caches, was the target of Operation Enduring Freedom. U.S. forces removed the Taliban from power and began to scour the Afghan countryside, destroying camps, weapons, and terrorist command and control centers dug into caves.

After determining that Saddam Hussein supported terrorists and was at risk for providing those organizations with weapons of mass destruction (nuclear, chemical, or biological), the United States began pushing for a full account of Iraq's weapons stockpile and its compliance with a litany of United Nations Resolutions.

On March 19, 2003, President Bush gave the order to begin Operation Iraqi Freedom to liberate the Iraqi people, remove Hussein from power, and account for Iraqi weapons of mass destruction. F-117A Stealth Fighters and Tomahawk cruise missiles began the battle, targeting a compound where Hussein and members of his family and regime were thought to reside. From this single, coordinated attack, Coalition forces streamed into Iraq to free the Iraqi people.

On April 1, 2003, the Coalition Forces, led by the United States, demanded the unconditional surrender of Hussein and his Ba'ath Party government. Without a word from Hussein, Coalition Forces continued their march on Baghdad. Meanwhile, in the rest of the world, the hunt for terrorists continues—led by America's *Defenders and Avengers*.

In the fight against terrorism, a fleet of fixed- and rotary-wing, as well as manned aerial vehicles, is used to seek out and destroy the enemy. This book provides a visual reference to the aircraft that serve the U.S. Military, ranging from planes developed during the Vietnam War, to those taking flights now. These aircraft and the crews that build, fly, and support them are the defenders of our shores and the avengers of our fallen citizens.

PART I

"We've got total dominance of the air. It is not air superiority, it's dominance."
Secretary of Defense Donald Rumsfeld, on Operation Iraqi Freedom. March 26, 2003

AIR FORCE

Secretary Rumsfeld's comments on the opening days of Operation Iraqi Freedom described an enemy air arm that had suffered tremendous punishment in strikes by U.S. and Coalition fighters and bombers. Air strikes quickly eliminated any threat the Iraqi Air Forces might pose. This quick elimination was a scene repeated from the 1991 Gulf War. Dominance of the skies over Iraq had been achieved by aircraft from the U.S. Army, Air Force, Navy, and Marine Corps, with the help of our allies, chiefly Britain and Saudi Arabia.

The primary service tasked with maintaining air superiority over an enemy is the U.S. Air Force. The service grew out of the Army Air Forces of World War II. In the early months of 1939, the Army Air Corps, as it was then known, had several hundred aircraft nearing obsolescence. However, by 1945, the Army Air Forces had grown to become the most formidable and technologically advanced aerial armada the world had ever seen. Two years later, the functions of the army and the Army Air Forces were separated when President Harry S. Truman signed the National Security Act of 1947 into law. On September 18, 1947, the U.S. Air Force became a separate military service, tasked to "defend the United States and protect its interests through aerospace power."

Since its inception, the air force's command reporting structure has changed as the U.S. military complex has grown. Administratively, the air force is managed by the secretary of the air force, appointed by the president of the United States. The secretary of the air force is responsible for all operations of the air force, but maintains control of all interactions with Congress, other government agencies, and the public. Military operations of the air force, army, and navy report to each service's chief of staff, who together form the joint chiefs of staff. The joint chiefs report to the secretary of defense, who reports to the commander in chief of the armed forces, the president of the United States.

The air force's chain of command from the chief of staff to the airman has nine separate reporting commands. Each command controls a specific function within the service; for example, the air force Materiel Command manages the development, acquisition, testing, and evaluation of everything from aircraft to weapons systems to new information technology systems.

War fighting commands such as the Air Combat Command (ACC), Air Mobility Command (AMC), Pacific Air Forces (PACAF), Air Force Space Command (AFSPC), Air Force Special Operations Command (AFSOC), and the United States Air Force in Europe (USAFE) are composed of numbered air forces, wings, groups, squadrons, and flights. Wings are the command element that takes air force units into combat.

Tank killer! It was nearly 15 years after entering operational service that the A-10 fired its first shot in anger and began to earn the reputation it already carried. This A-10A 78-0712 is assigned to the Bulldogs of the 354th FS at Davis-Monthan AFB, Arizona. *Jim Dunn*

This lineup of A-10s belongs to the famous Flying Tigers of the 74th FS based at Pope AFB, North Carolina. *Greg L. Davis*

Believing that future wars will require the U.S. Air Force to respond to numerous conflicts around the globe, the service initiated the Expeditionary Aerospace Force (EAF) concept in August 1998. EAFs will be expected to deploy rapidly, operate from forward bases, and leverage air force assets by tailoring what weapons types will be deployed and when. The air force states that EAFs are "lighter, leaner, and more lethal." Each major war-fighting command supplies components to the EAF, such as fighters, bombers, tankers, and reconnaissance aircraft, which deploy to support the EAF's mission. This concept enables commanders to tailor which assets are required to meet different types of threats, including the removal of a terrorist-supporting dictator as demonstrated in Operation Iraqi Freedom.

Aerial defense of America's borders was a critical issue during the Cold War. After the fall of the Soviet Union, that mission was relaxed. Patrolling the air defense intercept zones of the United States had always been the responsibility of the Air National Guard (ANG), which was alerted for patrols after the September 11, 2001, terrorist attacks. Under Operation Noble Eagle, ANG aircraft flew combat air patrols (CAP) over many major U.S. cities, 24 hours a day, in the four months following the attacks. Airborne alert patrols are still maintained, although at a reduced rate.

After the fall of the Soviet Union and the liberation of Kuwait, defense budgets declined and bases were closed and transitioned to civilian uses. At the same time, aircraft have aged, and advances in technology are changing how an aerial campaign is conducted.

Some Boeing B-52s are nearing 40 years of service, and the Lockheed C-5 Galaxy is not far behind. Yet these aircraft are slated to remain in frontline service with the air force past the year 2025.

While some systems undergo modification programs, other air force programs are maturing, including the CV-22 Osprey tilt-rotor, the F/A-22 Raptor, and the F-35 Joint Strike Fighter. The CV-22 will replace a variety of helicopters and will enable the rapid deployment of troops to over-the-horizon landing zones. The F/A-22 will replace the F-15 in the air superiority fighter role and will most likely take up the Stealth Fighter's strike role as existing F-117s age.

With technological advances in unmanned aerial vehicles, such as the RQ-1 Predator and RQ-4 Global Hawk, the United States will be able to put more reconnaissance sensors above the battlefield without endangering the lives of aircrews. The Predator's extended loiter time, missile-firing capability, and its ability to down-link sensor information add a new dimension to how the U.S. military will prosecute future armed conflicts. Recent tests demonstrated that multiple X-45 unmanned combat air vehicles (UCAV) can destroy high-priority targets, such as enemy air defense missile sites, thus clearing the way for manned aircraft to strike. An advanced UCAV system based on the X-45 is expected to be fielded in the year 2008.

The air force is a service undergoing change, dictated by budget constraints, management philosophy, and advances in technology. The dynamics of change will produce a "lighter, leaner, and more lethal" air force for the twenty-first century.

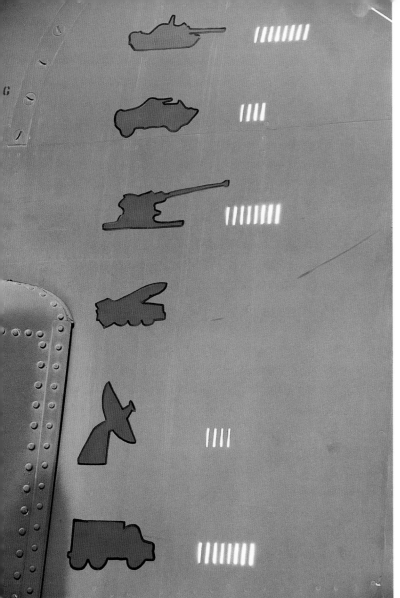

Retired due to battle damage suffered in Operation Desert Storm and now displayed at the McClellan Aviation Museum, A-10A 76-540 *Fist* served with the 706th TFS at NAS New Orleans. *Jim Dunn*

U.S. AIR FORCE COMMANDS

Air Combat Command, Langley Air Force Base (AFB), Virginia

Air Education and Training Command, Randolph AFB, Texas

Air Force Materiel Command, Wright-Patterson AFB, Ohio

Air Force Reserve Command, Robins AFB, Georgia

Air Force Space Command, Peterson AFB, Colorado

Air Force Special Operations Command, Hurlburt Field, Florida

Air Mobility Command, Scott AFB, Illinois

Pacific Air Forces, Hickam AFB, Hawaii

United States Air Forces in Europe, Ramstein AB, Germany

Only three active-duty A-10A squadrons are based outside of the continental United States: one squadron each in Germany and South Korea. The only Warthog squadron assigned to PACAF is the Fighting Falcons of the 355th FS based at Eielson AFB, Alaska. *Jim Dunn*

ATTACK AIRCRAFT AND FIGHTERS

A-10/OA-10 Thunderbolt II

Whether tank busting, convoy strafing, or serving in the Fast FAC (forward air control) mission, the Fairchild/Republic A-10 Thunderbolt II represents the air force's ultimate ground-support aircraft. Conceived in the late 1960s, the A-10 was to be a force equalizer to offset the three-to-one advantage in main battle tanks the Soviets enjoyed over NATO. America's and NATO's defensive strategy was to have A-10s, working in conjunction with helicopter gunships, loitering over the battlefield and destroying thousands of Soviet tanks before they could overrun Western Europe.

To deliver its lethal cargo, the A-10 was built around the General Electric GAU-8/A seven-barrel, 30mm Gatling gun, capable of firing 1,174 armor-piercing projectiles; 11 hardpoints for bombs or missiles; and a pair of General Electric TF-34-GE-100 turbofan engines. The aircraft's twin tails, twin shoulder-mounted engines, and Gatling gun barrels protruding from the aircraft's nose and resembling a snout, earned the A-10 the nickname "Warthog." A total of 715 of the airborne tank killers were constructed, and the first was delivered in October 1975. The first squadron of A-10s became operational in March 1976.

Although the threat of a Soviet invasion was very real through the end of the 1980s, the aircraft's first real test occurred during Operation Desert Storm. After Iraq invaded Kuwait on August 2, 1990, A-10s were deployed to the Gulf region during the build-up phase, known as Operation Desert Shield. When air operations by Coalition Forces began on January 17, 1991, Desert Shield shifted to Operation Desert Storm. In the battle to liberate Kuwait, A-10s were tasked with destroying dug-in Iraqi troop positions, armor, and vehicles. Warthogs were particularly effective at destroying Iraqi troop concentrations and thin-skinned vehicle columns by using Mk-20 Rockeye II cluster bombs.

A typical A-10 underwing and fuselage load for a mission against Iraqi forces consisted of a pair of AIM-9 missiles (air-to-air missiles for self-defense against Iraqi fighters); four 500-pound bombs (laser designated, general purpose, incendiary, or cluster types); a pair of AGM-65 Maverick missiles (air-to-surface missiles adept at destroying tanks and anti-aircraft sites); and either the ALQ-119 or ALQ-131 electronic countermeasures pod. Carrying such loads enabled A-10 pilots to attack Iraqi tanks, which were often dug into revetments. An A-10 pilot could quickly destroy two or even three tanks using Maverick missiles, then destroy two or three additional armored vehicles with the aircraft's GAU-8/A Gatling gun. On February 25, 1991, one day after the ground attack began, two A-10 pilots from the 23rd Tactical Fighter Wing's (TFW) 76th Tactical Fighter Squadron (TFS) destroyed a record 23 tanks in a single day.

In all, 194 A-10s and FastFAC OA-10s participated in Operation Desert Storm, and only five were lost, with two pilots killed. The type flew 8,100 sorties and destroyed more than 1,000 Iraqi tanks, over 2,200 vehicles, and dozens of antiaircraft missile launch sites. Current air force plans call for the A-10 to serve until the year 2028.

Although the F-35 JSF has been chosen to replace the A-10, the USAF is no longer in a rush to see the Warthog go. A proposal to re-engine the A-10, along with other upgrades, may keep it in service for another 25 years. *Greg L. Davis*

There are just over 100 A-10As currently serving in six ANG squadrons including A-10A 78-619, assigned to the 190th FS Idaho ANG at Gowen Field, Boise. The other five states that have a Warthog squadron are Connecticut, Maryland, Massachusetts, Michigan, and Pennsylvania. Another 239 Warthogs serve with active-duty and AFRC squadrons. *Jim Dunn*

A-10/OA-10 THUNDERBOLT II

Mission: A-10—close air support, OA-10—airborne forward air control
Builder: Fairchild Republic Co.
Powerplant: Two General Electric TF34-GE-100 turbofans rated at 9,065 pounds thrust per engine
Length: 53 feet, 4 inches
Height: 14 feet, 8 inches
Wingspan: 57 feet, 6 inches
Weight: 51,000 pounds maximum takeoff
Speed: 420 miles per hour (Mach 0.56)
Range: 800 miles (695 nautical miles)
Armament: One 30mm GAU-8/A seven-barrel Gatling gun and up to 16,000 pounds of ordnance
Crew: One
Unit Cost: $8.8 million
Date Deployed: March 1976
Inventory:

       Active Force — 189
       Air National Guard — 100
       Reserve — 50

A-10/OA-10 THUNDERBOLT II

UNITS ASSIGNED

UNIT	NICKNAME	TAIL CODE
74th FS	Flying Tigers	FT
75th FS	Sharks	FT
118th FS	Flying Yankees	CT
131st FS	Death Vipers	MA
172nd FS	Mad Ducks	BC
103rd FS	Black Hogs	PA
104th FS		MD
354th FS	Bulldogs	DM
357th FS	Dragons	DM
358th FS	Lobos	DM
190th FS		ID
303rd FS	KC Hawgs	KC
47th FS	Termites	BD
706th FS	Cajuns	NO
355th FS	Fighting Falcons	AK
25th FS	Assam Dragons	OS
81st FS	Panthers	SP
422nd TES	Green Bats	OT
A-10 DIV		WA

F-15 A, B, C, D

America's primary air superiority fighter is the F-15 Eagle. The F-15 was conceived in the late 1960s to combat new generations of Soviet fighters such as the MiG-23 and MiG-25. War planners envisioned the Eagle destroying vast numbers of technologically inferior Soviet Bloc fighters in an air war over Europe. The F-15 Eagle was designed as a highly maneuverable, single-seat fighter, capable of a maximum speed near Mach 2.5, that would replace the F-4 Phantom II in the air superiority role.

McDonnell Douglas (now Boeing) was awarded a contract for seven test aircraft in December 1969. The prototype was rolled out at the factory in St. Louis and then shipped to Edwards AFB, where it took its maiden flight on July 17, 1972. Production F-15As quickly demonstrated the aircraft's agility, breaking time to climb records set by Soviet fighters.

Air superiority Eagles have been built in the single-seat F-15A and F-15C models and the tandem-seat F-15B and F-15D models. Externally, the A and C are nearly identical, except that the F-15C can be fitted with conformal external fuel tanks between the wings and the fuselage. Conformal fuel tanks cannot be dropped, but their contents can be vented overboard to lighten the aircraft for combat. While the F-15A was limited to maneuvers up to 7.33g, under certain conditions the C model is capable of 9g maneuvers at maximum gross weight.

Eagles are equipped with an internal M61A1 20mm Vulcan Gatling gun and carry up to eight air-to-air missiles. McDonnell Douglas built 384 F-15As and 61 F-15Bs, both versions powered by Pratt & Whitney F100-PW-100 turbofan engines capable of 14,870 pounds thrust each. F-15Cs (485 built) and D models (90 constructed) are capable of an increased maximum takeoff weight and incorporate all of the upgrades made to the F-15A/Bs in the field. F-15C/Ds have been fitted with the more reliable, although slightly less powerful, Pratt & Whitney F100-PW-220 engines.

The 1st Tactical Fighter Wing at Langley AFB, Virginia, became the initial operational F-15A unit in January 1976. Three years later, in September 1979, the first F-15Cs were delivered to the 18th Tactical Fighter Wing at Kadena Air Base, Okinawa. Foreign operators of the F-15 are Israel, Japan, and Saudi Arabia.

When Operation Desert Storm began, F-15Cs of the 1st Tactical Fighter Wing were deployed to Saudi Arabia, arriving on August 7, 1990. In all, 125 F-15Cs would take part in Desert Shield/Desert

Based at Otis ANGB, F-15A 77-100 is part of the 101st FS (also called the Cape Cod unit) of the Massachusetts ANG. *Jim Dunn*

Since the terror attacks of September 11, 2001, homeland defense is the most important mission for the USAF. Photographed over the Pentagon on November 17, 2001, F-15C 81-035 from the Fighting Eagles of the 27th FS at Langley AFB, Virginia, is seen on a combat air patrol (CAP) as part of Operation Noble Eagle. *Greg L. Davis*

Storm. U.S. Air Force Eagles flew 5,667 sorties, principally guarding AWACS and other electronic warfare aircraft and sweeping the skies of Iraqi aircraft. During the war, F-15Cs claimed 35 Iraqi military aircraft destroyed in aerial combat (see Appendix III, *Aerial Victory Credits*).

In March 1999, F-15Cs scored four additional kills in the skies over Kosovo. In Operations Enduring Freedom and Iraqi Freedom, Eagles constantly maintained combat air patrol in the skies over U.S. troops and guarded AWACS and other high-value reconnaissance systems operating in high-threat environments.

The air force plans a number of upgrades to its F-15C/D fleet to keep the type in frontline service past the year 2020. Eagles were designed for a life span of 12,000 flying hours, which could be extended through a structural life-extension rebuild program. Current Eagle retrofits include the upgraded Raytheon APG-63(V)1 radar (expected installations to be completed in 2006), the installation of the Joint Helmet-Mounting Cuing System for targeting of the AIM-9X air-to-air missile (upgrades completed by 2007), and upgrades of the Eagle's engine to the Pratt & Whitney F100-PW-220E series.

During Operation Desert Storm, the 58th FS was credited with 16 air-to-air victories, which was nearly half of the total number of USAF victories in the war. To maintain their skills, the unit frequently attends exercises at Nellis AFB, where F-15C 85-100 is seen getting an end-of-runway (EOR) check prior to takeoff. *Jim Dunn*

F-15 A, B, C, D

Mission: Tactical fighter
Contractor: McDonnell Douglas (Boeing)
Powerplant: Two Pratt & Whitney F100-PW-220 or 229 afterburning turbofan engines rated at 23,450 pounds each engine (C/D models)
Length: 63.8 feet
Height: 18.5 feet
Wingspan: 42.8 feet
Speed: 1,875 miles per hour
Maximum gross takeoff weight (MGTOW): 68,000 pounds (C/D models)
Ceiling: 65,000 feet
Range: 3,450 miles ferry range with conformal fuel tanks and three external fuel tanks on wing attach points
Armament: One internally mounted M-61A1 20mm six-barrel cannon with 940 rounds of ammunition; four AIM-9L/M Sidewinder; four AIM-7F/M Sparrow air-to-air missiles, or eight AIM-120 AMRAAMs, carried externally.
Crew: F-15A/C: One. F-15B/D: Two
Unit Cost: A/B models, $27.9 million; C/D models, $29.9 million
Date Deployed: July 1972
Inventory:
    Active Force – 396
    Air National Guard – 126

F-15 A, B, C, D

UNITS ASSIGNED

UNIT	NICKNAME	TAIL CODE
1st FS	Fightin' Furies	TY
2nd FS	Second to None	TY
12th FS	Dirty Dozen	AK
19th FS	Gamecocks	AK
27th FS	Fighting Eagles	FF
44th FS	Vampires	ZZ
58th FS	Gorillas	EG
60th FS	Fighting Crows	EG
67th FS	Fighting Cocks	ZZ
71st FS	Ironmen	FF
85th TES	Skulls	OT
94th FS	Hat-In-The-Ring	FF
95th FS	Mr. Bones	TY
101st FS	Eagle Keepers	MA
110th FS	Lindbergh's Own	SL
114th FS	Eager Beavers	No tail code, Klamath Falls, OR
122nd FS	Bayou Militia	JZ
123rd FS	Red Hawks	No tail code; Portland International Airport (IAP), OR
159th FS	Jaguars	No tail code; Jacksonville IAP, FL
199th FS		HH
390th FS	Wild Boars	MO
422nd TES	Green Bats	OT
445th FLTS		ED
493rd FS	Grim Reapers	LN
F-15 DIV		WA

F-15E Strike Eagle

Developed from the F-15 air superiority fighter's robust design, the F-15E Strike Eagle is a tandem, two-seat, supersonic, all-weather, air-to-air and air-to-ground fighter. Strike Eagles can drop conventional bombs or, when fitted with LANTIRN (Low-Altitude Navigation and Targeting Infrared for Night) pods, can strike with precision, laser-guided munitions. The aircraft, which has a pilot in the front seat and a weapons system officer in the rear, replaced the FB-111 as the air force's long-range, all-weather medium bomber.

The first F-15E flew on December 11, 1986, and was first delivered to the 405th Tactical Training Wing at Luke AFB, Arizona, in April 1988. The air force has taken delivery of 227 F-15Es, and the Republic of Korea is now acquiring 40 of the type (designated F-15K).

A typical weapons load for an F-15E includes: 500 rounds for the aircraft's 20mm cannon; 4 AIM-9 air-to-air missiles; either 8 GBU-12s (500 pound), 4 GBU-10s (2,000 pound), or 6 cluster bombs (CBU-87 or 89); or 6 Mk-20 Rockeye bombs.

With the Raytheon (Hughes) APG-70 ground-mapping radar, the F-15E's crew can identify large targets such as bridges or airfield hangars from up to 80 miles and smaller targets such as trucks at closer range. In air-to-air mode, the APG-70's Doppler-shift radar has "look-down, shoot-down" capabilities of detecting low-flying aircraft against background clutter such as terrain or cityscapes. When in air-to-air mode, the APG-70 can detect aircraft as far out as 100 miles. To keep the F-15E's crew aware of the situation around it at all times, the APG-70 will sweep the ground, freeze the radar image, and sweep the air around the aircraft in a matter of seconds to prevent situational blindness.

During Operation Desert Storm, Strike Eagles assisted A-10 Warthogs in destroying tanks and other armored vehicles. Using GBU-12 laser-guided bombs, F-15Es sought armor targets, primarily in Kuwait. F-15Es flew 949 tank-busting sorties. At night, Strike Eagles were also sent after bridges, communications infrastructure, and ammunition dumps. Working in conjunction with both AWACS (aerial surveillance) and JSTARS (ground surveillance) aircraft, 391 F-15E "Scud Hunt" sorties were flown against the mobile missile sites. Strike Eagle crews flew at altitudes between 12,000 and 15,000 feet, monitoring the area using the aircraft's forward-looking infra red (FLIR) system and the plane's synthetic aperture radar to detect the heat and radar signatures of Scud launchers and the associated support vehicles. In all, 2,172 Strike

Part of the Air Education and Training Command (AETC), the 325th FW based at Tyndall AFB, Florida, is the active-duty training unit for the F-15. Its three squadrons are the 1st FS (red), 2nd FS (yellow), and 95th FS (blue). *Jim Dunn*

Known as the Heritage Flight, the air force allows a few qualified civilian pilots to fly their vintage warbirds in formation with select USAF pilots at various airshows around the county. Though only 32 years separates the first flight of the North American P-51 Mustang from the McDonnell Douglas F-15 Eagle, the evolution in fighter aircraft is stark. *Jim Dunn*

These two Strike Eagles from the Bold Tigers of the 391st FS Mountain Home AFB, Idaho, demonstrate their fighter/bomber capabilities with a weapons load of four AIM-120 AMRAAMs and two AIM-9 Sidewinders for the fighter role, and two GBU-15 2,000-pound guided bombs for the strike mission. *Greg L. Davis*

One important component giving the F-15E its day/night all-weather strike capability is the low-altitude navigation and targeting infrared for night (LANTIRN) system carried in the two pods under the engine intakes. The AN/AAQ-14 targeting pod below the left intake features an infrared sensor with laser designator, while the AN/AAQ-13 navigation pod has the terrain-following forward-looking infrared radar. *Lou Drummond*

Eagle sorties attacked 2,124 targets in Iraq and Kuwait with two aircraft lost; one crew perished, and the other crew was taken prisoner and later returned to the United States.

During Operation Enduring Freedom, Strike Eagles were extensively employed in destroying Taliban arms caches stockpiled in caves. Using laser-guided 2,000-pound GBU-24 bombs, the Strike Eagle's weapons system officers often directed bombs straight into the mouths of Afghan caves, igniting huge secondary explosions as stored weapons were destroyed. F-15Es also played an important role in Operation Iraqi Freedom. The air force expects to operate the F-15E past the year 2030 and plans to enhance its war fighting capabilities with improved targeting pods and laser designators with increased range.

Gunfighters 366th wing badge carried on F-15E 87-0210 of the Bold Tigers of the 391st FS, Mountain Home AFB, Idaho. *Jim Dunn*

Seen here at RAF Lakenheath, England, F-15E 88-1705 is part of the Eagles of the 334th FS, one of the two Strike Eagle training squadrons in the USAF. *Joe Sadler*

Even though the backseat weapons systems officer (WSO) is not pilot-rated, the F-15E (like other tandem-seat USAF aircraft) is fitted with flight controls in the rear cockpit. Using four cathode ray tube (CRT) displays, the WSO controls the radar, navigation, targeting, and defensive systems for the aircraft. *Jim Dunn*

Returning to the ramp, F-15E 91-327 is assigned to the 57th WG Fighter Weapons School, Nellis AFB. On the vast test ranges of southern Nevada, virtually any type of real-world operational mission can be duplicated using advanced electronic simulators along with a highly skilled adversary squadron flying F-16s. *Jim Dunn*

F-15E STRIKE EAGLE

Mission: Air-to-ground attack aircraft

Builder: McDonnell Douglas (Boeing)

Powerplant: Two Pratt & Whitney F100-PW-220 or 229 afterburning turbofan engines capable of 25,000 to 29,000 pounds thrust each

Length: 63.8 feet

Height: 18.5 feet

Wingspan: 42.8 feet

Speed: 1,875 miles per hour (Mach 2.5-plus)

MGTOW: 81,000 pounds (36,450 kilograms)

Range: 2,400 miles ferry range with conformal fuel tanks and three external fuel tanks

Armament: One 20mm Gatling gun mounted internally with 500 rounds of ammunition. Four AIM-7F/M Sparrow missiles and four AIM-9L/M Sidewinder missiles, or eight AIM-120 AMRAAM missiles. Any air-to-surface weapon in the air force inventory (nuclear and conventional)

Crew: Two (pilot and weapon systems officer)

Unit Cost: $31.1 million

Date Deployed: April 1988

Inventory:

       Active Force – 217

F-15E STRIKE EAGLE

UNITS ASSIGNED

UNIT	NICKNAME	TAIL CODE
85th TES	Skulls	OT
90th FS	Pair O' Dice	AK
333rd FS	Lancers	SJ
334th FS	Eagles	SJ
335th FS	Chiefs	SJ
336th FS	Rocketeer	SJ
391st FS	Bold Tigers	MO
422nd TES	Green Bats	OT
445th FLTS		ED
492nd FS	Madhatters	LN
494th FS	Panthers	LN
F-15E DIV		WA

Shown here on a test mission, F-15E 92-366 of the Green Bats, 422nd TES, Eglin AFB, carries a weapons load of one AIM-120 AMRAAM and two AGM-65 Mavericks during test flights from Nellis AFB. *Jim Dunn*

F-16 A, B, C, D

The F-16 was developed from a February 18, 1972, air force proposal for an inexpensive (under $3 million each), lightweight, agile fighter capable of Mach-2 flight for use primarily in daytime dogfighting to supplement the F-15. Both General Dynamics and Northrop were granted contracts for the construction and demonstration of two prototype aircraft. General Dynamics delivered the YF-16 Fighting Falcon, a single-seat, single-engine, single-tail fighter equipped with a 20mm M61A1 Gatling gun and a pair of wing-tip-mounted AIM-9L Sidewinder air-to-air missiles. The YF-16, called the Viper by air force crews, flew its first official flight on February 2, 1974. The F-16 featured a blended wing/body, fly-by-wire controls activated through a side-stick controller, and an ejection seat that reclined 30 degrees to enable the pilot to endure maneuvers up to 9 gs (nine times the force of gravity acting upon the pilot and aircraft). General Dynamics won the fly-off. Northrop, partnering with McDonnell Douglas, took its design, the YF-17, to the navy; that aircraft later went into production as the F/A-18 Hornet.

The first F-16A, the single-seat model, took its maiden flight on August 7, 1978, followed by the tandem, two-seat B model four months later. Room for the installation of the B model's second seat required that fuselage fuel tanks be removed, reducing internal fuel capacity from 6,972 pounds to 5,875 pounds. Both aircraft featured the Westinghouse APG-65 radar and two wingtip and seven underwing/fuselage hardpoints, capable of carrying two 370-gallon fuel tanks, or up to 15,000 pounds of ordnance.

Upgrades to the aircraft for all-weather attack capabilities included the APG-68 radar, a new heads-up display, and the LANTIRN (Low Altitude Navigation Targeting for Infra Red at Night) system, as well as the ALQ-165 jamming system. These aircraft were redesignated F-16C, and the two-seat version became known as F-16D.

USAF active-duty fighter squadrons are assigned either 18 or 24 aircraft, while AFRC and ANG squadrons each have 15 fighters assigned. The active-duty Black Widows of the 421st FS based at Hill AFB, Utah, have a total of 18 Fighting Falcons assigned. *Jim Dunn*

This pair of F-16ADFs from the 178th FS—one of the few ANG squadrons still operating that type—seen flying a Noble Eagle combat air patrol (CAP) in the days after September 11, 2001. *Greg L. Davis*

In times of conflict, nose art was a frequent addition to fighter aircraft. Occasionally you will see nose art featuring a female form on a jet, although the USAF has discouraged that type of design. *Cold Steel* adorns F-16C 85-448 from the Lobos of the 175th FS South Dakota ANG. *Jim Dunn*

Fighting Falcons are built-in blocks, which signify an aircraft's capabilities and configuration. For example, any F-16 with a block number ending in zero is an aircraft fitted with a General Electric F110-GE-100/129 engine, and a block number ending with a two signifies a Pratt & Whitney F100-PW-200/220/229 engine installation. The F-16 Block 30/32 features an engine bay that will accommodate either manufacturer's engine.

During the Gulf War, 248 Fighting Falcons took part in operations over Kuwait and Iraq. The largest F-16 raid of the war took place on January 16, 1991, when 56 Fighting Falcons struck the Baghdad Nuclear Research Center. During the conflict, F-16s flew 13,087 sorties comprising four mission types: day visual attacks, anti-Scud missions, fast forward air controller (FastFAC), and ground support. F-16s completed 2,912 day visual sorties against bridges, oil refineries, communications targets, and ammunition storage facilities. When engaged in Scud missile destruction, GPS/LANTIRN-equipped F-16s flew at night and dropped cluster bombs for maximum destructive power. In the FastFAC mission, F-16s located Iraqi targets and coordinated attacks by other strike aircraft. And F-16s flew 8,258 sorties in support of Coalition ground forces. Three F-16s were lost in combat and five were destroyed by other means.

While Fighting Falcon is the official USAF nickname for the F-16, to its crews it is known as the Viper. This F-16C carries a lethal mix of AMRAAMs and Sidewinders along with its M61A1 20mm cannon. *Greg L. Davis*

Seen on the transient line at Hill AFB, Utah, F-16C 86-0291 *By Request II* wears special markings from the Sun Devils 302nd FS based at Luke AFB, Arizona. Hill AFB serves as the logistics/maintenance depot for the F-16. *Paul Negri*

A decade later, after the terrorist attacks of September 11, 2001, Air National Guard F-16s scrambled to provide combat air patrols over most major U.S. cities. F-16s also were used extensively in Operation Southern Watch, enforcing the "No-Fly Zone" over southern Iraq, and Operation Allied Force, the air action in Yugoslavia. Allied Force F-16CJs (Block 50/52), configured for the Wild Weasel anti-radar mission, have fired HARM missiles to destroy enemy air defense radar and surface-to-air missile sites. During Operation Enduring Freedom, the anti-terrorist campaign in Afghanistan, F-16s supported ground forces by dropping precision-guided munitions.

F-16s are built for an 8,000-hour life cycle, and they will remain in the U.S. Air Force's inventory past the year 2025. The Fighting Falcon is also flown by, or has been ordered by, Bahrain, Belgium, Denmark, Egypt, Greece, Indonesia, Israel, Jordan, The Netherlands, New Zealand, Norway, Pakistan, Portugal, the Republic of Korea, Saudi Arabia, Singapore, Taiwan, Thailand, Turkey, the United Arab Emirates, and Venezuela.

This pair of MiG aggressors is assigned to the 414th Combat Training Squadron at Nellis AFB. Part of the Air Warfare Center 57th WG, these F-16C/Ds are flown by pilots from the Red Flag Adversary Tactics Division as part of the Red Forces during training exercises over the ranges of southern Nevada. *Jim Dunn*

Another mission that the F-16 has been adapted for is that of a Wild Weasel. Designated F-16CJ (Block 50), these late-model Falcons replaced the venerable F-4G in the suppression of enemy air defense (SEAD) missions using the AGM-88 high-speed antiradiation missile (HARM). *Jim Dunn*

F-16 A, B, C, D

Mission: Multi-role fighter

Builder: Lockheed Martin Corp.

Powerplant: F-16C/D – one Pratt and Whitney F100-PW-200/220/229 or

General Electric F110-GE-100/129 capable of 27,000 pounds thrust

Length: 49 feet, 5 inches

Height: 16 feet

Wingspan: 32 feet, 8 inches

Speed: 1,500 miles per hour (Mach 2 at altitude)

MGTOW: 37,500 pounds

Range: 1,740 nautical miles

Armament: One M-61A1 20mm Gatling gun with 500 rounds; external stations can carry up to six air-to-air missiles, conventional air-to-air and air-to-surface munitions, and electronic countermeasure pods

Crew: F-16C, one; F-16D, one or two

Unit Cost: F-16A/B, $14.6 million; F-16C/D, $18.8 million

Date Deployed: January 1979

Inventory:

Active Force – 732

Air National Guard – 579

Reserve – 70

F-16 A, B, C, D

UNITS ASSIGNED

UNIT	NICKNAME	TAIL CODE
4th FS	Fightin' Fuugins	HL
13th FS	Panthers	WW
14th FS	Samurais	WW
18th FS	Blue Foxes	AK
21st FS	Gamblers	LF
22nd FS	Stringers	SP
23rd FS	Fighting Hawks	SP
34th FS	Rude Rams	HL
35th FS	Pantons	WP
36th FS	Flying Fields	OS
55th FS	Fighting 55th	SW
61st FS	Top Dogs	LF
62nd FS	Spikes	LF
63rd FS	Panthers	LF
77th FS	Gamblers	SW
78th FS	Bushmasters	SW
79th FS	Tigers	SW
80th FS	Juvats	WP
85th TES	Skulls	OT
93rd FS	Makos	FM
107th FS	Red Devils	MI
112th FS	Stingers	OH
111th FS	Ace in the Hole	EF

UNITS ASSIGNED CONTINUED

UNIT	NICKNAME	TAIL CODE
113th FS	Racers	TH
119th FS	Jersey Devils	AC
120th FS	Cougars	CO
121st FS	Capital Guardians	DC
124th FS	Hawkeyes	IA
125th FS	Tulsa Vipers	OK
134th FS	Green Mountain Boys	VT
138th FS	Cobras	NY
148th FS	Kickin' Ass	AZ
149th FS	Rebel Riders	VA
152nd FS	Tigers	AZ
157th FS	Swamp Foxes	SC
160th FS	Snakes	AL
162nd FS	Sabres	OH
163rd FS	Marksmen	FW
170th FS	Flyin' Illini	SI
174th FS	Bats	HA
175th FS	Lobos	No tail code; Sioux Falls, SD
176th FS	Badgers	WI
178th FS	Happy Hooligans	ND
179th FS	Bulldogs	MN
182nd FS	Lone Star Gunfighters	SA
184th FS	Flying Rezorbacks	FS
186th FS	Big Sky	No tail code Great Falls IAP, MT
188th FS	Tacos	NM
194th FS	Griffins	No tail code; Fresno IAP, CA
195th FS	Warhawks	AZ
301st FS	Red Tail Angels	LF
302nd FS	Sun Devils	LR
308th FS	Emerald Knights	LF
309th FS	Wild Ducks	LF
310th FS	Top Hats	LF
389th FS	Thunderbolts	MO
414th CTS		WA
416th FLTS		ED
421st FS	Black Widows	HL
422nd TES	Green Bats	OT
425th FS	Black Widows	LF
428th FS	Buccaneers	CC
457th FS	Spads	TX
466th FS	Diamondbacks	HI
510th FS	Buzzards	AV
522nd FS	Fireballs	CC
523rd FS	Crusaders	CC
524th FS	Hounds	CC
555th FS	Triple Nickel	AV
F-16 DIV		WA
USAFADS		WA
AATC		AZ

Seen returning to Tonopah, F-117A 80-0786 was the second production aircraft. During the Gulf War it was named *War Pig* and flew 24 combat sorties in that conflict. It remains operational with the 49th FW. *Lockheed*

F-117 Nighthawk

No other aircraft or weapons system has captured the imagination of the press or the American public like the F-117A Nighthawk. Whenever the Stealth Fighter is in action, it is big news. Military leaders around the world sit in awe of the aircraft's ability to strike a target undetected.

The F-117A was conceived by engineers at Lockheed's Advanced Development Projects group, the famed "Skunk Works," in response to a 1974 DARPA (Defense Advanced Research Projects Agency) contract for aircraft designs with reduced radar cross sections (RCS). DARPA's study lead to the Experimental Survivability Testbed (XST) program, where Lockheed and Northrop submitted full-scale mock-ups of proposed aircraft with low RCS. Lockheed won the design contest, and its aircraft design proceeded under the program codename "Have Blue." Two Have Blue aircraft were built and used to test the principles that went into building the F-117A. Satisfied that Lockheed was on the right track, the government awarded the company a contract for five aircraft under the program name "Senior Trend." Developed in complete secrecy, the first F-117A took to the skies on June 18, 1981. In addition to the five development aircraft, Lockheed delivered 59 Senior Trend planes to the air force, which provided that service with two 18-aircraft operational squadrons, aircraft for training, and a reserve of planes to replace those lost in combat. The first F-117A was delivered on August 23, 1982, and the last on July 12, 1990.

The term "Fighter" in Stealth Fighter is a misnomer; the aircraft is not equipped to carry any air-to-air weapons. Nighthawks are employed in the tactical strike/attack role when deep penetration behind enemy lines is required. The aircraft's minimal radar signature enables it to defeat enemy air defense radars and drop its bombs before detection. Once the bombs are on their way, the F-117A can fly beyond the range of a target's antiaircraft defenses.

In order to maintain secrecy, Lockheed built the F-117A using off-the-shelf aircraft components. To this end, the F-117A was fitted with General Electric F404-GE-F1D2 engines used on the F/A-18, minus the afterburner; the aircraft's unique boat-tail

Under the management of the Defense Advanced Research Projects Agency (DARPA), the famous Lockheed Skunk Works first flew the proof-of-concept Have Blue aircraft in December 1977. This design led to a contract for five full-scale development (FSD) aircraft, designated YF-117s. First flown on December 18, 1981, FSD 3 YF-117A 79-10782 *Scorpion 3* is the oldest active stealth in the inventory, and is assigned to the 410th FLTS at Edwards AFB. *Jim Dunn*

Powered by two non-afterburning General Electric F-404-GE-F1D2 turbofans, the F-117A is equipped with auto throttle and an automatic recovery system. *Lou Drummond*

Viewed high over the Atlantic en route to RAF Fairford, these two F-117As will stick close to their KC-10 tanker. *Lou Drummond*

exhaust, which reduces the aircraft's infrared signature, will not accommodate an afterburner. The F/A-18 also yielded most of the cockpit fittings, while the F-15 contributed landing gear, and the F-16's flight computers manage the aircraft in the air.

Seven years after the first F-117A was delivered to the air force, the Pentagon acknowledged the aircraft's existence on November 10, 1988. Six F-117As dropped bombs on the night of December 19–20, 1989, during the attack on Panama known as Operation Just Cause.

Special Delivery

The Nighthawk is capable of delivering the GBU-10 Paveway II LGB (Laser-Guided Bomb), GBU-27 Paveway II LGB mated to either a Mk-84 2,000-pound bomb or a 2,000-pound BLU-109B penetrator bomb. In addition, the F-117A eventually will carry the AGM-154A JSOW (Joint Stand-Off Weapon), a 1,500 pound bomb that can be launched against a target from more than 15 miles (low-level release) or 45 miles out (high-level release). The AGM-154A delivers approximately 150 CEBs (combined effects bomblets) that can destroy tanks or parked aircraft.

Stealth Fighter at War

Less than a month after the Iraqi invasion of Kuwait on August 2, 1990, the U.S. Air Force deployed 22 F-117As from the 415th Tactical Fighter Squadron (37th Tactical Fighter Wing) to King Khalid Military City, Saudi Arabia. The F-117As of the 416th

Tactical Fighter Squadron followed in December, and a number of Nighthawks from the 417th arrived in Saudi Arabia in January 1991. A total of 45 F-117As participated in what became known as the Gulf War.

F-117 NIGHTHAWK

Mission: Strike/Attack
Builder: Lockheed Martin
Powerplant: Two General Electric F404-GE-F1D2 (non-afterburning) 10,800-pound static thrust each
Length: 63 feet, 9 inches
Height: 12 feet, 9.5 inches
Wingspan: 43 feet, 4 inches
Weight: 52,500 pounds
Speed: 600 knots (high subsonic); Cruise: 500 knots
Range: 600 nautical miles (unrefueled), unlimited with air refueling
Armament: 4,000 pounds of bombs targeted with an IRADS (Infrared acquisition and targeting system)
Crew: One
Unit Cost: $45 million
Date Deployed: 1982
Inventory:

Active force – 55

F-117 NIGHTHAWK

UNITS ASSIGNED

UNIT	NICKNAME	TAIL CODE
8th FS	Black Sheep	HO
9th FS	Flying Knights	HO
410th FLTS		ED

When the Iraqi leader failed to withdraw from Kuwait, the Allied Coalition launched Operation Desert Storm at 12:22 A.M. (local time) on January 17, 1991, with a strike of ten F-117As against a command and control site at Nukhayb, as well as Iraqi Air Force Headquarters and other targets in the capital city of Baghdad. The F-117A's stealthy characteristics enabled the aircraft to bomb targets in heavily defended downtown Baghdad and return without damage. The prowess of the Stealth Fighter was shown nightly on television. Bomb-strike footage showed the laser-guided bombs of the F-117A penetrating command centers and bunkers with the resulting explosion blowing out the sides of the structure.

When President George H. W. Bush declared a cease-fire on February 28, 1991, the F-117 Nighthawks had flown 1,271 sorties and dropped more than 2,000 tons of bombs, scoring 1,669 direct hits (or 80 percent) on the 2,087 targets attacked. Lessons learned in the 1991 Gulf War were used to improve Stealth Fighter tactics and advance the development of laser-guided bombs to increase the weapon's accuracy.

During the air war in the skies above Kosovo and Yugoslavia in the early months of 1999, Nighthawks dropped the CBU-94. This cluster bomb dispenses carbon-graphite wire bundles that fan out. When the bundles make contact with a city's electrical infrastructure, the wires short-circuit power lines, shutting down power plants and putting target cities and enemy command centers in the dark. The only F-117A lost in combat occurred during the NATO campaign in Kosovo. This aircraft was brought down by a Soviet-built air-to-air missile that exploded near the F-117A. The pilot was forced to eject but was rescued six hours later. Of the millions of antiaircraft projectiles and missiles launched at Stealth Fighters during Desert Storm and Kosovo, one was bound to strike home, yet it is stealth technology and the skills of the pilots and crews that prevented more losses.

The F-117A stands as an example of American industrial achievement and military strength. The Stealth Fighter can take the battle to an enemy's doorstep, and put a bomb through it.

F/A-22A Raptor

In November 1981, the U.S. Air Force began planning for the eventual replacement of the highly successful F-15 family of fighters and to meet the Soviets' anticipated next generation of fighter aircraft. After a design proposal and evaluation competition, industry

When the Lockheed YF-22 prototype first flew in September 1990, no one could foresee that 13 years later, the winner of the Advanced Tactical Fighter competition still had not started operational testing. The Lockheed/General Dynamics/Boeing team won a contract for nine F-22As in August 1991, and the first of these Engineering and Manufacturing Development (EMD) aircraft took to the air in September 1997. *Jim Dunn*

After its first flight in September 1997, F-22A 91-001, along with the second EMD aircraft 91-002, conducted virtually all of the flight testing during the next three years. *Jim Dunn*

F/A-22 A RAPTOR

Mission: Air superiority fighter, attack

Builder: Lockheed Martin

Powerplant: Two Pratt & Whitney F119-PW-110 thrust vectoring turbofans rated at 35,000 pounds thrust each

Length: 62 feet, 1 inch

Height: 16 feet, 5 inches

Wingspan: 44 feet, 6 inches

MGTOW: 60,000 pounds (estimate)

Speed: 763 miles per hour (Mach 2-plus maximum)

Armament: AIM-120 AMRAAM and AIM-9 air-to-air missiles, plus a
pair of GBU-32 JDAMs and a 20mm Gatling gun carried internally,
plus four external hardpoints

Crew: One

F/A-22 A RAPTOR

UNITS ASSIGNED:
Expected deployment in 2005;
currently under test and evaluation

411th FLTS, AFB ED
422nd TES, Green Bats OT

teams headed by Northrop and Lockheed were each awarded $818 million demonstration and concept validation contracts in October 1986. Lockheed's F-22 design was the winner of the Advanced Tactical Fighter competition, in which the YF-22 went head-to-head against Northrop's YF-23. The prototype YF-22 was first flown on September 29, 1990, by company test pilot Dave Ferguson. Seven years later, on September 7, 1997, the first F-22 Raptor, *Spirit of America*, was flown from the runway at the company's Marietta, Georgia, factory by company test pilot Paul Metz.

On September 17, 2002, the F-22 was redesignated F/A-22 to better reflect the Raptor's perceived new combat roles. The F/A-22's low radar cross-section (RCS) is expected to give the aircraft the ability to defeat surface-to-air missile-tracking radar. This will enable the F/A-22 to penetrate and attack heavily defended targets such as static or mobile missile sites and other priority enemy infrastructure.

Aside from its stealthy characteristics, the F/A-22 is set apart from other modern fighters by its ability to "super cruise." New Pratt & Whitney F-119-PW-110s were developed specifically for the F/A-22 that enable the plane to fly supersonic without an afterburner. These engines feature low RCS inlets and exhaust nozzles, thrust-vectoring exhaust nozzles, and lower maintenance support requirements (40 percent fewer parts that require 60 percent fewer specialized tools).

The heart of the F/A-22's information system is the AN/APG-77 multimode radar, which is built as an integral part of the aircraft. The ANAPG-77 unit is coupled with the weapons management system and the electronic warfare suite; information from all three systems is integrated and then presented to the pilot to provide the most up-to-the-minute situational information. The radar unit is capable of scanning 120 degrees to either side of the aircraft's nose and acquiring and tracking multiple targets beyond visible range. In addition, the F/A-22 has infrared search and track capabilities. Being able to see enemy fighters before their radar can acquire the F/A-22 gives the Raptor a tremendous advantage in air-to-air combat.

The Raptor is being evaluated at Edwards AFB by the 412th Logistics Group's 411th Flight Test Squadron and by Air Combat Command, 57th Wing, 422nd Test and Evaluation Squadron at Nellis AFB, Nevada. In all, the 422nd will receive eight aircraft for use at the U.S. Air Force's Air Warfare Center at Nellis. Currently, the air force plans to acquire 339 F/A-22s, and will eventually replace its F-15 fleet with Raptors.

F-35A Joint Strike Fighter

In the 1980s, the Defense Advanced Research Projects Agency (DARPA) began focusing its efforts on a follow-on aircraft to the Advanced Tactical Fighter, which became the F-22. Using technologies developed for the F-22, such as its high-thrust engines, DARPA set out specifications for a Short Take-Off, Vertical Landing (STOVL) aircraft to meet navy and Marine Corps requirements. Lockheed and McDonnell Douglas each received contracts in 1993 to develop a Conventional Take-Off and Landing (CTOL) variant for carrier operations and a STOVL model for the marines.

Simultaneously, the air force started looking toward a new technology replacement for its F-16. The air force's needs were to be met through the Common Affordable Lightweight Fighter (CALF), which was administered under the Joint Advanced Strike Technology (JAST) program. In the early months of 1994, the navy/Marine Corps CTOL and STOVL development efforts were added to the JAST program that was intended to provide a common aircraft that, depending upon engine configuration, would serve the navy, marines, and air force. This single airframe would replace the F-16 Fighting Falcon, AV-8 Harrier, and F/A-18 Hornet. A request for proposals was released to the aerospace industry in March 1996, and the Joint Strike Fighter was born.

Boeing developed the X-32, which featured a delta-wing shape and deep body, while Lockheed entered the competition with the X-35, a sleek but conventional-looking fighter. Both designs featured low radar cross-sections and the ability to employ precision-guided munitions. In addition, the Joint Strike Fighter will be able to downlink sensor information about a target from E-8C Joint Stars and other reconnaissance platforms.

On October 26, 2001, Lockheed and the Department of Defense announced the Lockheed team (with major partners Northrop/Grumman and BAE Systems) as winner of the $25 billion system development and demonstration contract that calls for the construction of 22 aircraft (14 flight test and 8 ground test). Once

F-35A JOINT STRIKE FIGHTER

Mission: Air superiority fighter, STOVL fighter/attack
Builder: Lockheed Martin
Powerplant: one Pratt & Whitney JSF119-611 afterburning turbofan
Length: 45 feet
Wingspan: 36 feet
MGTOW: 50,000 pounds
Speed: Mach 1-plus
Range: 600 miles
Crew: One

The navy plans to order a version of the F-35A with the capability to operate from aircraft carriers. This version would replace early model Hornets. The marines are also set to order the F-35B short takeoff/vertical landing (STOVL) to replace their Hornets and Harriers. *Jim Dunn*

the developmental phase is over, the air force plans on an initial operating capability for the F-35 beginning in 2011.

Current plans call for the air force to acquire 1,763 F-35As, while another 1,239 will be produced for the U.S. Navy (F-35C—carrier landing variant) and Marine Corps, as well as the air force of the United Kingdom (F-35B STOVL—short-takeoff/vertical landing capable). Squadron deliveries are slated to begin in 2008. If all 3,002 aircraft are built, the program is estimated to be worth more than $200 billion.

Three active-duty units are operating B-1Bs at Dyess AFB, and B-1B 83-0071 *Spit Fire* is assigned to the Bats of the 9th BS. *Jim Dunn*

BOMBERS

B-1B Lancer

The B-1's developmental history officially began in July 1963 as part of the Advanced Manned Strategic Aircraft (AMSA) program. Requests for proposals were issued to Boeing, General Dynamics, and North American Rockwell in November 1963. During the Kennedy and Johnson presidencies, AMSA received only limited funding because of the belief that Intercontinental Ballistic Missiles were the strategic weapon of the future. After Richard Nixon's election in 1968, newly appointed Defense Secretary Melvin Laird revamped the air force's bomber acquisition plans. The following year, AMSA was renamed the B-1 (B-1A), and new requests for proposals were issued in November 1969. On June 5, 1970, North American

Rockwell and General Electric were awarded contracts for airframe and engine development, respectively.

Three pre-production B-1As had flown by the end of 1976, but President Carter cancelled both the airframe and engine contracts on June 30, 1977, essentially dooming the project. However, the

With its wings at their forward 15-degree position for takeoff, B-1B 85-0082 of the 419th FLTS lifts off from its home at Edwards AFB. *Jim Dunn*

5

The bomber that almost wasn't has now been in operational service since October 1986. First flown in December 1974, the Rockwell B-1A program was canceled by President Carter in June 1977, only to be resurrected by President Reagan as the B-1B (shown here) in October 1981. The first B-1B made its debut flight in October 1984. *Jim Dunn*

Carter Administration did grant $442 million to build and equip a fourth B-1A with full offensive and defensive electronics systems. All four B-1As flew until funding ran out on April 30, 1981. The aircraft were stored at Edwards AFB pending final disposition.

Ronald Reagan defeated Carter in 1980 on a platform advocating a strong U.S. defense. Reagan reinstated the B-1 program on October 2, 1981, as a bridge between the B-52 and the Advanced Technology Bomber (which became the B-2). The B-1's blended wing/body, variable-geometry wings, four afterburning General Electric F-101-GE-102 turbofan engines, and AN/ASQ-184 offensive avionics system enables the B-1B to fly to the target at nap-of-the-earth heights to deliver its payload, whether conventional or nuclear.

Combat Veteran Lancers

B-1Bs were designed as strategic bombers capable of penetrating Soviet airspace to deliver nuclear weapons. Lancers remained on alert to deliver nuclear weapons, and thus did not directly participate in Operation Desert Storm. With the collapse of the Soviet Union and a decrease in strategic threats against the United States, B-1Bs stood down from the nuclear alert mission in 1997.

On December 17, 1998, B-1Bs got their first taste of combat in Operation Desert Fox. Launching from bases in Bahrain, B-1Bs from Dyess AFB, Texas, and Ellsworth AFB, South Dakota, destroyed Republican Guards barracks deep inside Iraq. From April to June of 1999, B-1Bs were deployed to RAF Fairford, Gloucestershire, England, during Allied bombing raids over Kosovo, known as Operation Allied Force. This operation was the first time the U.S. Air Force used the B-1, B-2, and B-52 in the same campaign. Although the B-1Bs only flew two percent of the combat sorties during Operation Allied Force, the type dropped more than 20 percent of all bombs during the conflict.

Most recently, B-1Bs retaliated against the Taliban for harboring known terrorists after the September 11, 2001, attacks. Known as Operation Enduring Freedom, B-1Bs dropped the type's first bombs over Afghanistan on October 7, 2001, less than one month after the terrorist attacks in New York and Washington, D.C.

B-1B 85-0067 *On Defense* is assigned to the Mohawk Warriors of the 28th BS at Dyess AFB, Texas. This squadron is responsible for aircrew training in the B-1B, and is part of the 7th BW. *Jim Dunn*

Its role as a conventional bomber has not meant an end to the debate about the future service of the bomber. In 2002, one active-duty and both of the ANG squadrons operating the B-1B had their mission eliminated. This resulted in the retirement of 33 aircraft and the relocation of the Thunderbirds of the 34th BS from the 366th BW at Mountain Home AFB to the 28th BW at Ellsworth AFB, South Dakota. *Greg L. Davis*

B-1Bs Beyond the New Millennium

The air force's B-1 fleet has been undergoing a reduction in force since a consolidation plan for the type was announced in June 2001. Aircraft based at McConnell AFB, Kansas; Mountain Home AFB, Idaho; and Robins AFB, Georgia, have been consolidated at Ellsworth AFB and Dyess AFB. Another 24 aircraft are slated for storage at the Aerospace Maintenance and Regeneration Center (AMARC) at Davis-Monthan AFB, Arizona. Fourteen of those B-1s will be stripped of usable parts, which will be returned to the air force's inventory. The money saved by parking two-dozen aircraft and reclaiming their usable parts will be used to upgrade the current fleet. Modifications to the B-1s, known as Block E upgrades, involve fitting the Lancers with new avionics computers and new armament capabilities, including the ability to deploy the Wind-Corrected Munitions Dispenser, the Joint Air-to-Surface Standoff Missile (JASSM), and the AGM-154 Joint Standoff Weapon. The 60 B-1Bs in the air force's fleet are expected to serve past the year 2023.

B-1B

Mission: Strategic bomber, tactical bomber
Builder: North American Rockwell/Boeing
Powerplant: Four General Electric F-101-GE-102 turbofan engines, each producing more than 30,000 pounds thrust with afterburner
Length: 146 feet
Height: 34 feet
Wingspan: 137 feet (extended forward), 79 feet (swept aft)
Weight: 190,000 pounds
Speed: 900-plus miles per hour (Mach 1.2 at sea level)
Armament: Three internal weapons bays—84 Mk-82 general purpose bombs or Mk-62 naval mines, 30 CBU-87/89 cluster munitions or CBU-97 Sensor Fused Weapons, and up to 24 GBU-31 JDAM GPS-guided bombs or Mk-84 general-purpose bombs
Crew: Four (aircraft commander, copilot, offensive systems officer, and defensive systems officer)
Unit Cost: $281 million per aircraft
Inventory:
      Active force – 54
      Air National Guard – 6

B-1B

UNITS ASSIGNED		
UNIT	**NICKNAME**	**TAIL CODE**
9th BS	Bats	DY
13th BS	Grim Reapers	DY
28th BS	Mohawk Warriors	DY
34th BS	Thunderbirds	EL
37th BS	Tigers	EL
419th FLTS		ED

Rolling out on runway 03L at Nellis AFB, B-2A 89-0128 *Spirit of Nebraska* was delivered as a Block 10 aircraft. This standard, which encompassed the first 16 B-2s, allowed for the delivery of freefall nuclear and conventional bombs in the traditional role of a strategic bomber. *Jim Dunn*

B-2A Spirit

Conceived during the height of the Cold War, Northrop's B-2 Spirit, more commonly known as the stealth bomber, provides the air force with a strategic bomber capable of penetrating deep into enemy territory. The B-2 can deliver conventional or nuclear weapons to high-value, strategic targets by avoiding detection from enemy air defense radar. Enemy radar is defeated through the bomber's minimal radar cross section, low-observable aerodynamic lines, radar-absorbent coating, and the use of composite materials that do not reflect radar energy, allowing the aircraft to fly virtually undetected.

Developed in complete secrecy in the late 1970s and early 1980s, the B-2A began life under the Advanced Technology Bomber

All 21 of the B-2As have now been upgraded to Block 30 standard. These aircraft have a maximum weapons payload of 50,000 pounds that are carried in side-by-side weapons bays, each equipped with a rotary launcher. *Jim Dunn*

The B-2 earned the distinction of conducting the longest combat mission in aviation history when, during the first three days of Operation Enduring Freedom in October 2001, six B-2s flew from Whiteman AFB to hit targets in Afghanistan. All of the aircraft landed at Diego Garcia before returning to Whiteman. *Lou Drummond*

Refueling from a 60th AMW KC-10, B-2A 82-1067 *Spirit of Arizona* was the second B-2 produced. *Lou Drummond*

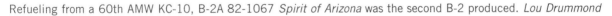

program. The air force had originally sought a fleet of 132 stealth bombers, but cost concerns and a redefinition of manned bomber mission profiles caused that number to be reduced to 75, then further down to 15 aircraft. The aircraft purchase was increased to 21 planes to enable the air force to field two squadrons of the advanced technology bomber, and to use one aircraft for an extended testing period. The B-2A Spirit was unveiled to the public on November 22, 1988, at air force Plant 42 in Palmdale, California. The B-2 took to the sky for the first time on July 17, 1989.

The B-2 carries a crew of only two: the pilot sits in the left seat and the mission commander in the right, with one additional crew or observer's seat. The crew sits forward of the twin bomb bays, which are inboard of the bomber's engines. The aircraft's flying wing shape is 69 feet long, about the length of an F-15, with a wing span of 172 feet, nearly equal to that of the B-52. To keep the aircraft stable in flight, the B-2 features an advanced fly-by-wire control system.

Stealth bombers have been delivered to the air force in three different series: Block 10, Block 20, and Block 30. Block 10 aircraft (production aircraft numbers 2 through 16) were capable of delivering B83 nuclear bombs or 16 Mk-84 2,000 gravity bombs. All Block 10 aircraft have been upgraded, and all B-2s will be Block 30 configured.

Block 20 stealth bombers (numbers 17 through 19) can deliver B61 nuclear weapons and have been retrofitted with the GATS/GAM (GPS-Aided Targeting System/GPS-Aided Munition) system, which dispenses up to 16 GAMs from bomb bay rotary launchers. Block 20 B-2s can also deploy CBU-87/B combined effects munition cluster bombs from low altitudes. To aid the pilots, a Terrain Avoidance/Terrain Following (TA/TF) flight control system has been added for low-level missions.

Block 30 B-2s (numbers 20 and 21, plus earlier upgraded aircraft) feature the Raytheon AN/APQ-181 radar suite with improved TA/TF system, a new radar warning receiver, and the Lockheed/Martin AN/APR-50 Defensive Management System, and can drop the new GBU-30 Joint Direct Attack Munition (JDAM) and Joint Stand Off Weapon I (JSOW), as well as a contrail elimination system for use in high-altitude flight. All aircraft will be modified to Block 30 standards by the end of fiscal year 2005.

The first B-2 was delivered to the 509th Bomb Wing at Whiteman AFB, Missouri, on December 17, 1993. The B-2 fleet received its first combat orders in March 1999 in support of Operation Allied Force in Kosovo. The air force reports that 509th Bomb Wing B-2s, flying from Missouri to Kosovo and back, "destroyed 33 percent of all Serbian targets in the first eight weeks."

B-2As from the 509th Bomb Wing also participated in Operation Enduring Freedom to rid Afghanistan of the Taliban regime and the Al Qaeda terrorist network. Stealth bombers dropped GPS-guided GAM-113 5,000-pound ground-penetration bombs against underground bunkers and cave complexes. The aircraft would depart Whiteman AFB and refuel en route to targets halfway around the globe in Afghanistan. After dropping their bombs, the B-2s would land at the U.S. base on the island of Diego Garcia in the Indian Ocean before returning to the United States.

B-2 crews from the 509th were part of the 40th Expeditionary Operations Group's 393rd Expeditionary Bomb Squadron for combat duty in Operation Iraqi Freedom. Beginning March 21, 2003, B-2s played a major role in striking strategic targets in Iraq using laser-guided munitions. For B-2s attacking targets in Iraq, it was a 35-hour, round-trip flight from Whiteman AFB.

Recently, the air force has deployed a new, transportable B-2 hangar system that enables the aircraft to operate from forward bases. The B-2 shelters are 126 feet long, 250 feet wide, and 55 feet tall. A number of B-2 transportable hangars have been erected at RAF Fairford, England, and at Diego Garcia. B-2s can deploy to Anderson AFB, Guam, where they can be maintained in existing air force hangars. The air force has determined that the B-2A will have a structural service life of 40,000 flying hours, which should keep the stealth bomber in frontline service until the year 2027.

B-2A SPIRIT

Mission: Strategic bomber

Builder: Northrop Grumman Corp.

Powerplant: Four General Electric F-118-GE-100 engines with 17,300 pounds thrust each

Length: 69 feet

Height: 17 feet

Wingspan: 172 feet

Weight: 336,000 pounds

Cruising Speed: 625 miles per hour (Mach 0.85)

Range: Intercontinental with aerial refueling

Armament: 40,000 pounds of conventional or nuclear weapons

Crew: Two pilots

Unit Cost: $1.3 billion

Date Deployed: December 1993

Inventory:

Active force — 21

B-2A SPIRIT

UNITS ASSIGNED

UNIT	NICKNAME	TAIL CODE
325th BS	Alley Oop	WM
393rd BS	Tigers	WM
419th FLTS		ED

High over the Indian Ocean en route to Afghanistan on an Enduring Freedom mission, this B-52H based on Diego Garcia carries 1,000-pound CBU-89 Gator cluster bombs under both wings. *Lou Drummond*

B-52H Stratofortress

Although the B-52's lineage can be traced directly to a June 1945 memo from the Army Air Force to the Air Material Command, the G and H model Stratofortresses serving the U.S. Air Force are substantially newer and significantly different from the original models. The XB-52 first flew on October 2, 1952, and production versions quickly followed. Early production models included 3 B-52As; 50 B-52Bs (27 were modified to RB-52B reconnaissance-capable configuration); 35 B-52Cs; 170 B-52Ds; 100 B-52Es; and 89 B-52Fs.

B-52D and F models, and later B-52Gs, formed the backbone of the U.S. bombing campaign in North Vietnam. During Operation Linebacker II (December 18–29, 1972) B-52s flew 729 sorties against 34 targets in North Vietnam. More than 15,000 tons of bombs rained down on industrial targets, rail yards, airfields, petroleum processing and storage facilities, as well as the enemy's electric power generating plants. To defend against the B-52s, the North Vietnamese launched 884 surface-to-air missiles, hitting 24 bombers and destroying 15.

Boeing's Seattle, Washington, and Wichita, Kansas, factories both produced aircraft through the F model. After the last B-52F

was delivered from the Seattle plant in November 1958, Boeing transferred all engineering and manufacturing responsibilities for the aircraft to their Wichita factory.

Boeing Wichita built 193 G model Stratofortresses, which also underwent combat in Vietnam, before switching production to the B-52H. The H model is equipped with eight Pratt & Whitney TF-33-P-3 turbofan engines capable of 17,000 pounds thrust each, developing 50 percent more thrust at takeoff, and 20 percent more at cruising speeds as compared to the B-52G. New engine nacelles, wider in the front to accommodate the TF-33's two-stage fan section, make the H model readily identifiable.

In addition to the engine change, the other noticeable external difference between the H and previous models is the defensive armament. Earlier B-52s carried a stinger tail turret with four .50-caliber machine guns, while the H model was introduced with the new AN/ASG-21 fire control radar and a General Electric six-barrel M61A1 Vulcan 20mm cannon.

Internally, the B-52H features terrain-avoidance radar for nape-of-the-earth penetration missions, as well as night-vision

Besides being able to carry a wide variety of unpowered, freefall munitions under its wings, the B-52H is the only aircraft in the inventory that can carry either nuclear or conventional air-launched cruise missiles (ALCM/CALCM). *Greg L. Davis*

goggle capabilities and forward-looking infrared and low-light-level TV for low-altitude flight and target acquisition. The final B-52H was delivered to the 4137th Strategic Bomb Wing based at Minot, North Dakota, signaling the end of the B-52 line, in which 744 aircraft of all variants had been built.

During Operation Desert Storm, B-52Gs from the 2nd Bomb Wing (BW) (homebased at Barksdale AFB, Louisiana), 42nd BW (Loring AFB, Maine), 93rd BW (Castle AFB, California), 97th BW (Eaker AFB, Arkansas), 379th BW (Wurtsmith AFB, Michigan), and the 416th BW (Griffiss AFB, New York), participated in the aerial

The vast majority of the B-52H fleet still retains the capability to deliver nuclear weapons. An advanced cruise missile, the AGM-129, with either a 5 or 150 kiloton warhead, can be employed. A single B-52H can carry 12 of these weapons. *Jim Dunn*

Five crewmembers are crammed into a two-level workspace on the B-52. The pilot, co-pilot, and electronic warfare officer are on the upper level; the radar navigator/bombardier and route navigator are on a lower deck. *Greg L. Davis*

Old Crow Express II, B-52H 60-0055 from the Bomber Barons of the 23rd BS at Minot AFB, North Dakota, salutes B-52G 57-6492, a veteran of 51 Desert Storm missions. *Jim Dunn*

campaign. On January 16, 1991, hours before the war against Iraq began, seven 2nd BW B-52s took off from Louisiana in darkness to arrive within range of Iraq mid-morning on January 17. Flying more than 35,000 miles round-trip in 14 hours, the B-52s flew to a point in northwest Saudi Arabia and fired 35 conventional air-launched cruise missiles (CALAM) at eight targets. The Al Musayyib Thermal Power Plant was the B-52's primary target, and a number of CALAMs struck command, control, and communications (C3) and telecommunications infrastructure targets.

After the CALAM mission, a number of B-52s flew low-level bombing raids, and on the third night of the air war, they attacked the oil refinery complex at Uwayjah. One B-52 was damaged by an Iraqi SA-3 surface-to-air missile during the raid, and the decision was made to fly all future B-52 raids at altitude.

In the ensuing days, B-52s flew 99 strikes against the Iraqi Air Force infrastructure, such as airfields and aircraft on the ground. Another 303 strikes by B-52s hit oil refineries and storage areas, command and control targets, missile sites, and locations where weapons of mass destruction were suspected of being manufactured.

As the war progressed, B-52s deployed to RAF Fairford, United Kingdom; Moron Air Base, Spain; Jeddah (King Abdul Aziz International Airport), Saudi Arabia; and the American air base on Diego Garcia in the Indian Ocean. With bases closer to the front lines, B-52s were tasked with attacking Iraq's Republican Guard—its men, armor, and supply dumps. Known as area targets, men and tanks were susceptible to the B-52's ability to rain down bombs from 50,000 feet, carpeting an area with explosives. In all, B-52s

The Devil's Own (B-52H 60-0059) is assigned to the Red Devils of the 96th BS at Barksdale AFB, Louisiana. *Jim Dunn*

Deployed at no higher than 135 knots, the 44-foot drag chute aids in braking the BUFF. *Jim Dunn*

flew 1,741 sorties during the Gulf War, averaging 41 missions per day, and dropping 72,000 bombs, or 30 percent of all bombs dropped in the Gulf War.

After the September 11, 2001, terrorist attacks on the United States, B-52Hs flew missions over Afghanistan from Diego Garcia in support of Operation Enduring Freedom. In addition to attacking terrorist targets with various types of bombs, the B-52s participated in the air force's psychological war by dropping M129 leaflet bombs. In February and March 2003, B-52s began deploying from Minot AFB, North Dakota (23rd Bomb Squadron), as well as Barksdale AFB (2nd BW) in preparation for the second war with Iraq.

Currently, the B-52H is expected to serve the U.S. Air Force until the year 2025. Design studies have looked at the feasibility of changing the aircraft's engines. In April 2003, a Defense Science Board recommended replacement of the B-52's TF-33 engines, citing age, fuel consumption, and the cost of aerial refueling—$17.50 per gallon—as reasons to accelerate the retrofit program.

B-52H STRATOFORTRESS

Mission: Strategic Bomber
Builder: Boeing Military Aircraft Co.
Powerplant: Eight Pratt & Whitney TF33-P-3/103 turbofan engines rated at 17,000 pounds thrust each
Length: 159 feet, 4 inches
Height: 40 feet, 8 inches
Wingspan: 185 feet
MGTOW: 488,000 pounds
Speed: 650 miles per hour (Mach 0.86)
Range: Unrefueled 8,800 miles (7,652 nautical miles)
Armament: 70,000 pounds of bombs, missiles, and naval mines; M-61A-1 20mm Gatling gun in the tail for defense
Crew: Five (aircraft commander, pilot, radar navigator, navigator, and electronic warfare officer)
Unit Cost: $74 million
Date Deployed: May 9, 1961 (B-52H)
Inventory:

        Active force – 85
        Reserve – 9

B-52H STRATOFORTRESS

UNITS ASSIGNED

UNIT	NICKNAME	TAIL CODE
11th BS	Mr. Jiggs	LA
20th BS	Buccaneers	LA
96th BS	Red Devils	LA
23rd BS	Bomber Barons	MT
93rd BS	Indian Outlaws	BD
419th FLTS		ED

The first KC-135A Stratotanker was delivered to the U.S. Air Force in 1957. Today, the re-engined KC-135E and R models are still the backbone of the USAF aerial refueling fleet. While the crew of KC-135E 58-0080, from the 191st ARS of the Utah ANG, doesn't expect any receivers at this altitude, they get an A+ for a great photo flyby. *Jim Dunn*

TANKERS AND TRANSPORTS

KC-135 Stratotanker and C-135 Stratolifter

For more than 40 years, the mainstay of America's aerial refueling force has been the Boeing-built KC-135 Stratotanker. Developed from the company's model 367-80, the aircraft features a 35-degree swept wing developed from the aerodynamic lessons learned from the B-47 and B-52. Initially, the KC-135 and its transport version, the C-135 Stratolifter, were powered by four Pratt & Whitney J57P-59W water-injected engines. It flew its maiden flight on August 31, 1956, with squadron deliveries beginning the following June.

The Stratotanker's main deck can carry passengers or cargo pallets, which are loaded through a port-side, up-swinging cargo door located forward of the wing. Filling the lower compartments of the aircraft are gas tanks for off-loading fuel through the flying boom, controlled by the boom operator at the rear of the aircraft. Highly trained flying boom operators lie face-down on a cot, looking through a large window giving a 140-degree field of vision. Reaching below the cot, the operator controls the flying boom's movements with a joystick. Buttons on the joystick enable the operator to change approach lights under the tanker to signal the receiver aircraft to move forward or backward, left or right. This method of communication is used when radio silence is the utmost concern.

This view from the cockpit of a KC-10 give the receiver's perspective on refueling from a KC-135E. While the pilot of the receiving aircraft maneuvers into position with help from guide lights on the forward underside of the KC-135, the tanker's boom operator extends the probe into position and flies the boom into the receptacle on the receiving aircraft. *Jim Dunn*

Fifty former KC-135Qs, models that were given separate tanks to carry JP-7 fuel for the SR-71, have been re-designated as KC-135Ts. Most of these aircraft, including KC-135T 60-0337, are assigned to the 92nd ARW at Fairchild AFB, Washington. *Jim Dunn*

Nose art is popular and widespread throughout the tanker fleet, while tail codes are only seen on tankers in ACC and PACAF. Perhaps the most unique tail marking in use is the square D, which is carried on the KC-135Rs of the 100th ARW at RAF Mildenhall, England. It pays tribute to the famous World War II B-17 unit, the Bloody 100th Bomb Group. *The Latest Rumor* (KC-135R 63-8017) is with the 351st ARS of the 100th ARW. *Jim Dunn*

With an executive white-over-blue color scheme and the title "United States of America," KC-135E 57-2589 serves with Special Missions Hawaii, 65th AS, to support Commander Pacific Air Forces. The KC-135R 61-0320 provides support for test missions at Edwards AFB with the 452nd FLTS. *Jim Dunn*

ABOVE AND RIGHT: The U.S. Navy receives a great deal of its aerial refueling support from USAF KC-10s and KC-135s. Photographed off of Hawaii during RIMPAC 2000, this KC-135E from the 116th ARS Washington ANG provides support for an F-14 of Carrier Air Wing Fourteen from the USS *Abraham Lincoln*. *Richard Vander Muelen*

The first major upgrading of the KC-135 involved the addition of Pratt & Whitney JT3D engines (similar to the military TF33-PW-102). The program began in 1982, and the more than 200 aircraft receiving this engine retrofit were redesignated KC-135E. The airframe of the KC-135E has the ability to serve in the fleet well past the year 2040, but the technology of its engines may limit the aircraft's service life. Currently, the air force and Department of Defense are considering the possibility of phasing out the KC-135E and leasing aerial refueling-equipped Boeing 767s.

To increase the KC-135's performance, the air force elected to retrofit its remaining A model Stratotankers with the 22,224-pound thrust CFM F108-CF-100 turbofan engines, similar to the commercial CFM56 that powers the Boeing 737-400. This modification program began in 1980, and those aircraft that have received F108 engines are redesignated KC-135R (formerly KC-135As) or 135T (formerly KC-135Qs, which were specially configured to off-load JP-7 fuel to the SR-71). First flight of a KC-135R took place in August 1982, and deliveries to Strategic Air Command Squadrons began in July 1984. The upgraded KC-135s can operate at a higher gross weight from shorter runways, and off-load fifty percent more fuel than the KC-135A. Stratotankers have also undergone service life extension programs to reskin the undersurface of the wings and rear fuselage areas. Some KC-135s have also been fitted with probe and drogue-refueling systems for operations with NATO and other Allied air forces.

The KC-135 fleet underwent a series of avionics upgrades in the 1990s. The Pacer CRAG (CRAG — Compass, Radio, and GPS) program was initiated to convert the KC-135, and other air force aircraft, from a three-person cockpit to a two-person configuration, eliminating the navigator. In addition, the cockpit was upgraded with GPS and an

KC-135 STRATOTANKER & C-135 STRATOLIFTER

Mission: Aerial refueling and cargo/personnel transport

Builder: Boeing

Powerplant: Four CFM F108-CF-100 turbofans rated at 22,224 pounds thrust each

Length: 136 feet, 3 inches

Height: 41 feet, 8 inches

Wingspan: 130 feet, 10 inches

Weight: 322,500 maximum takeoff

Speed: 530 miles per hour at 30,000 feet

Range: 1,500 miles with 150,000 pounds of transfer fuel; ferry mission, up to 11,015 miles

Armament: None

Crew: Three (pilot, co-pilot, boom operator)

Unit Cost: KC-135A, $26.1 million; KC-135R, $53 million

Date Deployed: August 1956

Inventory:

       Active force – 253

       Air National Guard – 222

       Reserve – 70

KC-135 STRATOTANKER & C-135 STRATOLIFTER

UNITS ASSIGNED

UNIT	NICKNAME	LOCATION
18th ARS	Kanza	McConnell AFB, KS
54th ARS	Jesters	Altus AFB, OK
55th ARS	Master of the Art	Altus AFB, OK
63rd ARS	Flying Jennies	Selfridge ANGB, MI
72nd ARS		Grissom ARB, IN
74th ARS		Grissom ARB, IN
77th ARS	Totin Tigers	Seymour Johnson AFB, NC
91st ARS		McDill AFB, FL
92nd ARS	Black Hawks	Fairchild AFB, WA
93rd ARS		Fairchild AFB, WA
96th ARS	Screaming Eagles	Fairchild AFB, WA
97th ARS		Fairchild AFB, WA
99th ARS		Robins AFB, GA
106th ARS	Rebels	Birmingham IAP, AL
108th ARS		Scott AFB, IL
116th ARS	Ace of Spades	Fairchild AFB, WA
117th ARS	Kansas Coyotes	Forbes Field, KS
126th ARS		Gen. Mitchell ARS, WI
127th ARS	Jayhawks	McConnell AFB, KS
132nd ARS	Maineiacs	Bangor IAP, ME
133rd ARS		Pease ANGB, NH
136th ARS	New York's Finest	Niagara Falls IAP, NY
141st ARS	Tigers	McGuire AFB, NJ
145th ARS	Jazz	Rickenbacker ANGB, OH
146th ARS		Pittsburgh IAP, PA
147th ARS		Pittsburgh IAP, PA
150th ARS		McGuire AFB, NJ
151st ARS		McGhee Tyson ANGB, TN
153rd ARS	Magnolia Militia	Key Field ANGB, MS
166th ARS	Sluff	Rickenbacker ANGB, OH
168th ARS		Eielson AFB, AK
173rd ARS	Huskers	Lincoln ANGB, NE
191st ARS	Salty Guard	Salt Lake City, UT
196th ARS	Grizzlies	March AFB, CA
197th ARS	Copperheads	Phoenix Sky Harbor, AZ
203rd ARS		HH
314th ARS	Warhawks	Beale AFB, CA
336th ARS	Rats	March AFB, CA
344th ARS	Ravens	McConnell AFB, KS
349th ARS	Blue Knights	McConnell AFB, KS
350th ARS	Red Falcons	McConnell AFB, KS
351st ARS		RAF Mildenhall, England
384th ARS	Square Patches	McConnell AFB, KS
465th ARS	Okies	Tinker AFB, OK
905th ARS	Rhinos	Grand Forks AFB, ND
906th ARS	Dakrats	Grand Forks AFB, ND
909th ARS	Young Tigers	ZZ
911th ARS	Red Eagles	Grand Forks AFB, ND
912th ARS	Vipers	Grand Forks AFB, ND

Of the 732 KC-135s delivered to the USAS, 161 aircraft belonging to the Air Force reserve and ANG were upgraded with TF-33-PW-102 engines obtained from retired 707 airliners purchased by the USAF. These aircraft were designated KC-135E and entered service in July 1982. *Jim Dunn*

off-the-shelf TCAS (Traffic Collision Avoidance System) used by the airlines, thus reducing avionics maintenance issues and increasing safety during formation flying. Also included in the modification are a flight data recorder, cockpit voice recorder, and emergency locator transmitter (ELT). Pacer CRAG modifications save the air force approximately $10 million per year in maintenance costs.

A number of Stratolifters serve in the VIP transport role. The C-135B/C/E and EC-135E/K/N are used to transport military staffs as well as the commander in chief of the U.S. Special Operations Command. It is reported that these VIP variants will soon be phased out in favor of smaller, more economical aircraft.

In preparation for the Gulf War, an Atlantic and a Pacific Air Refueling Bridge was established. More than 70 KC-135s flew from

nine countries to help more than 1,000 aircraft deploy to the region. During that air campaign, 193 KC-135A, E, Q, and R were in the theater. Another 69 were flying in direct support of the air war by tanking aircraft en route to the Gulf region or returning. Tankers gave battlefield commanders the flexibility to reassign targets without strike planes having to return to base for more fuel. Stratotankers in theater flew 13,587 missions, off-loading more than 517 million pounds of fuel during Operation Desert Storm. In addition, Stratotankers carried 4,817 short-tons of cargo and delivered 14,208 passengers during the war.

As America hunts for terrorists in Operation Enduring Freedom, KC-135s are playing a major role, enabling aircraft to strike at the heart of Afghanistan and Iraq.

KC-10A Extender

One lesson the United States learned from its support of Israel during the 1973 Yom Kippur War was that the U.S. Air Force needed an additional refueling and cargo-carrying aircraft, and it had to be capable of refueling in flight. A request for proposals was released for an Advanced Tanker Cargo Aircraft (ATCA). Both Boeing and McDonnell Douglas presented versions of aircraft already in production; Boeing offered a military version of its 747 freighter, and McDonnell Douglas presented its DC-10-30CF (convertible freighter). The DC-10-based proposal was selected because it could carry a heavier load from a shorter runway than the 747.

McDonnell Douglas' winning design was designated KC-10A Extender, and orders eventually totaling 60 aircraft were issued. The Extender shares 88 percent of the parts that make up commercial DC-10s. The KC-10A made its first flight on July 12, 1980, and during air-to-air refueling tests tanked its first aircraft, a C-5, on October 30, 1980. Strategic Air Command received its first aircraft on March 17, 1981, and the initial aircraft was delivered to Barksdale AFB, Louisiana. On September 17, 1987, KC-10A serial number 82-0190 was destroyed by fire, marking the type's only serious incident.

Forty KC-10s were modified with wingtip-mounted drogue refueling pods that enable three receiving aircraft to tank simultaneously. The flying boom can transfer 1,100 gallons per minute, while the drogue system can off-load 470 gallons per minute. In addition, the aircraft can carry 75 soldiers and 170,000 pounds of cargo 4,400 miles. Unlike the cramped quarters of the KC-135 boom operator, the KC-10A provides a seat for the aerial refueling operator (ARO), an instructor's seat and control panel, plus a third seat for another student.

Once the KC-10 became operational, it quickly established high standards of performance. On June 21, 1982, a KC-10 transferred a record 67,400 pounds of fuel to a C-141 only 750 miles from the South Pole in support of Operation Deep Freeze. The following year, KC-10s flew in support of Operation Early Call, the monitoring of Libyan airspace by E-3A AWACS aircraft.

The KC-10s answered the call to battle during Operation Urgent Fury, the assault to liberate the island of Grenada. Beginning on October 22, 1983, KC-10s and KC-135s refueled transports en route to and from the island. Extenders also refueled aircraft during the April 1986 Operation El Dorado Canyon, when the United States struck targets in Libya in response to numerous terrorist acts traced to that African nation. That same year, KC-10s participated in Operation Just Cause, the ouster of Panamanian dictator Manuel Noriega. KC-10s and KC-135s transferred more than 12 million pounds of fuel to more than 100 aircraft during 256 sorties in Operation Just Cause.

During Operation Desert Storm, 46 KC-10s were busy tanking U.S. and Coalition aircraft. Combat in the Gulf region involved extensive use of the KC-10's probe and drogue refueling system to accommodate U.S. Navy and Marine Corps aircraft as well as planes from our allies. During Desert Storm, KC-10 crews flew

The Cadillac of the heavies in the USAF inventory is the McDonnell Douglas KC-10A Extender. Based on the DC-10-30CF McDonnell Douglas was awarded the contract in the Advanced Tanker Cargo Aircraft competition in 1977 over a modified Boeing 747. A total of 60 KC-10As were delivered to the USAF between 1981 and 1988. *Lou Drummond*

Forty Extenders have been modified to receive underwing-mounted hose-and-drogue pods, which make it possible to refuel three aircraft at a time. Navy and Allied aircraft equipped with refueling probes can receive 400 gallons a minute from this system, while the main boom can also have an extended hose-and-drogue pumping 600 gallons a minute. *Jim Dunn (above) and Lou Drummond (below)*

Besides its duties as an aerial refueler, the KC-10 is a major airlift asset for the USAF. With a strengthened main desk and a 11 foot, 8 inch by 8 foot, 6 inch cargo door, the KC-10 can be loaded with 27 standard pallets or vehicles such as these Humvees that are about to be loaded. Airline type seating for up to 75 passengers can also be installed. *Jim Dunn*

3,278 sorties and off-loaded 283,616,000 pounds of fuel. After the Gulf War, in 1996 and 1998, KC-10s again supported the deployment of F-117A Stealth Fighters and B-52s to the Persian Gulf, during attempts by the United States to convince Saddam Hussein to allow United Nations weapons inspectors to complete their jobs. Again in 2003, KC-10s refueled aircraft operating against Iraq.

KC-10A EXTENDER

Mission: Aerial refueling, transport
Builder: McDonnell Douglas (now Boeing)
Powerplant: Three General Electric CF6-50C2 turbofans rated at 52,500 pounds thrust each
Length: 181 feet, 7 inches
Height: 58 feet, 1 inch
Wingspan: 165 feet, 4.5 inches
MGTOW: 590,000 pounds
Speed: 619 miles per hour (Mach 0.825)
Range: 4,400 miles (3,800 nautical miles) with cargo; 11,500 miles (10,000 nautical miles) without cargo
Off-loadable Fuel: 200,000 pounds
Crew: Four (aircraft commander, pilot, flight engineer, and boom operator)
Unit Cost: $88.4 million
Date Deployed: March 1981
Inventory:
        Active force – 59

The KC-10 was designed for a service life of 30,000 hours, which should see the aircraft flying through the year 2043. The determining factor for the KC-10's long life will be the availability of spare parts. In the post-September 11, 2001, economic downturn, many commercial carriers elected to park their DC-10 fleets. If these aircraft and their associated spare parts inventories are scrapped, it will severely limit the air force's long-term access to replacement parts. Currently, the 60th and 349th Air Mobility Wing (AMW) Travis AFB, California, and the 305th and 514th AMW, McGuire AFB, New Jersey operate KC-10As.

KC-10A EXTENDER

UNITS ASSIGNED		
UNIT	**NICKNAME**	**BASE**
2nd ARS	Second to None	McGuire AFB, NJ
6th ARS		Travis AFB, CA
9th ARS	Universal	Travis AFB, CA
32nd ARS	Capt. Shreve Sqn	McGuire AFB, NJ
70th ARS		Travis AFB, CA
76th ARS	Freedom's Spirit	McGuire AFB, NJ
78th ARS		McGuire AFB, NJ
79th ARS		Travis AFB, CA

From its status as the first jet airlifter to leading airborne assaults and low-level special operations missions, as well as performing thousands of humanitarian missions on every continent, the Starlifter was for the USAF the right aircraft at the right time. When the final chapter is written after more than 40 years of service, the C-141 will be listed as one of the most valuable airlifters to ever serve. *Jim Dunn*

C-141 Starlifter

Lockheed's C-141 Starlifter began life in December 1960 as Logistics Transport System 476L at a time when the air force's cargo-carrying aircraft fleet was composed entirely of piston-powered planes. The C-141 was designed as a medium-range, all-jet transport capable of carrying up to 60,000 pounds of strategic cargo over 3,500 nautical miles, hauling/dropping supplies within a combat theater, or deploying airborne troops.

Lockheed's C-141A competed against designs from Boeing, Convair, and Douglas. The Starlifter won that competition, and the first aircraft rolled out in August 1963. It featured a 70-foot long, 10-foot, 4 inch-wide by 9-foot, 1.25-inch-tall fuselage cross-section.

A major upgrade to the flight deck and defensive systems produced the first of 64 C-141Cs in October 1998. These aircraft featured a digital glass cockpit, GPS, and updated flight controls. Defensive countermeasurers against shoulder-launched surface-to-air missiles were also installed. All of the C-141Cs will be assigned to either AFRC or ANG squadrons. *Jim Dunn*

The Starlifter was used extensively in Vietnam, transporting everything from men and munitions into the theater to the repatriation of 500 prisoners of war and the delivery of 949 Southeast Asian orphans back to the United States. After the war, the air force contracted with Lockheed to modify its 271 C-141A models to B model configuration with a fuselage extension of 23 feet, 4 inches, as well as in-flight refueling capabilities. This fuselage extension, comprising a 13-foot, 4-inch plug inserted ahead of the wing and a 10-foot plug aft of the main wing, increased the aircraft's

C-141 STARLIFTER

Mission: Strategic airlift

Builder: Lockheed

Powerplant: Four Pratt & Whitney TF33-P-7 turbofan engines rated at 21,000 pounds thrust each

Length: 168 feet, 3.5 inches

Height: 39 feet, 3 inches

Wingspan: 159 feet, 11 inches

MGTOW: 323,000 pounds

Speed: 425 miles per hour

Range: Intercontinental with aerial refueling

Crew: Five

Unit Cost: $42.3 million (Fiscal Year 1998 dollars)

Date Deployed: October 1964 (C-141A); December 1979 (C-141B)

Inventory:

Active force — 35

Air National Guard — 16

Reserve — 40

C-141 STARLIFTER

UNITS ASSIGNED

UNIT	NICKNAME	BASE
6th AS	Bully Beef Express	McGuire AFB, NJ
89th AS	Rhinos	Wright-Patt. AFB, OH
155th AS	Memphis Belle	Memphis IAP, TN
183rd AS	Wings of the Deep South	Jackson IAP, MS
356th AS		Wright-Patt. AFB, OH
729th AS	Pegasus	March AFB, CA
730th AS	First Associate Reserve	March AFB, CA
732nd AS	Rams	McGuire AFB, NJ
756th AS		Andrews AFB, MD

internal carrying volume 75 percent, to 11,399 cubic feet. The C-141B's 93-foot-long fuselage can accommodate 208 ground troops, 168 fully equipped paratroopers, or 103 litter patients plus attendants, or a combination of seats, cargo pallets, and vehicles.

Combat came quickly for the B model, as C-141s from Charleston, Travis, McChord, McGuire, and Norton AFBs supported Operation Urgent Fury to rescue American citizens from the island of Grenada in August 1983. Next, in Operation Just Cause, 63 C-141s participated in the initial assault on Panama, during which more than 2,000 men of the 82nd Airborne Division were airlifted from their base in the Carolinas and parachuted into combat. Once fighting had ended, C-141s began flying humanitarian aid into Panama.

During Operation Desert Shield, airlift operations were code named Operation Volant Wind. Troops were airlifted to Saudi Arabia via Rhein-Main Air Force Base, Germany, or Torrejon and Zaragoza Air Bases, Spain. The flight took 15 hours, and Starlifter crews would change at the stops en route.

During Operation Desert Storm, C-141s flew 1,766 sorties, averaging 55 per day. Starlifters transported 482,000 passengers into and out of the Gulf region, delivered 15 air-transportable hospitals with a capacity of 750 beds, and moved 513,000 tons of cargo. To accomplish this, more than 80 percent of the Starlifters in service supported Operation Desert Storm.

Immediately after the September 11, 2001, terrorist attacks, Starlifter crews from the 445th Airlift Wing at Wright-Patterson AFB, Ohio, transported California's Task Force 3, from Menlo Park, and Washington Task Force 1, from the Puget Sound area, to McGuire AFB, New Jersey, for deployment to assist in rescue and recovery at the World Trade Center and the Pentagon. Starlifters supported Operation Enduring Freedom in 2003, and a number of the aircraft transported what the Department of Defense calls "hard-core terrorists that have demonstrated a willingness to escape, take their own lives, or kill others." C-141 crews are making the 15-hour flights from the Gulf region to Camp X-Ray at Guantanamo Bay, Cuba, where the terrorists are detained and interrogated for information about future planned attacks on the United States and American citizens. In addition, a number of C-141s deploy men and equipment in the Special Operations, Low Level support role.

The air force's fleet of Starlifters will soon mark its 40th year of service to the air force. With age comes fatigue, and a number of flight restrictions have been placed on the C-141.

The aging fleet of Starlifters will be retired from the air force's inventory by 2006 and be replaced by the Boeing-built C-17, which is larger and more economical to operate. Designed for a life of 30,000 flying hours, the C-141 fleet has served its country well; most aircraft have flown more than 28,000 hours, and high-time examples have surpassed 40,000—a testament to the aircraft's designers and the crews that fly and maintain the Starlifter.

C-5A/B/C Galaxy

To many people throughout the world, the United States is represented by the awesome size and power of the air force's Lockheed C-5 Galaxy. When America sends relief supplies to a war-torn nation, or one suffering from a natural disaster, those supplies traditionally arrive in a C-5 Galaxy. To project power, the C-5 has been the primary airlifter that has delivered troops and their outsized equipment to distant bases.

In the early 1960s, the Military Air Transport Service (MATS) was searching for an all-jet-powered replacement aircraft that could carry oversized loads that were then being flown in Douglas' C-133 Cargomaster. The Department of Defense's specific operational requirement for the C-5, released in June 1963, called for an aircraft that could carry between 100,000 and 130,000 pounds of cargo 4,000 miles, at a speed of 506 miles per hour, and above the weather at 30,000 feet. The aircraft had to be able to operate from unimproved airstrips. The air force wanted the new airlifter ready for squadron service in June 1970. In June 1964, the air force Systems Command awarded contracts for its CX-HLS (Cargo Experimental – Heavy Logistics System) to Boeing, Douglas, and Lockheed.

This C-5 is about to be returned to service after a 21-day refurbishment that included inspection and replacement of worn parts, repair of minor damage, and touch-up painting. *Jim Dunn*

A pair of C-5As, 68-0213 and 68-0216, was modified to accept special payloads in support of Space Shuttle missions. Designated C-5Cs, both aircraft are based with the 60th AMW at Travis AFB. *Jim Dunn*

Lockheed won the design competition, and rolled out the first C-5A, serial number 68-8303, on March 2, 1968. The aircraft made its first flight three months later, on June 30, 1968, and the 443rd Military Airlift Wing received the first operational aircraft in December 1969. A total of 81 C-5As were built. Two C-5As had their rear upper deck seating area removed so the aircraft could accommodate outsized loads in support of the Space Shuttle Program. After undergoing the conversion to space container transport system (SCTS) configuration, both aircraft were redesignated C-5C.

The Galaxy's cavernous interior is 121 feet, 1 inch long by 19 feet wide, and 13 feet, 6 inches tall. The nose and tail ramps add another 23 feet, 6 inches of floor space, giving the interior 34,795 cubic feet of storage capacity. The C-5's enormous fuselage can accommodate 6 AH-64 Apache helicopters or 6 M-2/M-3 Bradley infantry vehicles. If loaded with cargo only, the C-5 can carry loads on its 36 cargo pallet positions.

Although the C-5 was designed to operate from unimproved airstrips, its cargo-carrying capacity proved too large for intra-theater operations. The C-5 flew its first mission to Vietnam on July 9, 1970, delivering supplies to Cam Ranh Bay. The plane's cargo had to be off-loaded and repalletized to fit into C-130s, which transshipped the materiel to the front lines. In 1972, when Da Nang was under siege, C-5s delivered 1.6 million pounds of equipment, ranging from tanks and helicopters to food and ammunition. Each Galaxy was unloaded and back in the air in less than 40 minutes.

By 1973, as the war in Vietnam wound down, C-5s began flying the first humanitarian airlift operations of their careers. On January 23, 1973, all 5,300 residents of the island of Heimaey, Iceland, were forced to evacuate when a volcano erupted. For nearly 60 days, cargo aircraft, including C-5s, flew in emergency supplies, heavy equipment, and relief workers, and flew out hospital patients and evacuees. In August and September of that year, C-5s and C-141s delivered more than 2,400 tons of relief supplies to flood victims in Pakistan.

The C-5 has internal ramps that allow cargo to be rolled on and off, and it can also kneel to adjust to the height of the ground equipment that is available. *Jim Dunn*

In 1981, all C-5As were retrofitted with new wing boxes to eliminate a cracking problem. In the following year, the air force contracted with Lockheed to build an additional 50 aircraft with the strengthened wing box, new 43,000-pound thrust General Electric TF39-GE-IC engines, and a series of avionics improvements. These new aircraft were designated C-5B, and the first aircraft was rolled out at Lockheed's Marietta, Georgia, factory on July 12, 1985.

During Operations Desert Shield/Desert Storm, C-5s flew 42 percent of the cargo and 18.6 percent of the passenger missions to supply the operation. During the actual war, from January 16 to February 28, 1991, C-5s flew 740 sorties, which is an

The C-5 is one of the few remaining USAF aircraft requiring a flight engineer, a position essential to the operation of the complex systems on the aircraft. *Jim Dunn*

The C-5's ability to handle outsize loads, from mobile hospitals to mobile bridging systems, makes it an extremely valuable airlifter. *Jim Dunn*

Between 1983 and 1987, the air force ordered 50 C-5Bs with uprated TF39-GE-1C turbofan engines and a strengthened wing box. *Jim Dunn*

impressive number, considering that most Galaxy missions flown from the United States to the Gulf region averaged 16 hours. In addition, C-5s helped form an "air bridge" from the United States to B-52 bases in Spain, the United Kingdom, and Diego Garcia, transporting supplies of bombs for the offensive against Iraq.

The air force plans to operate the C-5 Galaxy until the year 2040. To meet this goal, the aircraft will undergo a series of modernizations. The first phase of the upgrade program focuses on the cockpit with a new digital flight control system that incorporates seven 6-inch by 8-inch liquid crystal flat-panel displays, the addition of global positioning capabilities to the inertial navigation system, and the installation of a TCAS (Traffic Collision and Avoidance System) and enhanced ground proximity warning system. The TCAS upgrade, which can track up to 50 aircraft within 80 nautical miles, has been completed in all 126 of the air force's C-5As and Bs.

In December 2001, Lockheed Martin Aeronautics Company won a system development and demonstration contract for the C-5's reliability enhancement and re-engining program (RERP), the second phase of the C-5 modernization. Valued at $1.1 billion, RERP calls for new General Electric CF-6-80-C2 engines supported by newly designed Goodyear Aerospace engine pylons. A system development and demonstration contract calls for Lockheed Martin to complete engine upgrades on four aircraft by the year 2007.

C-5A/B/C GALAXY

Mission: Strategic Airlift
Builder: Lockheed Martin
Powerplant: Four General Electric TF39-GE-IC capable of 43,000 pounds thrust each
Length: 247 feet, 8 inches
Height: 65 feet, 1 inch
Wingspan: 222 feet, 8 inches
MGTOW: 840,000 pounds (wartime)
Speed: 518 miles per hour
Range: 6,320 miles (empty), global with inflight refueling
Crew: Seven (pilot, copilot, two flight engineers, three load masters)
Unit Cost: $179 million (C-5B)
Date Deployed: 1980 (C-5B)

C-5A/B/C GALAXY

UNITS ASSIGNED

UNIT	NICKNAME	BASE
3rd AS		Dover AFB, DE
9th AS	Pelicans	Dover AFB, DE
21st AS	Beeliners	Travis AFB, CA
22nd AS	Mulies	Travis AFB, CA
56th AS	Jumbo Country	Altus AFB, OK
68th AS		Kelly Field, TX
137th AS	Fearless Ones	Stewart ANGB, NY
301st AS		Travis AFB, CA
312th AS		Travis AFB, CA
326th AS	Flying Bunnies	Dover AFB, DE
337th AS		Westover ARB, MA
709th AS		Dover AFB, DE

C-17A Globemaster III

Operations in Vietnam required an aircraft with the hauling capability of the C-141 and the ability of the C-130 to land at unimproved airstrips near the battle's front lines. Unfortunately, an airlifter with such performance did not exist at the time.

To meet the army's and Marine Corps' need for a tactical airlifter with tremendous hauling capabilities, the air force contracted with Boeing and McDonnell Douglas to develop proof-of-concept aircraft under the Advanced Medium Short Takeoff/Landing Transport (AMST) program. Both manufacturers met the air force's goals, Boeing delivering the YC-14 and McDonnell Douglas the YC-15, and the planes served as proof-of-concept vehicles for powered lift devices that dramatically reduced takeoff and landing distances. From the lessons learned in the AMST program, the air force announced the C-X airlifter program in 1980.

McDonnell Douglas' C-X airlifter entry was selected for production on August 28, 1981 and designated C-17 Globemaster III. (The company had previously built the C-74 Globemaster and the C-124 Globemaster II.) The 17th Airlift Squadron, Charleston AFB, South Carolina, became the first operational C-17 squadron on January 17, 1995. Two years later, Boeing acquired McDonnell Douglas, and the aircraft became the Boeing C-17.

The C-17's impressive performance is largely a result of its externally blown flaps, which provide tremendous lift. Fixed-vane, double-slotted flaps are lowered into the engine's exhaust stream, which deflects the engine's thrust downward, thereby producing lift. Exhaust blown over the top of the flap also creates lift, known as the Coanda Effect, which decreases the C-17's takeoff roll and allows for a lower minimum controllable air speed, steeper descents onto shorter runways, and reduced landing roll. High-lift devices and thrust reversers that blow engine exhaust forward and upward enable the C-17, with a 160,000-pound payload, to land in only 3,000 feet. When loaded with the maximum payload of 170,400 pounds, the C-17 can take off in 7,740 feet. The C-17's size and performance have given the U.S. military an aircraft the size of the C-141, which can indeed operate from airfields that are normally the domain of the C-130.

New avionics technologies have reduced the C-17's crew requirements to just a pilot, copilot, and loadmaster, who oversees the aircraft's cargo compartment, which has a loadable width of 18 feet, a floor length of 68 feet, 2 inches, and can carry 18 cargo pallets. A unique feature of the C-17 is its 54 permanent, fold-down troop seats (27 on each side of the cargo compartment). Using palletized passenger seats, the aircraft can accommodate an additional 100 passengers. In its aeromedical evacuation configuration, the C-17 can carry 48 litter and 102 ambulatory patients.

In 1995, Globemaster IIIs supported NATO's Operation Deliberate Force in Bosnia, and in 1999, supported Operation Allied Force in Yugoslavia, where the initial bombing attack took place on March 24, 1999. Soon after, C-17s began flying military equipment to NATO forces in the Balkans and also delivered thousands of meals, blankets, and tents to Serbian refugees.

C-17s provided airlift capabilities to U.S. and international forces for Operation Enduring Freedom, the action to remove the Taliban from control of Afghanistan. To help alleviate hunger, C-17s played a major role in air dropping more than 2.4 million meals, 1,000 blankets, and packages of wheat to the impoverished Afghan population. When the U.S. Army's 101st Airborne Division deployed in Afghanistan in January 2002, C-17s from Charleston AFB were

The C-17 will replace the venerable C-141 Starlifter by 2006. *Jim Dunn*

The C-17 is very capable in tactical airlift missions. The ability of the C-17 to operate from semi-prepared dirt surfaces allows for the direct transport of supplies and equipment to a forward operation area. A C-17 98-0054 from the 62nd AW at McChord, AFB, Washington, lifts off the Holland LZ at Fort Bragg. *Jim Dunn*

Powered by four Pratt & Whitney F117-PW-100 turbofan engines, the C-17 is 174 feet in length with a wingspan of 171 feet, 3 inches. The composite winglets that increase lift and improve fuel efficiency are 8.9 feet fall, and the tail stands just over 55 feet in height. With an operating range of 2,300 miles when fully loaded, the ability to refuel in-flight is an essential feature. *Jim Dunn*

The C-17 can carry nearly double the load of the C-141. An even bigger advantage is in the dimensions of the cargo hold, which can accommodate a helicopter the size of a CH-53E. *Jim Dunn*

The C-17's cockpit features a fully digital fly-by-wire flight control system with fighter-like stick grips and heads-up display (HUD), as well as multi-functional CRT displays with conventional instruments as backup. *Jim Dunn*

loaded with 45 tons of men and equipment for the flight to forward operating areas. Performing a steep descent to the landing strip, the C-17s were quickly off-loaded while the engines ran, enabling the aircraft to depart immediately in a maximum-performance takeoff, which limited its exposure to enemy fire.

In the months before and during Operation Iraqi Freedom, C-17s pre-positioned men and equipment in Kuwait and Saudi Arabia in preparation for the assault on Iraq. On March 26, 2003, C-17s made their first combat paratroop drop when 15 aircraft dropped the 173rd Airborne Brigade into northern Iraq to begin a second front in the march to Baghdad.

A little over one year after the terrorist attacks on the United States, Boeing delivered its 100th C-17. The air force christened the plane *Spirit of Strom Thurmond*, after the veteran World War II

army combat veteran and U.S. senator from South Carolina. Fittingly, the 100th C-17 is assigned to the 437th Airlift Wing at Charleston AFB, South Carolina. As of the end of fiscal year 2002, the C-17 fleet had flown a total of 410,690 hours. Acquisition plans call for 12 C-17s to be delivered in 2003, 10 in 2004, 11 in 2005, 12 in 2006, 14 in 2007, and 9 in 2008 for a total of 180 Globemaster IIIs.

C-17A GLOBEMASTER III

Mission: Strategic airlift
Builder: Boeing
Powerplant: Four Pratt & Whitney F117-PW-100 turbofan engines capable of 40,440 pounds thrust each
Length: 174 feet
Height: 55 feet, 1 inch
Wingspan: 169 feet, 10 inches
MGTOW: 585,000 pounds
Speed: 450 knots at 28,000 feet (Mach 0.74)
Range: 2,400 miles; global with inflight refueling
Crew: Three (pilot, copilot, loadmaster)
Unit Cost: $236.7 million
Date Deployed: June 1993
Inventory:
    Active force – 100

C-17A GLOBEMASTER III

UNITS ASSIGNED		
UNIT	**NICKNAME**	**BASE**
4th AS	Fighting Fourth	McChord AFB, WA
7th AS	Willing and Able	McChord AFB, WA
8th AS	Soaring Stallions	McChord AFB, WA
14th AS	Pelicans	Charleston AFB, SC
15th AS	Global Eagles	Charleston AFB, SC
16th AS		Charleston AFB, SC
17th AS	AAA Moving	Charleston AFB, SC
58th AS	Moose	Altus AFB, OK
97th AS		McChord AFB, WA
300th AS		Charleston AFB, SC
313th AS		McChord AFB, WA
317th AS	First in Reserve	Charleston AFB, SC
701st AS	Turtles	Charleston AFB, SC
728th AS	Flying Knights	McChord AFB, WA
418th FLTS		Edwards AFB, CA

Currently assigned to the 418th FLTS of the 412th TW at Edwards, many of the tests that C-17 87-0025 conducts involve the airdrop mission. The larger the aircraft, the more difficult it becomes to safely airdrop personnel and equipment. Marked with a grid pattern for photographic purposes, this demonstration airdrop was conducted at Edwards in October 2002. *Jim Dunn*

Using its externally blown single-slotted Fowler flap system, and with thrust reversers fully deployed (shown below), a loaded C-17 can be brought to a stop in less than 3,000 feet. *Jim Dunn*

Operated by the 99th AS of the 89th AW based at Andrews AFB, C-9C 73-1682 is one of the three assigned for executive transport duties. *Jim Dunn*

C-9A/B/C Nightingale

The U.S. Air Force operates a fleet of 20 C-9A Nightingales aeromedical transports and 3 C-9Cs, VIP transports. Derived from the Douglas Aircraft Company's DC-9-32CF (DC-9, series 32, Convertible Freighter) commercial jetliner, these aircraft were built to convert from an all-passenger interior to that of a freighter. The C-9As were delivered with the 32CF's 81-inch-by-136-inch upward-swinging, port-side cargo door. When the cargo door is open, a self-contained stretcher-loading ramp can be deployed from the aircraft. The ramp enables stretchers and ambulatory patients to be loaded without having to climb the boarding ladder.

C-9As can be configured to seat 40 ambulatory patients plus 4 litter patients, or 40 on stretchers; it can also accommodate any combination depending upon transportation requirements. A pair of flight nurses and three aeromedical technicians care for patients. The interior of the Nightingale has provisions for hanging intravenous fluid drip bags, patient oxygen outlets, refrigerators for whole blood and other medical supplies, as well as a medical crew station for communication and monitoring of patients.

The 89th Airlift Wing's 99th Airlift Squadron based at Andrews AFB, Maryland, operates the air force's three C-9Cs. These aircraft

Assigned to the Conquistadors of VR-57, C-9B 159115 *City of San Diego* is based at NAS North Island. *Jim Dunn*

C-9A/B/C NIGHTINGALE

Mission: C-9A, Aeromedical Evacuation; C-9C, VIP transport

Builder: Douglas Aircraft Co. (Boeing)

Powerplant: Two JT8D-9s of 14,500 pounds thrust each

Length: 119 feet, 3 inches

Height: 27 feet, 5 inches

Wingspan: 93 feet, 3 inches

MGTOW: 108,000 pounds

Speed: 525 miles per hour at 33,000 feet

Range: 2,500 miles

Crew: C-9A: Two pilots, one flight engineer, five medical staff; C-9C: Two pilots, one flight engineer, communications system operator, four in-flight attendants

Unit Cost: C-9A, $15.9 million; C-9C, $21 million

Date Deployed: August 1968

Inventory:

        Active force — 20 (Air Material Command)

One of approximately 500 C-130 Hercules currently in service, C-130H 82-00059 is assigned to PACAF with the 144th AS Alaska ANG at Kulis ANGB, Anchorage. *Jim Dunn*

C-9A/B/C NIGHTINGALE

UNITS ASSIGNED

UNIT	NICKNAME	BASE/TAIL CODE
11th AS	Nightingales	Scott AFB, IL
30th AS		YJ
73rd AS		Scott AFB, IL
75th AS	Fightin' Roos	RS
C-9B • U.S. Marine Corps (see U.S. Navy/Marine Corps tail codes)		
VR-46	Peach Airliners	JS
VR-52	Taskmaster	JT
VR-56	Globemaster	JU
VR-57	Conquistador	RX
VR-61	Islanders	RS
VMR-1	Roadrunner	MCAS Cherry Point, NC
C-9C		
99th AS	Sam Fox	Andrews AFB, MD

C-130E/H/J Hercules and Variants

Lockheed's C-130 Hercules, affectionately known as the "Herc," was first flown on August 23, 1954, and since that date, more than 2,000 aircraft have been built and flown by more than 65 countries around the world. Initial models delivered to the U.S. Air Force included the C-130A, B, and D models, which have all been retired from the inventory. The air force currently operates the C-130E, an extended-range variant of the C-130B, and the C-130H, similar to the E model, except that it has been retrofitted with Allison T56-A-T5 turboprops, new outer wing sections, and upgraded avionics including terrain- and collision-avoidance features.

As the military's primary tactical airlifter, C-130s deploy cargo by landing at an airstrip and off-loading or through one of three aerial deployment methods: para-drop, where the load is pushed across the floor's pallet rollers and out the rear of the aircraft, and then parachutes are deployed using a static line from the aircraft; the container delivery systems (CDS), where bundles are deployed using parachutes on static lines; and the low altitude parachute extraction system, where the aircraft flies only 10 to 15 feet off the

This crew from the 36th AS lines up for another airdrop run over a remote Pacific island in support of the annual Operation Christmas Drop. Flying from Andersen AFB, Guam, they airdrop 250-pound boxes of donated food, supplies, and toys to a number of islands in Micronesia. *Jim Dunn*

are configured to transport 42 passengers in an executive arrangement and are often used to transport high-level military or government delegations.

Unlike the aeromedical mission of USAF C-9 Nightingales, the navy uses their 15 C-9Bs and 12 DC-9s for the movement of passengers and cargo. Operated by seven Naval Reserve fleet support squadrons, the chief difference between the two types is that the DC-9s do not have the forward cargo door found on the C-9Bs.

MAFFS-carrying C-130s can make multiple runs over a fire or release the entire 2,700-gallon load in five seconds if needed. *Jim Dunn*

The LC-130H is the largest aircraft equipped with a retractable ski-wheel system. Four LC-130Hs, including 83-0491, were delivered to the 139th AS in 1983, with an additional three LC-130Hs and two LC-130Rs now assigned to the unit. *Jim Dunn*

Operated by the 40th FLTS at Eglin AFB, Florida, NC-130A 55-0022 is the oldest Herk in USAF service, and it may be the oldest one still flying. A unique feature is the Airborne Seeker Evaluation and Test System (ASETS) carried in a retractable turret. ASETS is being used to develop new seeker warheads for smart weapons. *Paul Negri*

deck, and drogue chutes pull pallets out of the C-130's cargo hatch, landing the pallets on the ground.

The C-130 came into its own as a tactical airlifter during the Vietnam War. U.S. Air Force C-130s transported more than 446,000 tons between July 1965 and December 1971, with a peak of 63,442 tons between January and June 1968 at the height of the Tet Offensive.

During Operation Desert Storm, C-130s flew 149 tactical airlift missions. C-130s airlifted the entire XVIII Airborne Corps over 400 miles from King Fahd International Airport, Saudi Arabia, and nearby bases to Rafha, Saudi Arabia, a distance of over 400 miles.

When not supporting military airlift requirements, C-130s deliver humanitarian aid and even fight forest fires. C-130s equipped with MAFFS (Modular Airborne Fire Fighting System) have fought fires in most western states. MAFFS can be fitted into a C-130 in about two hours, and has the capacity to deliver 2,700 gallons of retardant. MAFFS-equipped C-130s are flown by the 731st AS based at Peterson AFB, Colorado.

The air force intends to retire its C-130E fleet, which will be replaced with H models transferred from units receiving the new C-130J.

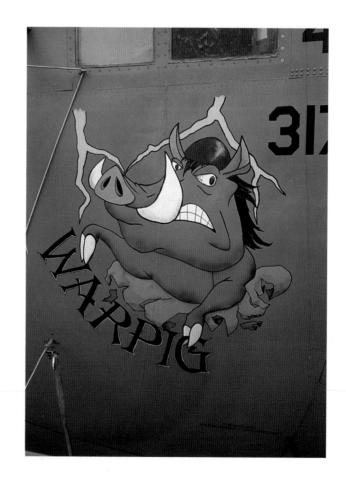

C-130H 74-1671 serves with the Screaming Eagles, 40th AS, Dyess AFB, Texas. *Jim Dunn*

The most distinctive feature of the C-130J is the six-bladed scimitar-shaped composite Dowty propellers attached to the four Rolls-Royce Allison AE21-00D3 engines. C-130J 01-1461 is assigned to the 115th AS of the California ANG at Channel Islands ANGB. *Jim Dunn*

J Model Super Hercules

Lockheed's C-130J Super Hercules looks very similar to the earlier E and H models, but its performance is substantially increased. The J model will be the U.S. military's intra-theater airlifter for most of this century, and will form the core of the army's Future Combat System concept. Instead of moving 70-ton tanks, which requires C-5 and C-17 transports, the army plans to build a new, 20-ton combat vehicle that will fit into a C-130J, which will carry the vehicle and troops 1,000 nautical miles.

The J model Super Hercules features a fully digital, night-vision-compatible cockpit with head-up displays and an automatic thrust control system, which reduces the crew demand to just the pilot and copilot, eliminating the need for a flight engineer and navigator. The loadmaster's tasks are greatly reduced by the addition of a computer-based Enhanced Cargo Handling System. The system enables the aircraft's cargo floor to be converted from cargo tie-down slots to pallet rollers, depending upon mission requirements. Externally, the C-130J is easily identified by its

---

C-130E/H/J HERCULES AND VARIANTS

Mission: Tactical and intra-theater airlift
Contractor: Lockheed Martin Aeronautics Company
Powerplant:
C-130E: Four Allison T56-A-7 turboprops; 4,200 shaft-horsepower
C-130H: Four Allison T56-A-15 turboprops; 4,591 shaft horsepower
C-130J: Four Rolls-Royce AE 2100D3 turboprops; 4,637 horsepower
Length: C-130E/H/J: 97 feet, 9 inches; CC-130J: 112 feet, 9 inches
Height: 38 feet, 3 inches
Wingspan: 132 feet, 7 inches
Cargo Compartment:
C-130E/H/J: length, 40 feet; width, 119 inches; height, 9 feet; rear ramp: length, 123 inches; width, 119 inches
C-130J-30: length, 55 feet; width, 119 inches; height, 9 feet; rear ramp: length, 123 inches; width, 119 inches
Speed:
C-130E: 345 miles per hour at 20,000 feet
C-130H: 366 miles per hour at 20,000 feet
C-130J: 417 miles per hour at 22,000 feet
C-130J-30: 410 miles per hour at 22,000 feet
MGTOW: C-130E/H/J: 155,000 pounds; CC-130J: 164,000 pounds
Maximum Allowable Payload: C-130E, 45,050 pounds; C-130H, 43,550 pounds; C-130J, 46,631 pounds; CC-130J, 46,812 pounds
Maximum Normal Payload: C-130E, 36,720 pounds; C-130H, 35,220 pounds; C-130J, 38,301 pounds; CC-130J, 38,812 pounds
Range at Maximum Normal Payload: C-130E, 1,838 miles; C-130H, 2,006 miles; C-130J, 2,729 miles; CC-130J, 2,897 miles
Crew: C-130E/H: Five (two pilots, navigator, flight engineer, and loadmaster)
C-130J/CC-130J: Three (two pilots and loadmaster)
Aeromedical Evacuation Role: Flight crew plus one flight nurse and two medical technicians
Unit Cost: C-130E, $11.9 million
C-130H, $30.1 million
C-130J, $48.5 million
Date Deployed: C-130A, December 1956; C-130B, May 1959; C-130E, August 1962; C-130H, June 1974; C-130J, February 1999
Inventory:
Active force – 186
Air National Guard – 217
Reserve – 107

4,637 shaft horsepower Rolls-Royce (Allison) AE2100D3 turboprop engines, which turn scimitar-shaped, six-blade Dowty Aerospace R391 propellers (13 feet, 6 inches diameter).

The C-130J is also being built in a stretched fuselage version, the CC-130J (formerly the C-130J-30), which has had a 180-inch fuselage plug added. The CC-130J can carry 128 combat-ready troops (versus 92 in the C-130J), 92 paratroopers (versus 64), or 97 litter patients (versus 74).

As of February 2003, Lockheed Martin has delivered 100 Super Hercules airlifters. The company has begun building the first of 60 C-130Js, 40 CC-130Js for the air force, and 20 KC-130J tankers for the Marine Corps, all of which will be delivered between 2003 and 2008. Additional air force Super Hercules variants include the WC-130J weather reconnaissance model and the EC-130J Commando Solo electronic warfare model.

UNITS ASSIGNED

UNIT	NICKNAME	BASE
2nd AS	Lancers	Pope AFB, NC
36th AS	Eagle Airlifters	Yokota AB, Japan
37th AS	Bluetail Flies	Ramstein AB, Germany
38th AS (P)		Ramstein AB, Germany
39th AS	Trail Blazers	Dyess AFB, TX
40th AS	Screaming Eagles	Dyess AFB, TX
40th FLTS		Elgin AFB, FL
41st AS	Black Cats	Pope AFB, NC
50th AS	Red Devils	Little Rock AFB, AR
53rd AS	Black Jacks	Little Rock AFB, AR
53rd WRS	Hurricane Hunters	Keesler AFB, MS
61st AS	Green Hornets	Little Rock AFB, AR
62nd AS	Blue Barons	Little Rock AFB, AR
95th AS	Flying Badgers	General Mitchell IAP, WY
96th AS	Flying Vikings	Minneapolis-St. Paul IAP, MN
105th AS	Old Hickory	Nashville IAP, TN
109th AS		Minneapolis-St. Paul, MN
115th AS		Channel Island IAP, CA
130th AS	Mountaineers	Charleston IAP, WY
135th AS	Baltimore's Best	Baltimore, MD
139th AS		Stratton ANGS, NY
142nd AS		New Castle, DE
143rd AS		Providence, RI
144th AS		Kulis ANGB, AK
156th AS	First in Flight	Charlotte IAP, NC
158th AS	Savannah Guard Dogs	Savannah IAP, GA
164th AS		Mansfield, OH
165th AS	Thoroughbred Express	Louisville IAP, TN
167th AS		Martinsburg, WY
169th AS		Peoria, IL
171st AS	Six Pack	Selfridge ANGB, MI
180th AS		St. Joseph, MO
181st AS		NAS Ft. Worth, TX
185th AS		Will Rogers Airport, Oklahoma City, OK
187th AS		Cheyenne, WY
189th AS		Boise, ID
192nd AS	High Rollers	Reno-Tahoe IAP, NV
198th AS	Buccaneers	Muniz ANGB, PR
204th AS		Hickam AFB, HI
327th AS		NAS Willow Grove, PA
328th AS		Niagara Falls IAP, NY
357th AS	Deliverance	Maxwell AFB, AL
517th As	Firebirds	Eielson AFB, AK
700th AS		Dobbins ARB, GA
731st AS		Peterson AFB, CO
757th AS	Blue Tigers	Youngstown, OH
773rd AS	Quiet Professionals	Youngstown, OH
758th AS		Greater Pittsburgh IAP, PA
815th AS	Jennies	Keesler AFB, MS

SPECIAL OPERATIONS AND ROTARY WINGS

AC-130H/U Gunship

While American involvement in the Vietnam War escalated, the U.S. Air Force found itself in need of an airborne gunship with greater firepower than its existing AC-47, nicknamed Spooky. On February 26, 1967, a C-130A, serial number 54-1626, was selected for conversion to the AC-130 Gunship II prototype configuration.

The C-130's cargo capacity was more than double that of the AC-47, which enabled the AC-130 to mount four 7.62mm miniguns (Gatling-type machine guns) and four M61 Vulcan 20mm cannons capable of firing 2,500 rounds per minute. The miniguns and Vulcans were mounted in pairs, one of each type forward of and behind the wing.

The prototype AC-130 helped determine the aircraft's crew, consisting of aircraft commander (pilot), co-pilot, flight engineer, loadmaster, navigator, navigator/sensor operator (night-vision sensors), navigator/infrared and radar sensor operator, armorer/scanner, armorer (7.62mm miniguns), and an armorer for the 20mm Vulcan cannons. The crew was later expanded to 14 when additional guns and sensors were installed during the aircraft's development.

The AC-130 prototype arrived in Vietnam on September 21, 1967. While there, the AC-130 flew close air support missions, armed reconnaissance, and interdiction strikes against North Vietnamese targets and convoys. Success of the AC-130A led to the conversion of 11 C-130Es to AC-130Es, which featured a single pair of Vulcans, a 40mm M1 cannon, and a 105mm M-102 cannon. Spectre became the call sign for the AC-130s during Vietnam, and has remained the aircraft's name ever since. While operating in Vietnam, AC-130s damaged or destroyed more than 10,000 North Vietnamese trucks and repelled countless enemy attacks with their tremendous firepower.

Refueling an HH-60G along the California coast, HC-130P 66-0221 is assigned to the 129th RQS, an ANG unit based at Moffett ANGS, California. *Rene J. Francillon*

Introduced to operational service in 1995, the ultimate gunship is the AC-130U. Using the new build AC-130H airframes, these gunships are equipped with a 105mm M102 howitzer, one 40mm L-60 Bofors cannon, and one 25mm General Electric GAU-12 Gatling gun. *Ghostriders* (AC-130U 89-0512) is one of 13 AC-130Us serving with the 4th SOS at Hulburt. *Jim Dunn*

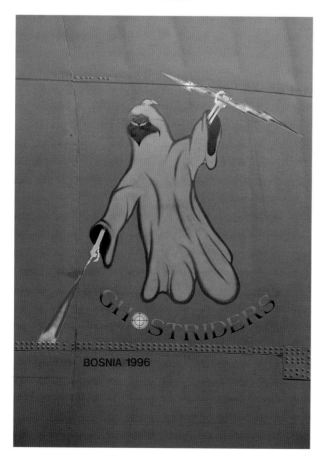

BOSNIA 1996

AC-130H/U GUNSHIP

Mission: Close air support and air interdiction
Builder: Lockheed (Boeing AC-130U modifications)
Powerplant: Four Allison T56-A-15 turboprop engines with 4,910 shaft horsepower thrust per engine
Length: 97 feet, 9 inches
Height: 38 feet, 6 inches
Wingspan: 132 feet, 7 inches
MGTOW: 155,000 pounds
Speed: 300 miles per hour
Range: 1,300 nautical miles, unlimited with aerial refueling
Armament: AC-130H/U: 40mm cannon and 105mm cannon; AC-130U: 25mm gun
Crew: AC-130U: Five officers (pilot, co-pilot, navigator, fire control officer, electronic warfare officer), flight engineer, TV operator, infrared detection set operator, loadmaster, four gunners
Unit Cost: AC-130H, $132.4 million; AC-130U, $190 million
Date Deployed: AC-130H, 1972; AC-130U, 1995
Inventory: Active force — 8 (AC-130H) and 13 (AC-130U)

AC-130H/U GUNSHIP

UNITS ASSIGNED

UNIT	NICKNAME	BASE
4th SOS	Ghostrider	Hulburt Field, FL
16th SOS	Spectre	Hulburt Field, FL

The MC-130H Combat Talon, including 88-0194 shown here, is equipped with features such as secure radios with data-burst transmission, AN/AAQ-15 FLIR in a retractable turret, and AN/APQ-170 multimode radar. *Greg L. Davis*

Spectres have also been employed in Grenada, Panama, Somalia, and Kosovo. During Desert Storm, the U.S. Air Force had 10 Spectres, 5 of which were stationed at King Fahd Airport, Saudi Arabia. One AC-130, on patrol to destroy Scud missile sites, maneuvered so violently while dodging surface-to-air missiles that it suffered structural damage and was returned to the United States for overhaul and repair.

Over the years, eight AC-130 gunships have been lost in combat—six in Vietnam, one in the fighting in Somalia, and one in Operation Desert Storm. An AC-130H, was destroyed on January 31, 1991, during Operation Desert Storm. The Spectre was providing air support to U.S. Marines when an Iraqi shoulder-fired surface-to-air missile struck the airplane. As a result of the subsequent crash, 14 U.S. servicemen lost their lives. More recently, an AC-130H was lost off the coast of Kenya while providing cover for U.S. troops in Mogadishu, Somalia.

Boeing and its subcontractor, Crestview Aerospace, are currently modifying four additional AC-130Hs to AC-130U Spooky II configuration. The U model features a new GPS-enabled navigation system, an electronics and countermeasures suite, and a night-vision system; it also incorporates the Hughes APG-180 radar system adapted from the F-15 Eagle fighter. The APG-180 tracks targets on the ground as well as where the aircraft's 40mm and 105mm rounds land. The system then automatically adjusts if the rounds miss their target. The 20mm cannons of the AC-130H have been replaced by 25mm GAU-12 Gatling guns fed by 3,000 rounds of ammunition. The four aircraft under conversion by Boeing/ Crestview Aerospace will be delivered in 2006.

MC-130E Combat Talon, MC-130H Combat Talon II, and MC-130P Combat Shadow

The MC-130E Combat Talon and MC-130H Combat Shadow aircraft give the U.S. Air Force the ability to insert or extract special operations personnel and equipment, while the MC-130P Combat Shadow provides low-level, limited-visibility aerial refueling to special operations helicopters.

During Operation Desert Storm, MC-130E Combat Talon crews inserted and resupplied special operations forces in the Iraqi desert. Most of these missions were flown at night to avoid exposing the positions of men on the ground. While the conflict raged, the staff of the 8th Special Operations Squadron (SOS) proposed that the Combat Talon be used to drop the Vietnam-era BLU-82 bomb. Essentially a 15,000-pound bomb intended for clearing landing zones and mine fields, it has a devastating effect on the enemy's morale—even if they are deep underground in bunkers. Iraqi surface-to-air threats required that the bombs be dropped from 16,000 to 21,000 feet, and on a number of occasions multiple BLU-82s were deployed simultaneously on the same target. The 8th SOS dropped 11 BLU-82s on Iraqi troop concentrations and mine fields during the war.

Combat Talon IIs have the capability to set up Forward Area Refueling Points behind enemy lines. The MC-130H lands at a predetermined location, deploys fuel hoses, and gasses up arriving helicopters. In an operation usually done at night, special operations helicopter crews fly in wearing night vision goggles to rendezvous for fuel, which is loaded while the helicopter's engines are kept running. Once the helicopters depart, the MC-130H departs the

MC130s

Mission: Infiltration, exfiltration, and resupply of special operations forces

Builder: Lockheed

Powerplant: Four Allison T56-A-15 turboprop engines capable of 4,910 shaft horsepower each engine

Length: 100 feet, 10 inches

Height: 38 feet, 6 inches

Wingspan: 132 feet, 7 inches

Speed: 300 miles per hour

Load: MC-130E: 53 troops, 26 paratroopers; MC-130H: 77 troops, 52 paratroopers or 57 litter patients

Ceiling: 33,000 feet

MGTOW: 155,000 pounds

Range: 2,700 nautical miles; unlimited with inflight refueling

Crew: MC-130E: Eight (two pilots, two navigators, electronic warfare officer, enlisted flight engineer, radio operator, and two loadmasters); MC-130H: Seven (two pilots, navigator, electronic warfare officer, flight engineer, and two loadmasters)

Date Deployed: MC-130E, 1966; MC-130H, June 1991

Unit Cost: MC-130E, $75 million; MC-130H, $155 million

Inventory:
Active force, MC-130H — 24
Reserve, MC-130E — 14

MC130s

UNITS ASSIGNED		
UNIT	**NICKNAME**	**LOCATION**
MC-130E		
8th SOS	Blackbirds	Duke Field, FL
MC-130 HP		
1st SOS	Stacy Goose Int'l	Kadena AB, Okinawa
5th SOS	Shadows	Eglin AFB, FL
7th SOS	Air Commandos	RAF Mildenhall, Eng
9th SOS	Night Wings	Eglin AFB, FL
15th SOS	Global Eagles	Hulburt Field, FL
17th SOS	Jackals	Kadena AB, Okinawa
39th RQS		Patricia AFB, FL
67th SOS	Night Owls	RAF Mildenhall, England
71st RQS	Kings	Moody AFB, GA
102nd RQS	ANG Oldest Unit	Gabresui ANGB, NY
129th RQS		Moffatt Fed AF, ANG, CA
303rd RQS		Portland, OR
550th SOS	Wolf Pack	Kirtland AFB, NM
711th SOS	Spectre	Duke Field, FL

refueling point at low level to avoid detection by enemy radar. Combat Talon IIs are equipped with the AN/APQ-170 terrain-following and terrain-avoidance radar, as well as the AN/APQ-175 adverse weather aerial delivery system for dropping soldiers and supplies at high speeds.

MC-130P Combat Shadows are used to refuel special operations force helicopters on long missions behind enemy lines. The aircraft are also used to airdrop commando units and their equipment, such as small boats, into sensitive areas. Paratroops can exit the Combat Shadow at altitudes as low as 500 feet.

MH-53J/M

Originally designed to meet a U.S. Marine Corps specification for a heavy-lift helicopter, the MH-53 series of Sikorsky helicopters is a direct descendant of the HH-3 Jolly Green Giant of Vietnam War fame. Sikorsky's MH-53J Pave Low III and MH-53M Pave Low IV are extensively modified for unconventional warfare, including the insertion and extraction of special operations forces and long-range rescues in hostile territory in any weather. Pave Lows can transport 38 fully equipped troops or 14 litter patients and suppress enemy ground fire with a combination of .50-caliber machine guns or 7.62mm Gatling guns.

MH-53J Pave Low IIIs are equipped with terrain-following/terrain-avoidance radar, forward looking infrared sensors, and an

The Pave Low III (Enhanced) program produced a total of 41 MH-53Js that combined the earlier features of INS, FLIR, and defensive countermeasures, with improved night and all-weather capabilities. The Black Knights of the 551st SOS operate several MH-53Js, including 66-14433 from Kirtland AFB, New Mexico. *Jim Dunn*

inertial navigation system with a GPS-enabled moving map display. Pave Low IVs feature the Interactive Defensive Avionics System/Multi-Mission Advanced Tactical Terminal (known as IDAS/MATT), which enables the Pave Low IV to receive threat assessment data from other aircraft in the area. IDAS allows the helicopter's crew to detect threats that are over the horizon.

In combat during Operation Desert Storm, three MH-53s lead a flight of AH-64s into Iraq 21 minutes before the war began. The helicopters destroyed two Iraqi radar sites, clearing the way for F-15Es to cross the border and search for Scud missile sites. After the 1991 Gulf War had ended, MH-53s played a large role in delivering relief supplies during Operation Provide Comfort.

Pave Lows have supported almost every military action from Operation Just Cause in Panama to the relief efforts in the Balkans, as well as in Operation Enduring Freedom and Operation Iraqi Freedom. The air force would eventually like to replace the MH-53 helicopter in the special operations role with the CV-22 Osprey tiltrotor, which will conceivably add more versatility, speed, and safety in inserting or extracting troops.

MH-53J/M

Mission: Long-range infiltration, exfiltration, and resupply of special operations forces in day, night, or marginal weather conditions
Builder: Sikorsky
Powerplant: Two General Electric T64-GE/-100 engines capable of 4,330 shaft horsepower per engine
Length: 88 feet, 3 inches
Height: 17 feet, 2 inches
Rotor Diameter: 72 feet, 3 inches
Speed: 165 miles per hour (at sea level)
Ceiling: 16,000 feet
MGTOW: 46,000 pounds (Emergency War Plan allows for 50,000 pounds)
Range: 600 nautical miles (unlimited with aerial refueling)
Armament: Combination of three 7.62 mini guns or three .50-caliber machine guns
Crew: Six (two pilots, two flight engineers, two aerial gunners)
Date Deployed: 1981
Unit Cost: $40 million
Inventory:
    Active force, 13 MH-53Js, 25 MH-53Ms

MH-53J/M

UNITS ASSIGNED

UNIT	NICKNAME	BASE
20th SOS	Green Hornets	Hurlburt Field, FL
21st SOS	Dust Devils	RAF Mildenhall, England
551st SOS	Black Knights	Kirtland AFB, NM

Developed from the Sikorsky UH-60A Blackhawk for the combat search and rescue (CSAR) mission, the HH-60G Pave Hawk is tasked with flying deep behind enemy lines to rescue downed aircrew. *Rene J. Francillon*

HH-60G and MH-60G Pave Hawk

The HH-60G and MH-60G Pave Hawk are the type of helicopter most often seen carrying out dramatic rescues and rendering humanitarian aid. Pave Hawks are based on the U.S. Army's UH-60 Blackhawk, modified with equipment to meet the air force's requirements. Pave Hawks are fitted with an aerial refueling probe that enables the helicopter to take on fuel from C-130s from any service. This capability limits the Pave Hawk's range to only the crew's endurance. HH/MH-60s are also fitted with additional internal fuel tanks, anti-icing capability, a winch capable of lifting 600 pounds, a forward-looking infrared sensor, color weather radar, a GPS-enabled inertial navigation system, and night-vision capabilities.

As Operation Desert Shield transitioned to become Desert Storm, MH-60s transported U.S. Navy SEAL teams on missions into Kuwait. When the war got underway, HH/MH-60s flew search and rescue missions as well. Pave Hawks were responsible for

HH-60G & MH60G PAVE HAWK

Mission: Combat search and rescue
Builder: Sikorsky
Powerplant: Two General Electric T700-GE-700 (or T700-GE-701) engines rated at 1,560 (or 1,630) shaft horsepower each
Length: 64 feet, 8 inches
Height: 16 feet, 8 inches
Rotor Diameter: 53 feet, 7 inches
MGTOW: 22,000 pounds
Speed: 184 miles per hour
Range: 445 miles, unlimited with aerial refueling
Armament: Two 7.62 mm miniguns
Crew: Four (two pilots, flight engineer, gunner or two pararescue jumpers)
Unit Cost: $9.3 million
Date Deployed: 1982
Inventory:
    Active force – 64
    Air National Guard – 18
    Reserve – 23

The MH-60G's first combat duty occurred when eight were deployed to Saudi Arabia to conduct special operations missions during Operation Desert Storm. In 1999, during Operation Allied Force, AFSOC MH-60Gs were credited with the rescue of two USAF F-16 and F-117 pilots shot down over Serbia. *Greg L. Davis*

rescuing a pair of downed pilots during Operation Allied Force in the Balkans.

The air force expects the Pave Hawk to serve through the year 2027 and plans a number of service-life extension programs that will see the helicopters fitted with missile defensive systems, such as radar jammers and flares.

HH-60G & MH60G PAVE HAWK

UNITS ASSIGNED		
UNIT	**NICKNAME**	**TAIL CODE**
33rd RQS		ZZ
41st RQS	Jolly Green	MY
56th RQS	Friends in Low Places	IS
66th RQS		WA
102nd RQS	ANG Oldest Unit	LI
129th RQS		CA
210th RQS		AN
301st RQS		FL
304th RQS		PD
305th RQS		DR
422nd TES	Green Bats	OT
512th RQS	Jolly	
HH-60 DIV		WA

The first of 79 UH-1Ns delivered to the USAF, 68-10772 now serves with the 40th HF of the 341st SW at Malmstrom AFB, Montana. *Jim Dunn*

UH-1N Iroquois

An outgrowth of the Bell HU-1A model, the U.S. Army's first turbine helicopter, delivered in 1956, the UH-1N was designed as an improved search and rescue platform for operations in Vietnam. Since that time, the UH-1N's role has expanded beyond search and rescue to include air force missile site support, disaster response, and VIP transport.

The helicopter is certified for single-pilot flight, although the normal crew allowance is a copilot and engineer. Depending upon the configuration, the helicopter can be outfitted to seat 11 passengers or transport 6 litter patients. The UH-1N is also used as a flight trainer and for aircrew survival training.

UH-1N IROQUOIS

Mission: Light-lift utility, priority transport
Builder: Bell Helicopter
Powerplant: Two Pratt & Whitney (Canada) T400-CP-400 turboshaft engines rated at 1,800 shaft horsepower each
Length: 42 feet, 5 inches
Height: 14 feet, 4 inches
Rotor Diameter: 48 feet
MGTOW: 10,500 pounds
Speed: 110 miles per hour
Range: 300 miles
Crew: Three (pilot, copilot, flight engineer)
Date Deployed: 1970
Inventory:
        Active force – 62

UH-1N IROQUOIS

UNITS ASSIGNED		
UNIT	**NICKNAME**	**TAIL CODE**
1st AS	First Heli	DC
35th RQF	St. Bernards	
37th HF		FE
40th HF		MM
54th HF	Nomads of the North	MT
76th HF		HV
459th AS	Orient Express	YJ
512th RQS	Jolly	NM

Descended from the famous Bell UH-1 Huey, the UH-1N is a larger twin-engined version that first entered USAF service in 1970. Assigned to the 76th Helicopter Flight (HF) of the 30th Space Wing (SW), UH-1N 69-6660 is used to patrol the missile range at Vandenberg AFB, California. *Jim Dunn*

Airborne Warning and Control Systems (AWACS) aircraft are the most important airborne asset in any engagement. Since first entering service in March 1977, the E-3 Sentry has given commanders the ability to oversee and direct their airborne forces, while at the same time providing those forces early warning of enemy threats. Today 33 of 34 E-3s delivered to the USAF serve as upgraded E-3B/Cs. *Jim Dunn*

RECON/ELINT/COMMAND AND CONTROL

E-3B/C Sentry AWACS

The key to successfully defeating an enemy force from the air is the attacking force's ability to control aircraft flying offensive missions and eliminate the enemy's ability to counterattack with aircraft. The Boeing-built E-3 Sentry AWACS (Airborne Warning and Control System) aircraft is the first line of defense against enemy aerial counterattack and the controller of the skies over the battlefield.

Based on the commercial 707-320B, AWACS aircraft are quickly recognized by the 30-foot-diameter, 6-foot-thick radome, which sits 14 feet above the aircraft's rear fuselage. From a distance of 200 miles, the AWACS radar can discern a low-flying target from background clutter such as hills or the ocean; this is termed "look-down" capabilities. The radar's detection range increases as the target gains in elevation.

The U.S. Air Force acquired 34 AWACS aircraft, including two EC-137D prototypes, with deliveries beginning in 1977. That total was reduced by one aircraft, when, on September 22, 1995, an E-3B and its entire crew of 24 perished in a bird-strike incident at Anchorage, Alaska. Great Britain, France, Saudi Arabia, and NATO have also purchased a total of 34 AWACS.

U.S. AWACS crews flew 379 sorties (5,052 hours) during the 1991 Gulf War. One E-3, either American or Saudi Arabian, was airborne in the Iraq-Kuwait-Saudi Arabia region at all times during the war, and a back-up E-3 crew was on alert, on the ground, or in the air, 24 hours a day. NATO E-3s controlled the airspace over the Mediterranean Sea to monitor and control aircraft flowing from the United States and Europe into the Gulf theater.

In addition to monitoring the airborne battlefield and tracking strike aircraft transitioning to and from the target, AWACS also keep close tabs on other signals-intelligence-gathering aircraft such as the RC-135 and EC-130. If an enemy aircraft ventures into the vicinity of an electronic warfare aircraft, AWACS controllers can direct fighters flying combat air patrol to intercept and destroy it. Of the 41 aircraft destroyed in air-to-air combat during Operation Desert Storm, 38 of the engagements were directed by AWACS controllers.

E-3s also perform a life-saving mission by orchestrating combat search and rescue missions to locate and recover downed airmen. The Gulf War's first pilot recovery directed by AWACS

The E-3 uses a new-build 707-320B airframe modified to support the rotating 30-foot diameter, disc-shaped dome that is its most distinctive feature. Rotating at 6 rpm the dome houses the AN/APY-2 radar that provides coverage out to more that 250 miles reaching from the surface of the earth into the stratosphere. The Sentry has 4 flight crew members and 16 mission specialists. *Jim Dunn*

occurred on January 21, 1991, when Lieutenant Devon Jones, pilot of a VF-103 F-14A (Plus), was downed by an Iraqi SA-2 surface-to-air missile. An E-3 guided two A-10s and an MH-53 Pave Low helicopter to Jones' position as an Iraqi patrol was closing in on the downed airman. The Iraqi vehicle was destroyed, and the Pave Low crew recovered Jones. Lieutenant Jones' radar intercept officer, Lieutenant Lawrence R. Slade, was captured by the Iraqis but released on March 3, 1991.

In the late 1990s, the E-3 fleet began a Radar System Improvement Program to upgrade the system's hardware and software, as well as its reliability. The final aircraft to undergo the RSIP retrofitting should be complete in fiscal year 2004.

E-3B/C SENTRY AWACS

Mission: Airborne surveillance, command, control, and communications
Builder: Boeing
Powerplant: Four Pratt & Whitney TF33-PW-100A turbofans capable of 21,000 pounds thrust each
Length: 145 feet, 6 inches
Height: 41 feet, 4 inches
Wingspan: 130 feet, 10 inches
MGTOW: 347,000 pounds
Speed: 360 miles per hour (cruise)
Endurance: 8 hours (unrefueled)
Crew: Four flight crew plus 12 to 19 specialists, depending upon mission
Unit Cost: $270 million
Date Deployed: March 1977
Inventory:
Active force – 33

E-3B/C SENTRY AWACS

UNIT	NICKNAME	TAIL CODE
\multicolumn{3}{c}{**UNITS ASSIGNED**}		
960th AACS	Viking Warriors	OK
961st AACS	Eyes of the Pacific	ZZ
962nd AACS	Eyes of the Eagle	AK
963rd AACS	Blue Knights	OK
964th AACS	Phoenix	OK
965th AACS	Falcons	OK
966th AACS	Ravens	OK
970th AACS		OK

Equipped with some of the most sophisticated communication systems known, the E-4B/C serves as the last line of communication for national leaders in emergencies. The four National Airborne Operations Center (NAOC) aircraft are assigned to the First Axe 1st ACCS of the 55th WG at Offutt AFB, Nebraska. At least one aircraft is maintained on a 24-hour ground alert at all times. *Greg L. Davis*

E-4B/C National Airborne Operations Center (NAOC)

Designed to meet the communications needs of a nation under nuclear attack, the E-4B National Airborne Operations Center is always standing by, but luckily has never been needed. Four E-4s have been delivered, each a modified 747-200 fitted out with advanced communications equipment to enable the United States to maintain an efficient governmental chain of command between the executive and military branches. A crew of up to 114 flies and operates the aircraft's systems and provides maintenance and security. The main cabin is separated into six compartments: a command center, conference room, briefing room, work and rest areas, as well a communications center. During the Cold War, one E-4 was always airborne. After the collapse of the Soviet Union, E-4 crews changed from a continuous airborne status to a 24-hour ground alert.

Three E-4As were delivered between 1974 and 1979; the first production-line-built E-4B was delivered in 1980. The three A models had all been upgraded to B configuration by 1985. An upgrade to C model configuration is currently being planned.

E-4B/C NAOC

Mission: National Airborne Operations Center
Builder: Boeing
Powerplant: Four General Electric CF6-50E2 turbofan engines rated at 52,500 pounds thrust each engine
Length: 231 feet, 4 inches
Height: 63 feet, 5 inches
Wingspan: 195 feet, 8 inches
Weight: 800,000 pounds
Crew: Up to 114
Unit Cost: $258 million
Date Deployed: January 1980
Inventory:
        Active force — 4

E-4B/C NAOC

UNITS ASSIGNED

UNIT	NICKNAME	TAIL CODE
1st ACCS	First Axe	OF

E-8C Joint STARS

Joint STARS stands for Joint (U.S. Air Force and Army) Surveillance Target Attack Radar System and is a stand-off-range, airborne command and control center. It is based on commercial 707-300 airframes that are extensively modified by Northrop Grumman.

The most notable external feature of the Joint STARS is the 40-foot-long under-fuselage radome, which houses a 24-foot-long, side-looking, phased array radar. The radar has five operating modes: wide-area surveillance, fixed target indication, synthetic aperture radar, moving target indicator, and target classification. On board the aircraft, one operator sits at the navigation and defensive systems station, and 17 others process information for sight path planning, cartographic data, radar management, surveillance and threat analysis, jammer locations, and the pairing of airborne weapons to ground targets. This information can be sent

Providing commanders with airborne battle management along with command and control, this Air Force/Army Joint Surveillance Target Attack Radar System (Joint STARS) is capable of tracking ground vehicles at ranges of over 150 miles. Developed by Grumman Aerospace the first two E-8 prototypes were in the middle of testing when they were deployed to support Operation Desert Storm. After 49 combat sorties they more than proved the value of this system. *Jim Dunn*

were able to track convoys and monitor enemy staging areas, as well as their paths of retreat.

On February 25, 2003, Northrop Grumman delivered the 15th E-8C, which is in Block 20 configuration, featuring commercial off-the-shelf computing and signal-processing capabilities. Northrop Grumman is also updating 10 previously delivered E-8Cs to Block 20 standards. These aircraft can provide moving target radar information through a secure datalink to the army's AH-64D Longbow Apache attack helicopters.

E-8C JOINT STARS

Mission: Airborne battle management
Builder: Boeing/Northrop Grumman
Powerplant: Four JT3D-3B turbojet engines capable of 18,000 pounds thrust each
Length: 152 feet, 11 inches
Height: 42 feet, 6 inches
Wingspan: 145 feet, 9 inches
MGTOW: 336,000 pounds
Speed: 0.84 Mach
Endurance: 11 hours; 20 hours with inflight refueling
Crew: Pilot, copilot, flight engineer, plus 18 mission specialists (normal)
Two pilots, two copilots, two flight engineers, plus 34 mission specialists (extended endurance missions)
Unit Cost: $244.4 million
Date Deployed: 1996
Inventory:
Active force — 14

E-8C JOINT STARS

UNITS ASSIGNED	
UNIT	**TAIL CODE**
12th ACCS	GA
116th AACS	GA
128th AACS	GA

through a secure satellite link to ground stations or via the JTIDS (Joint Tactical Information Distribution System) to tactical aircraft or AWACS planes.

The air force took delivery of its first E-8C on March 22, 1996. In November of that year, the E-8C provided support to U.S. forces in Kosovo. Two pre-production prototype E-8s flew missions in Operation Desert Storm from Riyadh. During the battle, the E-8s

While the Air Force operates several live-fire ranges for testing and training, the one that is subject to the greatest number of civilian incursions is located off of the Florida coast in the Gulf of Mexico. In order to conduct surveillance of these waters, and to exercise command and control over the drones and missiles being used, the Air Force uses two de Havilland Dash 8s designated E-9s that were ordered in 1984. *Rene J. Francillon*

E-9A

The U.S. Air Force inventory includes two Bombardier Aerospace E-9As, the military version of the de Havilland Canada Dash 8 turboprop airliner. E-9As have been fitted with the AN/APS-128D surveillance radar and externally mounted phased-array radar, which can track airborne targets, relay over-the-horizon missile telemetry data, and monitor ocean ranges during missile and drone tests. The 82nd Aerial Targets Squadron, Tyndall AFB, Florida, flies the E-9A.

E-9A

Mission: Telemetry relay

Builder: Bombardier Aerospace

Powerplant: Two Pratt & Whitney (Canada) PW120A turboprops rated at 2,000 shaft horsepower each

Length: 73 feet

Height: 24 feet, 7 inches

Wingspan: 85 feet

MGTOW: 34,500 pounds

Speed: 303 miles per hour (cruise)

Range: 800 miles

Crew: Four (two pilots, two system operators)

Inventory:

       Active force – 2

E-9A

UNITS ASSIGNED	
UNIT	**TAIL CODE**
82nd ATRS	TD

The only ANG squadron in the Air Force Special Operations Command (AFSOC) is the Quiet Professionals of the 193rd SOS of the Pennsylvania ANG at Harrisburg. This squadron operates foru EC-130E Rivet Rider aircraft, including 63-9817, in the Commando Solo mission. That involves psychological and civil affairs broadcasts. These aircraft are able to broadcast AM, FM, and shortwave radio signals and color VHF television signals and have been used extensively over Iraq. *Jim Dunn*

SPECIAL WARFARE C-130 HERCULES:
EC-130E/J Commando Solo and EC-130H
Compass Call

The rugged C-130 airframe has been adapted to a number of special use configurations, including psychological warfare and civil affairs broadcasts as well as electronic broadcast jamming. EC-130E Commando Solo and EC-130J Commando Solo II Hercs fly in the psychological warfare role, while EC-130H Compass Call Hercs provide communications jamming capabilities to theater commanders.

Introduced to USAF service in 1962, the C-130-3 remains in widespread use. Able to carry a larger payload over a much greater range than earlier models, the C-130E now took on longer logistical support missions. A total of 377 C-130Es were delivered to the USAF including 68-10937 that now serves with the 43rd AW at Pope AFB, North Carolina. *Jim Dunn*

Commando Solo

The Commando Solo mission began in 1967 during the Vietnam War. Air force C-121 Warning Stars were modified for psychological warfare operations and flew until 1978, when the mission was moved to the C-130E. In 1990, the C-130Es were upgraded with radio and TV (VHF and UHF) broadcasting systems capable of being received by nations in the Middle East. The planes are also capable of jamming enemy command and control communication networks and gathering intelligence. A typical Commando Solo mission calls for the aircraft to orbit near a target audience for the duration of the broadcast.

Four EC-130Es are now in service; two aircraft of that model have been converted to EC-130Js for the Commando Solo II mission by removing equipment from the E models and installing it into the J models. The first J model was delivered to the 193rd Special Operations Wing in Harrisburg, Pennsylvania, in mid-2001. An 11-member crew consisting of a pair of pilots, a navigator, flight engineer, loadmaster, mission control chief/electronic warfare officer, and 5 electronic communications specialists operates the EC-130E/Js.

C-130 HERCULES

Mission: Psychological warfare and electronic countermeasures
Builder: Lockheed Martin
Powerplant: Four Allison T56-A-15 turboprop engines rated at 4,910 shaft horsepower each
Length: 97 feet, 9 inches
Height: 38 feet, 8 inches
Wingspan: 132 feet, 6 inches
MGTOW: 155,000 pounds
Speed: 397 miles per hour (cruise)
Range: 2,835 nautical miles
Crew: 11 (EC-130E/J), 13 (EC-130H)
Inventory:
      Active force – 13 (EC-130H)
      Air National Guard – 6 (EC-130E/J)

C-130 HERCULES

UNITS ASSIGNED		
UNIT	**NICKNAME**	**TAIL CODE**
EC-130E/J		
193rd SOS	Quiet Professionals	No tail code; Harrisburg IAP, PA
EC-130H		
41st ECS	Scorpions	DM
43rd ECS	Bats	DM

The 193rd Special Operations Wing was busy during Operation Desert Storm, broadcasting messages urging Iraq's army to lay down their arms. The wing states that "more than 50 percent of the Iraqi POWs indicated that the message influenced their decision to throw down their arms." The 193rd also broadcast news and sports to Coalition forces in Saudi Arabia, earning the unit the title "Voice of the Gulf."

During Operation Iraqi Freedom, U.S. Special Operations forces operating Commando Solo aircraft flew from Camp As Sayliyah, Qatar, broadcasting to the Iraqi people that Coalition forces were coming to remove Saddam Hussein from power, and they were not hostile against Iraqi civilians. In addition, the programs feature American Top 40–style music, and last approximately one hour.

Compass Call

EC-130H Compass Call Hercs are dedicated to jamming an enemy's tactical command, control, and communications systems. Jamming such networks hinders the enemy's ability to respond to U.S. military actions, enabling air and ground forces to exploit any lack of a coordinated response. Thirteen members crew the EC-130H: two pilots, a navigator, flight engineer, mission control officer, cryptologic linguist, six analysis operators, and an airborne maintenance technician.

The air force's Compass Call assets are based at Davis-Monthan AFB, Arizona, and operate with the 41st and 42nd Electronic Combat Squadrons. Both squadrons operate a total of 13 aircraft, 6 in Block 20 and 7 in Block 30 configuration. All aircraft will be brought up to Block 35 standards by the end of fiscal year 2007, with modifications including an electronic countermeasures system to defeat enemy surface-to-air threats, new navigation and communication systems, and improved jamming equipment.

In Operation Desert Storm, Compass Call Hercs disrupted Iraqi air defense networks, preventing command and control centers from directing anti-aircraft fire. This was accomplished with the Compass Call aircraft flying outside of Iraqi airspace and safely away from enemy surface-to-air missiles. During the campaign, Compass Call C-130s flew 450 sorties, which gave 24-hour jamming of Iraqi tactical communications for 44 days in a row.

C-135 VARIANTS
OC-135B OPEN SKIES • RC-135S COBRA BALL • RC-135U COMBAT SENT •RC-135V/W Rivet Joint • TC-135S/W • WC-135W • EC-18B

The venerable KC-135 airframe has been an ideal platform for carrying large electronic suites. In the 1960s at the peak of the Cold War, when most electronics were vacuum-tube powered, the KC-135 was modified to perform a number of reconnaissance and monitoring missions. Many of the modified C-135 variants are undergoing engine upgrades to the CFM-56 powerplant. Crew training for the RC-135V and W are flown in three modified C-135Bs (redesignated TC-135S and W models).

RC-135 Rivet Joint communications intelligence gathering aircraft were used to monitor Iraqi military communications during

Operation Desert Shield. Intelligence gathered by the RC-135, which supported AWACS aircraft, was used to prevent a surprise attack by the Iraqis on Coalition bases in Saudi Arabia. When the war got underway, RC-135s monitored attacks to help Coalition commanders adjust to possible enemy counter-attacks. In all, RC-135s flew 197 sorties during Operation Desert Storm.

As Operation Iraqi Freedom ramped up in early 2003, two RC-135s from Offutt's 38th and 343rd Reconnaissance Squadrons were deployed to Saudi Arabia. The first aircraft departed on March 10 and was in theater ready for combat when the war began.

In support of the 1989 Open Skies Treaty, three WC-135Ws were modified to OC-135B configuration with four cameras; these aircraft engaged in treaty compliance flights over participating countries. Aside from the aircraft flight and maintenance crews, the Open Skies aircraft carry staff from the Department of Defense's Threat Reduction Agency as well as representatives from the country being over-flown. For low-level photography, the OC-135B has been fitted with three KS-87E cameras (one pointing vertically and two looking obliquely), and a KA-91C panoramic camera for photography at cruise altitudes around 35,000 feet. In addition to the cameras, OC-135Bs are fitted with synthetic aperture radar and video recording sensors. One OC-135B is kept in flyable storage, while the operating pair serves with Air Combat Command's 45th Reconnaissance Squadron, 55th Wing at Offutt AFB, Nebraska.

To monitor the behavior of other nations and their ballistic missile programs, the air force operates the RC-135S Cobra Ball. This aircraft can track a ballistic missile launch from outside a country's airspace using infrared telescopes and other sensors, including lasers used for range finding. The air force also operates a WC-135W for gathering air samples after nuclear tests.

The EC-18 advanced range instrumentation aircraft is flown from Edwards AFB, California. This aircraft is fitted with a seven-foot diameter parabolic telemetry antenna in a bulbous nose radome, as well as antennas in the wingtips. The EC-18 can be used to track air-to-air and cruise missiles, as well as theater and ballistic missiles.

C-135

	UNITS ASSIGNED	
UNIT	**NICKNAME**	**TAIL CODE**
EC-18B		
AFMC		Edwards AFB, GA
OC-135B		
45th RS	Sylvester	OF
RC-135		
38th RS	Fighting Hellcats	OF
45th RS	Sylvester	OF
82nd RS	Hog Heaven	OF (Kadena AB, Okinawa)
95th	Kickin' Ass	OF (RAF Mindenhall)
343rd RS		OF
TC-135		
45th RS	Sylvester	OF
WC-135		
45th RS	Sylvester	OF

C-135

RC-135

Mission: Surveillance

Builder: Boeing

Powerplant: Four CFM F108-CF-100 turbofans rated at 22,224 pounds thrust each

Length: 136 feet, 3 inches

Height: 41 feet, 8 inches

Wingspan: 130 feet, 10 inches

Weight: 322,500 maximum takeoff

Speed: 530 miles per hour at 30,000 feet

Range: 1,500 miles with 150,000 pounds of transfer fuel; ferry mission, up to 11,015 miles

Crew: Varies, depending upon mission

RQ-1A/B Predator

The RQ-1A Predator is an unmanned aerial vehicle (UAV) capable of aerial reconnaissance, target surveillance, and engagement, and is usually controlled by an in-theater commander. The Predator system is composed of 4 RQ-1As, a ground-control station with satellite uplink, and 55 personnel. The entire system is designed to be transported in a C-130 Hercules. A pilot flies the UAV while sitting in the ground station and obtaining visual cues from a color monitor that provides the view from the RQ-1's nose-mounted camera. The pilot is assisted by two sensor operators who monitor infrared and synthetic aperture radar sensors that can see at night or through clouds. RQ-1Bs are equipped with a turbocharged engine and deicing equipment. Nearly 90 RQ-1As have been delivered to the air force.

Used in conjunction with AC-130s in the skies over Afghanistan, Predators and their ground-based operators would identify and track targets, stream a video feed from the RQ-1A to the AC-130, and then hand that target off to the gunships. While the AC-130 was destroying the target, the Predator would range ahead to locate and track the next one.

RQ-1As have provided service over Kosovo, Afghanistan, and most recently in Operation Iraqi Freedom. Over Iraq, RQ-1As flew armed with an AGM-114 Hellfire missile for use against ground targets and a pair of Stinger air-to-air missiles for defense against close-range, airborne threats.

Equipped with a daylight TV camera, infrared sensors, and synthetic aperture radar, the Predator is an unmanned medium-altitude surveillance vehicle. At least 48 RQ-1s have been assigned to the 11th, 15th, and 17th Reconnaissance Squadrons operating from Indian Springs AAF, Nevada. *Jim Dunn*

While the air force learns new lessons with each Predator deployment, they have taken action to extend the UAV's capabilities. Under the Scathe Falcon program, the Predator's control station will be installed into a C-130, which will enable the UAV to be controlled in flight with the operator moving at a relative, safe distance. The U.S. Navy is investigating the potential of adding a Predator control station to a P-3 Orion. As the Predator shows its prowess in battle, a new, turboprop-powered version with an 86-foot wingspan is being tested by the air force. Known as Predator B, this UAV may carry medium-range AIM-9 Sidewinder and long-range AIM-120 air-to-air missiles and an increased sensor suite.

Current U.S. budget plans call for the air force to receive almost 20 RQ-1s in 2003 and nearly a dozen Predator Bs per year for the foreseeable future, beginning in 2004.

RQ-1A/B PREDATOR

Mission: Airborne surveillance
Builder: General Atomics Aeronautical Systems, Inc.
Powerplant: Rotax 914, four cylinder engine capable of 101 horsepower
Length: 27 feet
Height: 6 feet, 9 inches
Wingspan: 48 feet, 7 inches
MGTOW: 2,250 pounds
Speed: 84 miles per hour cruise, 135 maximum
Range: 454 miles
Armament: 450 pounds of missiles (currently Hellfire and Stinger)
Unit Cost: $40 million per system
Inventory:

> Active force – 48

RQ-1A/B PREDATOR

UNITS ASSIGNED	
UNIT	**TAIL CODE**
11th RS	WA (Indian Springs)
15th RS	WA (Indian Springs)
17th RS	WA (Indian Springs)

The RQ-4A Global Hawk is an unmanned high-altitude, long-endurance, aerial vehicle designed to provide field commanders near-real-time views over a wide area. It can survey up to 40,000 square nautical miles in a 24-hour period. *Jim Dunn*

RQ-4 Global Hawk

The U.S. military's need for near-real-time imagery of a battlefield or prolonged reconnaissance of a large geographic area drove the requirement for the RQ-4 Global Hawk. The ability to fly up to 12,000 miles, loiter over a target for up to 35 hours, collect data from 65,000 feet, and perform this mission in any weather gives military commanders an invaluable asset. The air force states that the RQ-4 can map 40,000 nautical square miles, an area the size of Illinois, in 24 hours.

While orbiting over enemy territory, the RQ-4 can protect itself by gathering threat information with its AN/ALR-89 radar warning receiver, its on-board radar jamming system, or by deploying its ALE-50 towed decoy system. For added protection, the RQ-4 and its aerial environment can be monitored by AWACS and JSTARS aircraft, or it can be escorted by a combat air patrol.

The RQ-4 uses a 10-inch reflecting telescope as the optical system for its infrared and electro-optical sensors, and the aircraft is equipped with synthetic aperture radar and a ground moving target indicator that can see through all weather to produce an image with a 1-foot resolution of clarity.

The RQ-4 program is currently in the engineering development phase and will soon enter low-rate, initial production, due to a $307

million contract that was awarded on February 3, 2003, to Northrop Grumman for six aircraft. Ten days later, the seventh RQ-4 was delivered to Edwards AFB. This aircraft is the last of the pre-production prototypes and features an integrated mission management computer for pre-programmed flight and navigation parameters. The U.S. Air Force plans to acquire 51 RQ-4s by 2010, and the navy has contracted for two aircraft, which will be delivered in 2005.

RQ-4 GLOBAL HAWK

Mission: Theater reconnaissance
Builder: Northrop Grumman (Ryan Aeronautical Center)
Powerplant: Allison AE3007H turbofan capable of 7,200 pounds thrust
Length: 44 feet, 4 inches
Height: 15 feet, 2 inches
Wingspan: 116 feet, 2 inches
MGTOW: 25,600 pounds
Speed: 389 miles per hour
Range: 12,000 nautical miles or maximum endurance of 42 hours
Inventory:
Test force — 6

RQ-4 GLOBAL HAWK

UNITS ASSIGNED	
UNIT	TAIL CODE
12th RS	BB
452nd FLTS	ED

In 1991, all TR-1As including 80-1099 were redesignated U-2Rs. Assigned to the 99th RS, of the 9th RW at Beale AFB, 80-1099 was the last of 25 TR-1As built. Its delivery marked the end of U-2 production. *Jim Dunn*

U-2S/TU-2S Dragon Lady

Developed in complete secrecy at Lockheed's famed "Skunk Works," the U-2 was first flown in August 1955. Referred to as the Dragon Lady for its flight handling characteristics, the plane performs strategic reconnaissance from altitudes above 65,000 feet. During the late 1950s, U-2s flying at high altitudes could not be intercepted by enemy fighters, which at the time had a ceiling of 58,000 feet.

On May 1, 1960, a U-2 flown by Francis Gary Powers was shot down over the Soviet Union, triggering an international incident when Powers was captured and tried for spying. In August 1962, a U-2 photographed Soviet-built SS-4 Sandal intermediate range ballistic missiles being positioned in Cuba, thus beginning the Cuban Missile Crisis.

The U-2R variant, introduced in the mid-1960s, featured a larger fuselage to accommodate additional sensor packages and

the J75-P-13B engine. In 1979, the air force contracted with Lockheed for the construction of additional U-2 airframes, although this batch of aircraft was designated TR-1 for Tactical Reconnaissance to avoid the stigma of buying more "spyplanes."

In the 40 years since the Cuban Missile Crisis, the U-2 has undergone numerous upgrades and retrofits. In May 1988, the air force and engine builder General Electric launched a program to retrofit the new F118-GE-101 engine to the U-2R/TR-1 airframe. The newly modified aircraft have been redesignated U-2S. The F118-GE-101 engine enables the U-2S to climb 3,500 feet higher, giving it a ceiling of 77,500 feet, a 1,200 nautical mile increase in range, longer mission endurance, and a 30 percent weight savings over the J75 engine.

Nine U-2s (four TR-1s and five U-2s) were in the Gulf region and ready for action at the beginning of Operation Desert Storm on January 16, 1991. Those aircraft flew 238 sorties during the war, flying both photographic and electronic intelligence (ELINT) missions, locating Scud missile sites, and providing bomb damage

Returning to its enclosure at Beale AFB, U-2S 80-1074 was originally delivered as a TR-1A. *Jim Dunn*

U-25/TU-25 DRAGON LADY

Mission: Photographic and electronic reconnaissance

Builder: Lockheed Martin

Powerplant: One General Electric F118-GE-101 engine capable of 17,000 pounds thrust

Length: 62 feet, 9 inches

Height: 16 feet

Wingspan: 103 feet

MGTOW: 40,000 pounds

Speed: 475-plus miles per hour

Range: 7,000 miles

Ceiling: 77,500 feet

Crew: One

Date Deployed: U-2, 1955; U-2R, 1967; U-2S, October 1994

Inventory:

Active force – 37

assessment imagery to theater commanders. The Dragon Lady provided half of all imagery used in Operation Desert Storm and 90 percent of the ground forces' targeting information. In Operation Allied Force, U-2s supplied more than 80 percent of the photo reconnaissance imagery used to select targets for future air strikes. The U-2 played an active part in Operation Iraqi Freedom, and the U.S. Air Force intends to fly the aircraft until the year 2050.

U-25/TU-25 DRAGON LADY

UNITS ASSIGNED

UNIT	NICKNAME	TAIL CODE
1st RS		BB
5th RS	Black Cats	BB (Osan AB, Korea)
99th RS		BB

rior that features a ball-roller cargo floor for handling cargo pallets.

In 1997, the air force ordered a pair of Gulfstream Vs, which have a range of 6,300 miles. Larger and with more powerful engines, the Gulfstream V has been designated C-37A. The aircraft is in service with the 89th Airlift Wing at Andrews AFB.

SPECIAL MISSION AIRCRAFT

C-20A/B/C • C-20H • C-37A Gulfstreams

C-20 is the military designation for the Gulfstream III executive jet. The air force has acquired three C-20As, seven C-20Bs, and three C-20Cs for transporting high-ranking military leaders. In 1990, two Gulfstream IVs were delivered to the air force and designated C-20Hs.

In U.S. Navy and Marine Corps service, the C-20D is the designation for the Gulfstream III, and C-20G denotes the Gulfstream IV. Navy C-20Gs are convertible from a passenger interior to a cargo inte-

VC-25A (Air Force One)

There is one aircraft that represents everything that the United States stands for, and which is readily identifiable by its paint scheme. That aircraft is *Air Force One*. For nearly 20 years, *Air Force One* was a Boeing 707-320B. The type carried Presidents Eisenhower, Kennedy, Johnson, Nixon, Ford, Carter, and Reagan on diplomatic missions all over the globe. The most memorable 707 *Air Force One* flights include Eisenhower's trip to Paris for talks with Nikita Khrushchev in May 1960, Kennedy's to Berlin in 1963, Johnson's to Vietnam in 1967, and Nixon's February 1972 trip to open relations with China.

C-20A/B/C, C-20J. C-37A

Mission: C-20A, operational support airlift; C-20B/H and C-37, special air missions

Builder: Gulfstream Aerospace Corp.

Powerplant: C-20A/B, two Rolls-Royce Spey Mark 511-8 turbofan engines of 11,400 pounds thrust each; C-20H, two Rolls-Royce Tay Mark 611-8 turbofan engines capable of 13,850 pounds each; C-37, two BMW/Rolls Royce BR710-48 high bypass ratio turbofan engines capable of 14,464 pounds thrust each

Length: C-20A/B, 83 feet, 2 inches; C-20H, 88 feet, 4 inches; C-37, 96 feet, 5 inches

Height: C-20A/B and C-20H, 24 feet, 6 inches; C-37, 25 feet, 11 inches

Wingspan: C-20A/B and C-20H, 77 feet, 10 inches; C-37, 93 feet, 6 inches

Speed: C-20A/B and C-20H, 576 miles per hour; C-37, 600 miles per hour

MGTOW: C-20A/B, 69,700 pounds; C-20H, 74,600 pounds; C-37 90,500 pounds

Range: C-20A/B, 4,250 miles; C-20H, 4,850 miles; C-37, 6,300 miles

Ceiling: C-20A/B and C-20H, 45,000 feet; C-37, 51,000 feet

Load: 12 passengers

Crew: Five (pilot, copilot, flight mechanic, communication system operator, flight attendant)

Unit Cost: C-20, all models $29.4 (fiscal year 1998 constant dollars); C-37, $36 million

Date Deployed: C-20A, 1983; C-20B, 1988; C-20H, 1992; C-37, 1998

Inventory: C-20A, Active force, 3; C-20B, Active force, 5; C-20H, Active force, 2; C-37, Active force, 2

C-20A/B/C, C-20J. C-37A

UNITS ASSIGNED

UNIT	NICKNAME	TAIL CODE
C-20		
76th AS	Sam Europe	no tail code, Ramstein AB, Germany
99th AS	Sam Fox	no tail code, Andrews AFB
VR-1	Star Lifters	JK (C-20D USN)
VR-48	Capital Skyliners	JR (C-20G, USN)
VR-51	Wind Jammers	RW (C-20G, USN)
H&HS		MCAS Kaneohe Bay, HI (C-20G, USN)
MASD(VM)5A		NAF Washington (C-20G, USMC)
(MASD=Marine Air Support Detachment)		
C-37		
99th AS	Sam Fox	no tail code, Andrews AFB
65th AS	Special Missions Hawaii	no tail code, Hickam AFB, HI
309th AS		Chievres AB, Belgium

The C-32As are designed to be used by the vice-president, cabinet, and members of Congress. With a crew of 16 and the maximum of 45 passengers, the C-32A is able to fly non-stop from Andrews AFB to Frankfurt, Germany. The cockpit is equipped with a military IFF, GPS, flight management system, and Traffic Collision Avoidance System (TCAS). *Ed Davies*

In 1990, the U.S. Air Force took delivery of the first of two VC-25As, which replaced the 707s for use in transporting the commander in chief. Based on Boeing's commercial 747-200B, the aircraft have become the new flying Oval Office. When the president is on-board, the VC-25A flies under the call sign Air Force One.

Each VC-25A is capable of being refueled inflight, they are quieter and more fuel efficient than the 707s they replaced, and have more than 250 percent more floor space. Interior accommodations include a presidential stateroom, offices, rest areas for the crew and the president's staff, a secretarial area, two galleys capable of seating for a small contingent of media representatives, and a communications center.

Due to the sensitive nature of its mission and the importance of its human cargo, the VC-25As can operate autonomously, without relying on the host airport's ground support equipment. The VC-25As have internal airstairs and cargo handling equipment. Although unarmed, both VC-25As are reportedly equipped with chaff dispensers, flares, threat assessment radar warning devices, and the ALQ-204 infrared countermeasures suite designed to defeat multiple heat-seeking missiles.

Both VC-25As are maintained and crewed by personnel from the Presidential Airlift Group, 89th Airlift Wing, Andrews AFB, Maryland.

VC-25A

UNITS ASSIGNED

Presidential Airlift Group, 89th Airlift Wing, Andrews AFB, Maryland

VC-25A

Mission: Presidential transport
Builder: Boeing
Powerplant: Four General Electric CF6-80C2B1 engines capable of 56,700 pounds thrust each
Length: 231 feet, 10 inches
Height: 63 feet, 5 inches
Wingspan: 195 feet, 8 inches
MGTOW: 833,000 pounds
Speed: 630 miles per hour
Range: 7,800 miles
Crew: 26 with seating for 70 passengers
Date Deployed: December 8, 1990
Inventory:
        Active force – 2

VC-32A

Although there are four VC-32As in the air force's inventory, the aircraft is most commonly seen as *Air Force Two*, the plane that transports the vice president of the United States. Other VC-32As are used to fly members of the Cabinet as well as members of Congress.

Boeing's successful 757-200ER (extended range) commercial airliner serves as the basis for the VC-32A. This jetliner is certified for ETOPS (extended-range twin engine operations), which means that if an engine has to be shut down in flight, while over water, the aircraft can fly to the nearest airport safely—even if the landing field is 180 minutes away.

The VC-32A's interior is divided into four main areas capable of seating 45 passengers. The aircraft is equipped with the latest, airliner-type flight management system, wind shear and ground proximity warning systems, TCAS (traffic alert and collision avoidance system), and a GPS system for non-precision-instrument approaches to landing. Crews from the 1st Airlift Squadron, 89th Airlift Wing, Andrews AFB, Maryland, fly and maintain these aircraft.

VC-32A

UNITS ASSIGNED

1st Airlift Squadron, 89th Airlift Wing, Andrews AFB, Maryland

VC-32A

Mission: Personnel transport

Builder: Boeing

Powerplant: Two Pratt & Whitney 2040 engines capable of 41,700 pounds thrust each

Length: 155 feet, 3 inches

Height: 44 feet, 6 inches

Wingspan: 124 feet, 8 inches

MGTOW: 255,000 pounds

Speed: 530 miles per hour

Range: 5,500 nautical miles

Crew: Two pilots plus up to 14 crew/staff depending upon mission type and duration

Date Deployed: June 19, 1998

Inventory:

        Active force – 4

AIR FORCE TAIL CODES

CODE	BASE
AC	Atlantic City ANGB, New Jersey
AF	U.S. Air Force Academy, Colorado
AK	Eielson AFB, Alaska
AL	Montgomery, Alabama (ANG)
AN	Kulis ANGB, Anchorage, Alaska
AV	Aviano AB, Italy
AZ	Tucson International Airport, Arizona
BB	Beale AFB, California
BC	Battle Creek ANGB, Michigan
BD	Barksdale AFB, Louisiana
CA	Moffett Federal Airfield ANGS, California
CB	Columbus AFB, Mississippi
CC	Cannon AFB, New Mexico
CI	Channel Islands ANGS, California
CO	Buckley AFB, Colorado
CT	Bradley ANGB, Connecticut
DC	Andrews AFB, Maryland
DE	New Castle County Airport, Delaware
DM	Davis-Monthan AFB, Arizona (355th Wing)
DR	Davis-Monthan AFB, Arizona (305th RQS)
DY	Dyess AFB, Texas
ED	Edwards AFB, California
EF	Ellington Field ANGB, Texas
EG	Eglin AFB, Florida (33rd Fighter Wing)
EL	Ellsworth AFB, South Dakota
EN	Sheppard AFB, Texas
ET	Eglin AFB, Florida (46th TW)
FE	F.E. Warren AFB, Wyoming
FF	Langley AFB, Virginia
FL	Patrick AFB, Florida
FM	Dade County/Homestead ARS, Florida
FS	Fort Smith, Arkansas (ANG)
FT	Pope AFB, North Carolina
FW	Fort Wayne International Airport, Indiana
GA	Robins AFB, Georgia (116th BW)
HA	Sioux City, Iowa (ANG)
HH	Hickam AFB, Hawaii
HI	Hill AFB, Utah (419th FW)
HL	Hill AFB, Utah (388th FW)
HO	Holloman AFB, New Mexico (49th FW)
HT	Holloman AFB, New Mexico (46th TG)
HV	Vandenberg AFB, California
IA	Des Moines, Iowa (ANG)
ID	Boise, Idaho (ANG)

CODE	BASE
S	NAS Keflavik, Iceland
JZ	NAS New Orleans Joint Reserve Base (JRB), Louisiana
KC	Whiteman AFB, Missouri
KS	Keesler AFB, Mississippi
LA	Barksdale AFB, Louisiana
LD	Lackland AFB, Texas
LF	Luke AFB, Arizona (56th FW)
LI	Gabreski ANGB, New York
LN	RAF Lakenheath, United Kingdom
LR	Luke AFB, Arizona (944th FW)
MA	Otis ANGB, Massachusetts (102nd FW)
MA	Barnes ANGB, Massachusetts (104th FW)
MD	Warfield ANGB, Maryland
MF	Greenville ANGB, South Carolina
MI	Selfridge ANGB, Michigan
MM	Malmstrom AFB, Montana
MN	Duluth, Minnesota (ANG)
MO	Mountain Home AFB, Idaho
MT	Minot AFB, North Dakota (5th BW and 91st SPW)
MY	Moody AFB, Georgia
NC	Douglas International Airport, Charlotte, North Carolina
ND	Hector International Airport, Fargo, North Dakota
NM	Kirtland AFB, New Mexico
NO	NAS New Orleans JRB, Louisiana
NY	Syracuse, New York (ANG)
OF	Offutt AFB, Nebraska
OH	Springfield, Ohio (ANG)
OK	Tinker AFB, Oklahoma
OK	Tulsa International Airport, Oklahoma
OS	Osan AB, Republic of Korea
OT	Eglin AFB, Florida (53rd Wing, 85th TES)
OT	Nellis AFB, Nevada (53rd Wing, 422nd TES)
PA	NAS Willow Grove JRB, Pennsylvania
PD	Portland, Oregon (ANG)
RA	Randolph AFB, Texas
RI	Quonset, Rhode Island (ANG)
RS	Ramstein AB, Germany
SA	Kelly AFB, Texas
SC	McEntire ANGS, South Carolina
SI	Springfield, Illinois (ANG)
SJ	Seymour Johnson AFB, North Carolina
SL	St. Louis, Missouri (ANG)
SP	Spangdahlem AB, Germany

AIR FORCE TAIL CODES CONTINUED

CODE	BASE
ST	Sheppard AFB, Texas
SW	Shaw AFB, South Carolina
TD	Tyndall AFB, Florida (53rd WEG)
TH	Terre Haute, Indiana (ANG)
TX	NAS Fort Worth JRB, Texas
TY	Tyndall AFB, Florida (325th FW)
VA	Richmond, Virginia (ANG)
VN	Vance AFB, Oklahoma
VT	Burlington, Vermont (ANG)
WA	Nellis AFB, Nevada (57th Wing)
WI	Madison, Wisconsin (ANG)
WM	Whiteman AFB, Missouri
WP	Kusan AB, Republic of Korea
WR	Robbins AFB, Georgia (93rd ACW)
WV	Marrtinsburg, West Virginia (ANG)
WW	Misawa AB, Japan
WY	Cheyenne Airport, Wyoming
XL	Laughlin AFB, Texas
YJ	Yokota AB, Japan
ZZ	Kadena AB, Japan

Notes: AB – Air Base; AFB – Air Force Base; ANGB – Air National Guard Base; ANGS – Air National Guard Station; NAS – Naval Air Station; RAF – Royal Air Force; RQS – Rescue Squadron.

PART II

NAVY & MARINE

U.S. Navy and Marine Corps Aviation

Eugene Ely was the first man to fly an aircraft off a ship on November 14, 1910, when he flew a Curtiss pusher biplane from a specially constructed wooden ramp off the bow of the cruiser *Birmingham*. The ensuing 92 years have seen dramatic changes in the U.S. Navy and the employment of naval aviation. The carrier battles of World War II showed that the age of surface ships engaging one another on the horizon and slugging it out with huge cannons was over. Control of the sky meant control of the sea. From early 1945, when carrier planes ranged over the Japanese home islands, naval aircraft have been used to project power and protect American interests abroad.

Today's navy boasts more than 4,000 planes, ranging from front-line fighters to patrol and early-warning aircraft. The navy is composed of approximately 55,800 officers and 321,400 enlisted men and women with an additional 150,000 serving in the U.S. Naval Reserve.

The navy's main fighting unit is the carrier strike group, often called a carrier battle group. The carrier forms the nucleus of the group and is surrounded by a pair of guided missile cruisers used to deliver Tomahawk cruise missiles to targets up to 1,000 miles away. Sailing in the anti-air warfare (AAW) role is a guided missile destroyer, which is accompanied by an antisubmarine warfare (ASW) destroyer and an ASW frigate. In addition, two attack submarines and a fleet oiler, which also carries ammunition and other stores support the group. Embarked on the carrier is the carrier air wing, the carrier battle group's primary strike weapon. Typically, a carrier air wing consists of 85 aircraft in one F-14 Tomcat squadron, three F/A-18 Hornet squadrons, an S-3B Viking sea control squadron, an EA-6B electronic warfare squadron, an E-2C Hawkeye airborne early warning command and control squadron, as well as one SH-60 squadron for plane guard and ASW patrols.

Currently, eight carriers are operational and two are under construction; all of them are nuclear powered, and together they comprise the Nimitz Class. They include the USS *Nimitz* (CVN 68) of San Diego, California; USS *Dwight D. Eisenhower* (CVN 69), Newport News, Virginia; USS *Carl Vinson* (CVN 70), Bremerton, Washington; USS *Theodore Roosevelt* (CVN 71), Norfolk, Virginia; USS *Abraham Lincoln* (CVN 72), Everett, Washington; USS *George Washington* (CVN 73), Norfolk, Virginia; USS *John C. Stennis* (CVN 74), San Diego, California; and the USS *Harry S. Truman* (CVN 75), Norfolk, Virginia. The navy is currently constructing two additional ships, *Ronald Reagan* (CVN 76), which will be commissioned in July 2003, and *George H. W. Bush* (CVN 77), which will sail in 2009.

The navy has moved into the concept design phase for a new class of aircraft carriers, designated CVN-21, and expected to join the fleet in the year 2014. They will be roughly the same size as the *Nimitz*-class carriers, with a complement of 5,500 crew and a 4.5-acre flight deck. CVN-21 air groups will encompass F/A-18 Super Hornets, the electronic warfare EA-18G Growler, the F-35C naval version of the Joint Strike Fighter, and the MH-60 series of helicopter for air-sea rescue and antisubmarine warfare.

CORPS

A number of F/A-18Ds serving in the VMFA (AW) squadrons do not have flight controls in the rear cockpit. These F/A-18Ds are equipped with two multi-functional displays and two sidesticks for control and guidance of weapons. *Richard Vander Meulen*

Assigned to the Maulers of VS-32 at NAS Jacksonville, S-3B 159762 is the CAG bird for the squadron. *Jim Dunn*

U.S. Marine Corps

For all intents, the Marine Corps is the U.S. Navy's land attack force. The Corps has its own potent air force, organized into air wings, which are assigned to Marine Expeditionary Units (MEUs) for forward deployments. Marine Air Wings can deploy aboard U.S. Navy carriers or Navy Amphibious Readiness Groups (ARGs).

Air elements of the Corps are controlled by either the Commander, U.S. Marine Corps Forces Atlantic (COMMARFORLANT),

stationed at Norfolk, Virginia, or Commander U.S. Marine Corps Forces Pacific (COMMARFORPAC), headquartered at Marine Corps Base Hawaii (Camp H. M. Smith) on the island of Oahu.

When deployed, Marine Expeditionary Units are assigned to amphibious assault ships that carry the unit's close air support AV-8B Harrier jets, as well as its rotary wing components, including AH-1 Cobras, UH-1N Hueys, CH-46E Sea Knights, and CH-53E

Assigned to HMLA-367 at Camp Pendleton, AH-1W 160821 displays the General Electric M197 20mm, three-barreled cannon mounted in the GTK4A nose turret. *Rene J. Francillon*

Super Stallions. In addition to deploying troops using helicopters, amphibious assault ships also carry one LCAC (Landing Craft, Air Cushion) and two LCU (Landing Craft, Utility).

The Marine Corps aircraft stable will change little over the next decade. New J model C-130s and the F/A-18E and F are being procured, but until the arrival of the Corps' F-35 Joint Strike Fighters, the service will concentrate on upgrading the systems of its existing aircraft. At this point in time, the Marines have a mix of fixed- and rotary-wing aircraft that perfectly suit its mission.

The purpose of the Marine Corps aviation is to provide close air support (CAS) to marine ground forces. The McDonnell Douglas AV-8B Harrier II is at the forefront of Marine CAS. Based at MCAS Yuma, Arizona, AV-8B 163688 is assigned to the Tomcats of VMA-311. *Rene J. Francillon*

Now in the twilight years of its service, the Grumman F-14 Tomcat still remains a potent and valuable asset to navy carrier-based aviation. This F-14D serves with the Tomcatters of VF-31 at NAS Oceana, Virginia. *Richard Vander Meulen*

FIGHTERS/STRIKE AIRCRAFT

F-14A/B/D Tomcat

Designed to replace the navy's successful F-4 Phantom II, the Grumman F-14 Tomcat came to be known as the ultimate air superiority fighter of the twentieth century. Capable of 1,544 miles per hour at 40,000 feet, the Tomcat's agility and its mission equipment make it nearly unbeatable in the sky. The F-14D's AN/APG-71 X-band, pulse-Doppler radar can simultaneously track and detect as many as 24 targets in any weather. The radar system can then direct AIM-54 Phoenix missiles toward 6 targets while monitoring the remaining 18 targets. Additional sensor systems include the AN/AVX-1 TV camera, AN/AAQ-14 LANTIRN (Low Altitude and Navigation Targeting Infrared for Night) pods, as well as the TARPS (tactical air reconnaissance pod system).

After the navy cancelled the swing-wing FB-111 contract in the 1960s, Grumman took many of the systems developed for that aircraft and incorporated them into a new design. The navy was very interested in Grumman's proposal and put the concept out for bid. Grumman won the contract for 6, later increased to 11, proof-of-concept aircraft. The Tomcat featured a variable geometry wing that is swept back for high subsonic and supersonic flight. The F-14A prototype first flew on December 21, 1970, and the Tomcat entered squadron service four years later. The Tomcat was built in the F-14A, B and D models. Eighteen F-14As were rebuilt to F-14D configuration, which features a pair of General Electric F100-GE-400 turbofan engines rated at 26,950 pounds thrust in afterburner.

Tomcats taught the Libyan Air Force not to antagonize the U.S. Navy, and they did it not once, but twice. On August 19, 1981, two VF-41 Black Aces Tomcats were flying combat air patrol (CAP) guarding the USS *Nimitz* near the coast of Libya. The flight of Black Aces F-14s was vectored to intercept a pair of Su-22s, when one fired an air-to-air missile at the Tomcats. The F-14s engaged the Libyan fighters with AIM-9 Sidewinder missiles, sending both aircraft into the gulf.

In January 1989, Libyan leader Muammar Al Qadhafi was rattling his sword once again. This time a pair of VF-32 Swordsmen Tomcats from the USS *John F. Kennedy* were airborne when a pair of Libyan MiG-23s attempted to engage. As the MiGs were running for the safety of the Libyan coast, one of the Tomcats fired an AIM-7 Sparrow that missed the lead aircraft. The second MiG was splashed by an AIM-7, and the flight leader's luck ran out when an AIM-9 ended his flying career.

In the first Gulf War, the Iraqi Air Force chose to defect to Iran, and very few air-to-air engagements occurred. F-14s flew CAP and barrier patrol missions for Coalition naval forces, provided battle damage assessment photos using TARPS pods, and ranged over Iraqi territory looking for Scud missile sites. In all, 109 Tomcats were based on board five carriers during the war, and they flew 4,005 sorties.

In the years following Desert Storm, Tomcats flew combat missions over Yugoslavia and in support of Operation Enduring Freedom. Four Tomcat squadrons participated in Operation Iraqi Freedom, including VF-154, flying A models from the USS *Kitty Hawk*, VF-103's F-14Bs from the USS *George Washington*, and F-

Launching from the USS *Abraham Lincoln*, these two new-build F-14Ds, 163413/107 and 164343/106, belong to the Tomcatters of VF-31 assigned to CVW-14. *Jim Dunn*

14Ds from both VF-31 on the USS *Abraham Lincoln* and VF-2 on board the USS *Constellation*.

When F-14D Tomcat purchases were cancelled in 1990 to fund future Naval fighter development programs, such as the ill-fated A-12 and multi-mission aircraft such as the F/A-18E/F, the Tomcat's service life became limited. The navy intends to keep the type flying until the year 2007, and the service is now retiring the A model.

F-14A/B/D TOMCAT

UNITS ASSIGNED		
UNIT	**NICKNAME**	**TAIL CODE**
VF-2	Bounty Hunters	NE
VF-11	Red Rippers	AG
VF-31	Tomcatters	NK
VF-32	Swordsmen	AC
VF-101	Grim Reapers	AD
VF-103	Jolly Rogers	AD
VF-143	Pukin' Dogs	AG
VF-154	Black Knights	NF
VF-211	Checkmater	NG
VF-213	Black Lions	NH
VX-23	Strike	SD
VX-30	Bloodhounds	BH
VX-9 DET	Evaluators	XF
NSAWC,	(NAS Fallon,	NV

F-14A/B/D TOMCAT

Mission: Multi-role strike fighter

Builder: Grumman Aerospace Corp.

Powerplant: Two General Electric F110GE-400 afterburning turbofan engines rated at 27,900 pounds thrust each

Length: 61 feet, 9 inches

Height: 16 feet

Wingspan: 64 feet (unswept), 38 feet (swept)

MGTOW: 72,900 pounds

Speed: 1,544 miles per hour at 40,000 feet

Range: 2,200 miles (ferry)

Armament: One M61 Vulcan cannon, 13,000 pounds of bombs and missiles

Crew: Two

Date Deployed: 1973

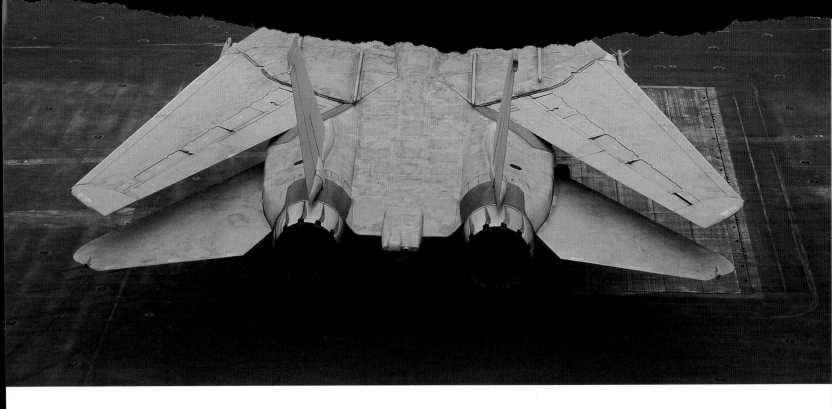

With a fuselage length of 62 feet, 8 inches, and an empty weight over 40,000 pounds, the F-14 is the largest and heaviest fighter aircraft in navy history. *Jim Dunn*

Just a few years ago, each carrier air wing had two F-14 squadrons assigned. Now some carriers are sailing without any Tomcats aboard, and final retirement for the type may come as early as 2005. The changing of the guard can be viewed on the deck of the *Lincoln* as F/A-18Es from VFA-115 make the first operational deployment with the type that will soon replace the Tomcat. *Jim Dunn*

First designed for the air combat role, the F/A-18 Hornet soon evolved into an attack aircraft. This F/A-18A serves with the Vampires of VX-9 at NAS China Lake, California. *Lou Drummond*

F/A-18 A/B/C/D Hornet

The F/A-18 Hornet traces its roots back to the Northrop Model P-530, P-600, and P-630—twin-engine, twin-tail fighter designs that competed, unsuccessfully, for the air force's mid-1970s air combat fighter program. When the navy announced its VFAX (lightweight, multi-mission fighter) competition, Northrop and McDonnell Douglas partnered to develop a naval version of the P-630. The joint design was tested as the navy's YF-17 prototype, and was contracted for production as the Fighter/Attack Model 18 (F/A-18) Hornet.

The prototype F/A-18 flew from McDonnell Douglas' St. Louis, Missouri, factory on November 18, 1978. The aircraft was fitted with the Hughes AN/APG-65 radar for both ground mapping and air-to-air target location and fire control, a pair of AIM-9s on the wing-tip rails, a pair of AIM-7s on fuselage hardpoints, and a 20mm M61 cannon in the nose. The aircraft were delivered in single-seat A model and two-seat B model configurations. Initial deliveries to the U.S. Navy began in May 1980 to VFA-125 at Naval Air Station Lemoore, California. The type became operational in 1983, with the marines on January 7 flying with VFMA-314, and the navy in October with VFA-113.

On September 3, 1987, the first F/A-18C flew, which incorporated new AIM-120 missiles and AN/ALQ-65 electronic countermeasures equipment. The two-seat D model flew on May 6, 1988. The C and D models were later fitted with AN/AAR-50 FLIR systems, night-vision goggle-compatible avionics, and AN/APG-73 radar enabling the aircraft to fight in all weather conditions and at night. The first night-strike Hornets were delivered to the fleet in November 1989.

VFA-81 Hornets claimed the type's first victories on the opening day of Operation Desert Storm. Four VFA-81 F/A-18Cs based aboard the USS *Saratoga* were en route to bomb an airfield in Iraq when they were directed to engage a pair of MiG-21s. Firing AIM-9M air-to-air missiles, Lieutenant Commander Mark Fox and

While F/A-18C 164645 from VFA-25 is positioned on the cat, F/A-18C 164634 from VFA-113 awaits its turn. *Jim Dunn*

Only 41 examples of the two-seat F/A-18B were produced. This example, 161714, is assigned to the NSAWC at NAS Fallon. *Jim Dunn*

Lieutenant Nicholas Mongillo were each credited with a kill. After the Iraqi MiGs fell, the flight of dual-role F/A-18s continued on to bomb the airfield.

The A- and C-model Hornets were put to the test in the 1991 Gulf War. Hornets flew suppression of enemy air defenses (SEAD) missions, attacked ground targets focusing on airfields and supporting infrastructure (offensive counter air, or OCA, missions), and conducted defensive counter air (DCA) escort missions. Hornets flew only 157 SEAD missions. As the Iraqi Air Force was quickly driven from the skies by the Coalition, there was a low number of OCA missions (217). Hornets also flew 2,129 escort sorties, known as DCA or defensive counterair. DCA missions typically escort strike packages into and from the target area. Occasionally, on DCA missions, F/A-18s would carry HARM anti-radiation missiles to destroy enemy ground radars.

Twelve F/A-18Ds were deployed during Operation Desert Storm. The two-seat Hornets flew in the forward air control and tactical air coordination roles, identifying targets and directing strikes for other aircraft. The dozen D models flew 557 sorties, firing more than 27,000 rounds of 20mm cannon ammunition and 2,325 rockets against and to mark ground targets.

During Operation Iraqi Freedom, troops ashore were supported by F/A-18Cs from the U.S. carriers *Kitty Hawk*, *Constellation*, *Nimitz*, and *Abraham Lincoln*. In addition to the United States Navy and Marine Corps, the air arms of Australia, Canada, Finland, Kuwait, Malaysia, Spain, and Switzerland fly the Hornet.

Throughout the 1990s, the capability of the Hornet was continuously improved with system upgrades and additions. Late models featured the uprated F-404-GE-402 afterburning engines, and the AN/APG-73 radar. *Richard Vander Meulen*

Assigned to the Vikings of VMFA (AW)-225 at MCAS Miramar, 165532 is an F/A-18D(CR) night attack/combat reconnaissance version of the Hornet. *Jim Dunn*

F/A-18 A/B/C/D HORNET

Mission: Strike fighter

Builder: Boeing (McDonnell Douglas)

Powerplant: Two F404-GE-402 turbofan engines rated at 17,700 pounds thrust each

Length: 56 feet

Height: 15 feet, 4 inches

Wingspan: 40 feet, 5 inches; 27 feet, 5 inches – folded

MGTOW: 51,900 pounds

Speed: Mach 1.7-plus

Endurance: Combat Air Patrol (150 nautical miles from ship) 1 hour, 45 minutes

Armament: One M61A1/A2 Vulcan 20mm cannon, 13,700 pounds of ordnance

Crew: A, C model: one; B, D model: two

Unit Cost: $29 million

Date Deployed: A, B models: October 1983; C, D models: September 1987

U.S. MARINE CORPS

UNIT	NICKNAME	TAIL CODE
VMFAT-101	Sharpshooters	SH
VMFA-112	Cowboys	MA
VMFA-115	Silver Eagles	VE
VMFA (AW)-121	Green Knights	VK
VMFA-122	Crusaders	DC
VMFA (AW)-124	Bengals	WK
VMFA-142	Flying Gators	MB
VMFA-134	Smoke	MF
VMFA-212	Lancers	WD
VMFA (AW)-225	Vikings	CE
VMFA-232	Red Devils	WT
VMFA (AW)-242	Bats	DT
VMFA-251	Thunderbolts	DW (AB)
VMFA-312	Checkerboards	DR (AC)
VMFA-314	Black Knights	VW (NG)
VMFA-321	Hells Angels	MG
VMFA-323	Death Rattlers	WS (NE)
VMFA (AW)-332	Moonlighters	EA
VMFA (AW)-533	Hawks	ED

F/A-18 A/B/C/D HORNET

UNITS ASSIGNED

UNIT	NICKNAME	TAIL CODE
VFA-15	Valions	AJ
VFA-22	Fighting Redcocks	NH
VFA-25	First of the Fleet	NK
VFA-27	Royal Maces	NF
VFA-34	Blue Blasters	AA
VFA-37	Bulls	AC
VFA-81	Sunliners	AA
VFA-82	Marauders	AB
VFA-83	Rampagers	AA
VFA-86	Sidewinders	AB
VFA-87	Golden Warriors	AJ
VFA-94	Mighty Shriker	NH
VFA-97	Warhawks	NH
VFA-105	Gunslingers	AC
VFA-106	Gladiators	AD
VFA-113	Stingers	NK
VFA-125	Rough Riders	NJ
VFA-131	Wildcats	AG
VFA-136	Knighthawks	AG
VFA-137	Kestrels	NE
VFA-146	Blue Diamonds	NG
VFA-147	Argonauts	NG
VFA-151	Vigilantes	NE
VFA-192	Golden Dragons	NF
VFA-195	Dambusters	NF
VFA-201	Hunters	AF
VFA-203	Blue Dolphins	AF
VFA-204	River Rattlers	AF
VFC-12	Fighting Omars	AF
VX-23	Strike	SD
VX-31	Dust Devils, NAWA China Lake	CA
VX-9	Vampires	XE
NSAWC		NV
NFDS	Blue Angels, NAS Pensacola	FL

Launching from the *Lincoln*, F/A-18E 165781 was one of 12 Super Hornets from the Eagles of VFA-15 aboard during workups for the first-ever operational deployment of the type. On November 6, 2002, these aircraft dropped four GPS-guided JDAMs against SAM sites in southern Iraq during their first ever combat mission. *Jim Dunn*

F/A-18E/F Super Hornet

The multi-mission F/A-18E/F Super Hornet brings to the service a new airplane with state-of-the-art avionics and defensive systems, a more comfortable cockpit to reduce pilot fatigue with digital avionics, and one that has the same fuel capacity as the F-14D Tomcat. The Super Hornet has a larger wing and leading edge extension, more powerful General Electric F414-GE-400 turbofan engines rated at 22,000 pounds thrust each, and square-shaped engine inlets for increased air flow. The first F/A-18E flew on November 29, 1995, followed on April 1, 1996, by the first F/A-18F. Initial sea trials for the Super Hornet began on January 18, 1997, when the first F/A-18F landed on the USS *John C. Stennis*. Super Hornets embarked on the USS *Abraham Lincoln* on July 24, 2002, for their first tour, flown by VFA-115. During the cruise, on November 6, 2002, VFA-115's Super Hornets attacked targets in Iraq's "no-fly" zone. The aircraft were also deployed in support of Operation Southern Watch. In the fleet, Super Hornets have completely replaced the Tomcat aboard the USS *Nimitz*, the most visible step in phasing the F-14 out of service.

Here, F/A-18E 165787 is respotted on the deck of the *Lincoln* to ready it for the next mission. *Jim Dunn*

F/Z-18E/F SUPER HORNET

UNITS ASSIGNED		
UNIT	NICKNAME	TAIL CODE
VFA-14	Top Hatters	NH
VFA-41	Black Aces	NH
VFA-102	Diamondbacks	NG
VFA-115	Eagles	NK
VFA-122	Flying Eagles	NJ
VX-23	Strike	SD
VX-31	Dust Devils,	CA
	NAWS China Lake,	
VX-9	Vampires	XE

F/Z-18E/F SUPER HORNET

Mission: Strike fighter
Contractor: Boeing
Powerplant: Two General Electric F414-GE-400 turbofans rated at 22,000 pounds thrust each
Length: 60 feet, 1 inch
Height: 15 feet, 8 inches
Wingspan: 15 feet, 8 inches
Speed: Mach 1.8-plus
Maximum gross takeoff weight (MGTOW): 63,500 pounds
Endurance: Combat Air Patrol (150 nautical miles from ship) 2 hours, 15 minutes
Armament: One M61A1/A2 Vulcan 20mm cannon plus 17,750 pounds of ordnance
Unit Cost: $60 million
Date Deployed: September 2001

During Operation Iraqi Freedom, the Eagles of VFA-115 flew F/A-18Es from the USS *Abraham Lincoln*. The Top Hatters of VFA-14 flew E models, and the Black Aces of VFA-41 flew F models; both squadrons were flying from the USS *Nimitz*. F/A-18Fs aboard the *Nimitz* were the first of their type to see combat. Additionally, on April 1, 2003, four Super Hornets from VFA-41 deployed to the *Abraham Lincoln* to add flexibility to that ship's air wing.

One mission that Super Hornet pilots would prefer not to be assigned, or even talk about, is that of aerial refuelers. Returning from a refueling mission, F/A-18E 165789 is configured with four 480-gallon fuel tanks and a refueling pod on the centerline station. *Jim Dunn*

This AV-8B (NA) from VMA-311 is on a training mission over the Turtle Mountains Military Operating Area (MOA), California. The NA variant featured a FLIR system and cockpit upgrades. *Rene J. Francillon*

The Marines ordered a total of 300 AV-8Bs and 28 TAV-8B two-seat trainers. A Rolls-Royce Pegasus F402-RR-408A vectored-thrust turbofan engine powers the AV-8B. The first 166 AV-8Bs delivered were basic day-attack (DA) versions, and the next 107 were the night-attack (NA) variant. The final 27 aircraft were the stretched, radar-equipped Harrier II Plus variant. *Rene J. Francillon*

AV-8B Harrier II

The United States Marine Corps operates the AV-8B Harrier as a front-line ground attack aircraft. Capable of short takeoff and vertical landing (STOVL), the AV-8B can be flown from unimproved forward airstrips or from amphibious support ships. The Harrier is capable of fighting in all weather and at night, and it is also equipped for air-to-air combat.

The Harrier evolved from the Hawker (later British Aerospace) P.1127 Kestrel, which first flew on October 21, 1960, at the Royal Aircraft Establishment, Bedford, England. The marines' first 98

aircraft (90 AV-8A single seat, and 8 dual-control TAV-8As) were built in England, and they began arriving in the United States in January 1971. McDonnell Douglas license-built the improved AV-8B, the prototype of which flew for the first time on November 9, 1979. Known as Big Wing Harriers, these jets had a larger wing area, were capable of carrying additional fuel, and were equipped with lift improvement devices. The first production AV-8B flew on August 29, 1983. Subsequent upgrades to the Harrier have included night-attack capabilities with the addition of a FLIR system and night-vision-goggle compatibility beginning in 1987. The Hughes APG-65 pulse-Doppler radar was installed in Harriers beginning in 1992. Known as Harrier II Plus, they featured a nose radome modified to fit the APG-65 radar, a reshaped FLIR mounting, and a new wing leading-edge root extension for improved aerodynamics.

The GAU-12/U Equalizer cannon is standard equipment on all models of the Harrier II. This General Electric 25mm five-barreled Gatling gun is powered by bleed air from the engine, and it can fire up to 4,200 rounds per minute. *Rene J. Francillon*

Harriers employ two vectored thrust nozzles on each side of the aircraft for lift. Roll control thruster jets on the nose, tail, and wingtips provide attitude control at low speeds. The AV-8 has earned a somewhat nasty reputation, because it suffered a higher number of accidents per flight hour than its contemporaries. If the aircraft hovers at altitudes below 30 feet, it can ingest a ground vortex and hot exhaust gases, causing the engine to stall, with insufficient altitude to recover. The cure to the Harrier's problem was to instruct pilots that if they hover below 60 feet, they have committed themselves to land.

U.S. Marine Corps Harriers were not involved in battle until the 1991 Gulf War. Eighty-six AV-8Bs were deployed to the region, flying from King Abdul Aziz Air Base, Saudi Arabia; from the amphibious assault ships USS *Tarawa* and USS *Nassau*; and a forward base near Tanajib, 40 miles from the Kuwaiti border. The Marine Corps reports that the average turnaround time per Harrier mission was only 23 minutes. That's close air support! During Desert Storm, AV-8Bs flew 3,359 sorties against 2,585 targets, of which 2,241 were ground support missions.

Harriers participated in Operation Noble Anvil, the bombing campaign in Kosovo in 1999, based aboard USS *Kearsarge*. During Operation Iraqi Freedom in 2003, Marine Attack Squadron Harriers from VMA-211, VMA-231, VMA-233, VMA-311, and VMA-542 provided ground-support as Marines advanced into Iraq. Harriers will remain the Marine Corps' frontline attack aircraft until the F-35B comes on line around the year 2010.

AV-8B HARRIER II

Mission: Close air support
Contractor: Boeing (McDonnell Douglas)
Powerplant: One Rolls Royce F402-RR-408 turbofan, vectored-thrust engine rated at 23,400 pounds
Length: 47 feet, 7.5 inches
Height: 11 feet, 7 inches
Wingspan: 30 feet, 3 inches
Speed: 630 miles per hour
Range: 1,600 miles
Armament: One 25mm GAU-12 five-barrel Gatling gun plus 12,000 pounds of ordnance
Crew: One
Unit Cost: $23.7 million
Date Deployed: January 1985; AV-8B II Plus June 1993
Inventory: Active force – 128

AV-8B HARRIER II

UNITS ASSIGNED		
UNIT	**NICKNAME**	**TAIL CODE**
VMAT-203	Hawks	KD
VMA-211	Avengers	CF
VMA-214	Black Sheep	WE
VMA-223	Bulldogs	WP
VMA-231	Ace of Spades	CG
VMA-311	Tomcats	WL
VMA-513	Nightmares	WF
VMA-542	Flying Tigers	WH
VX-9	Vampires	XE
VX-23	Strike	SP

Introduced in 1986, the AH-1W serves in seven active-duty and two reserve squadrons. *Rene J. Francillon*

ROTARY WINGS

AH-1W/Z Super Cobra

The U.S. Marine Corps adopted Bell's Cobra gunship in September 1970 as the AH-1J. Marine Corps AH-1s were built as twin-engine helicopters, unlike those of the U.S. Army. The Cobra brought a dedicated close air support helicopter to the Corps, enhancing its ground fighting capabilities. Six years later, the improved AH-1T, capable of firing the AGM-71 TOW (Tube Launched, Optically-Tracked, Wire Guided) missile for use against enemy tanks, was introduced. All older Marine Corps Cobras were upgraded to fire the AGM-71 missile. The T model also featured an improved engine and transmission. The type flying with the Marines today is the AH-1W.

Marine Corps AH-1s have supported every operation from the invasions of Grenada and Panama, to both trips to Iraq. In Operation Desert Storm, Marine Corps AH-1s flew 1,273 sorties, each one averaging 2 hours and 15 minutes, escorting troop-carrying helicopters, flying armed reconnaissance missions, and destroying tanks. Ship-based AH-1s supported the Marines' drive to Baghdad in Operation Iraqi Freedom. Marine Light Attack Helicopter Squadron 167 (HMLA-167), HMLA-267, HMLA-269, and HMLA-369 were all deployed for the fight against Saddam Hussein.

The AH-1W fleet is now undergoing a major modification program to renew the helicopter's airframe; improve its avionics and weapons system; replace the drive train, rotor head, tail boom; and change to a four-blade main rotor. Cobras undergoing this rework program will be redesignated AH-1Z, and almost 85 percent of their parts will be interchangeable with the service's UH-1 Huey fleet. It is estimated that the remanufacture of both the UH-1 and AH-1 will save the Marine Corps nearly $3 billion over the helicopters' 30-year life spans. In addition, the inventory of spare parts to support both helicopter types carried on amphibious assault ships will be greatly reduced.

AH-1W/Z SUPER COBRA

Mission: Attack helicopter
Builder: Bell Helicopter Textron
Powerplant: Two General Electric T700-GE-401 engines rated at 1,775 shaft horsepower (continuous)
Length: 58 feet
Height: 14 feet, 2 inches
Rotor Diameter: 48 feet
Speed: 169 mile per hour
MGTOW: 14,750 pounds
Range: 294 miles
Armament: One three-barrel 20mm M197 Gatling gun in nose turret
Crew: Two
Unit Cost: $10.7 million
Date Deployed: 1986
Inventory: Active force – 147

AH-1W/Z SUPER COBRA

UNITS ASSIGNED		
UNIT	**NICKNAME**	**TAIL CODE**
HMLA-167	Warriors	TV
HMLA-269	Gunrunners	HF
HMLA-169	Vipers	SN
HMLA-267	Stingers	UV
HMT-303	Atlas	QT
HMLA-367	Scarface	VT
HMLA-369	Gunfighters	SM
HMLA-773	Red Dog	MP
HMLA-773 DET A	Nomads	MM
HMLA-775	Coyotes	WR
HMLA-775 DET A	Coyotes	WG
HX-21	Rotary Wings, NAS Patuxent River, MD	MD
VX-9	Vampires	XE

MV-22B Osprey

The Bell Boeing V-22 Osprey is the future of assault warfare. The Osprey is designed to replace most helicopters and has the capacity to transport 24 fully equipped troops or 20,000 pounds of cargo. The wing rotates and the rotor blades fold for shipboard storage aboard from aircraft carriers and amphibious assault ships.

The twin, tilt-rotor craft takes off and lands like a helicopter, but converts to conventional flight by rotating its engines forward 90 degrees. When the engines face forward, the V-22 has the same capabilities as any turboprop-powered aircraft; making it capable of speeds of 300 miles per hour, with a range of more than 500 miles. The capability to change from vertical to conventional flight and back enables the troop-carrying Osprey to depart from a ship like a helicopter, transition to forward flight, and fly over the horizon to a beachhead. There, the aircraft transitions back to vertical flight, lands vertically, and disembarks its troops. The V-22's speed allows the aircraft to make nearly three trips in the time it would take a single helicopter to make just one round trip. Redundancy has been designed into the Osprey. For example, if its engine were hit by ground fire, the opposite engine could drive both rotors through the plane's cross-coupled transmissions.

The Naval Air System Command is currently putting that service's V-22s through their paces, and they surpassed 500 hours in the air during June 2003. The Osprey program will begin full-rate production in 2005 for the U.S. Navy, Marine Corps, and the U.S. Special Operations Command.

MV-22B OSPREY

Mission: Assault transport
Builder: Bell Boeing
Powerplant: Two Allison T406-AD-400 engines rated at 6,150 shaft horsepower each
Length: 63 feet
Height: 21 feet, 9 inches
Wingspan: 83 feet, 10 inches
Speed: 316 miles per hour
MGTOW: 47,500 pounds (VTOL)
Range: 515 nautical miles with 24 troops
Crew: Two, plus 24 troop seats or 12 litters
Unit Cost: $40.1 million
Date Deployed: under development

MV-22B OSPREY

UNITS ASSIGNED

UNIT	NICKNAME	TAIL CODE
VMMT-204	White Knights	
	MCAS New River, NC	

The CH-46E is the mainstay of Marine Medium Helicopter (HMM) squadrons. Based at MCAS Miramar, California, CH-46E 154832 is assigned to the Greyhawks of HMM-161. *Rene J. Francillon*

CH-46E Sea Knight

The turboshaft-powered CH-46 was designed in the late 1950s and replaced the service's piston-powered Piasecki H-21 Flying Banana and Sikorsky S-56 Mojave. The helicopter is fitted with two General Electric T58-GE-16 engines and it carries 12 fully equipped troops, or 4,000 pounds of cargo. A rear-loading ramp allows for quick egress of assault troops from the 6-foot-wide by 6-foot-tall cargo compartment.

CH-46s have been in the middle of every Marine Corps assault since Vietnam and have proven themselves under fire. Most recently, Sea Knights were on the frontlines in Operation Iraqi Freedom.

Currently, the Marine Corps has 17 squadrons of CH-46s. In April 2003, the Corps began the initial phases of an engine reliability improvement program for the Sea Knight that will see new, uprated T58-GE-16A turboshaft engines installed. These engines will improve the aircraft's performance through a new engine compressor, turbine section, and combustion chamber. This engine upgrade will keep Marine Corps Sea Knights in service until 2017. Eventually, the Sea Knight will be replaced by the MV-22 Osprey.

On a combat mission, the CH-46E carries a maximum of 14 troops, or a maximum operational payload of 4,000 pounds. The Sea Knight will eventually be replaced by the MV-22B Osprey. *Rene J. Francillon*

CH-46E SEA KNIGHT

Mission: Vertical replenishment and medium lift assault helicopter
Builder: Boeing Vertol
Powerplant: Two General Electric T58-GE-16 engines rated at 1,770 shaft horsepower each
Length: 84 feet, 4 inches; 45 feet, 8 inches (rotors folded)
Height: 16 feet, 8 inches
Wingspan: 51 feet (rotors extended)
Speed: 166.75 miles per hour
MGTOW: 24,300 pounds
Range: 152 miles (land assault mission)
Crew: Four (pilot, copilot, crew chief, mechanic)
Date Deployed: 1964; D model: January 1978

Over 250 CH-46Es were obtained by the modification and upgrade of CH-46D and F models. In the late 1990s, a further Dynamic Component Update was undertaken to improve the reliability and safety of the Sea Knight by replacing powertrain parts. *Rene J. Francillon*

CH-46E SEA KNIGHT

UNITS ASSIGNED		
UNIT	**NICKNAME**	**TAIL CODE**
H&HS	Swamp Foxes	5B
H&HS		5G
HC-3	Packrats	SA
HC-5	Providers	RB
HC-6	Chargers	HW
HC-8	Dragon Whales	BR
HC-11	Gunbearers	VR
HMM-161	Grey Hawks	YR
HMM-162	Golden Eagles	YS
HMM-163	Ridgerunner	YP
HMM-165	White Knights	YW
HMM-261	Bulls	EM
HMM-262	Flying Tigers	ET
HMM-263	Red Lions	EG
HMM-264	Black Bulls	EH
HMM-265	Dragons	EP
HMM-266	Fighting Griffins	ES
HMM-365	Sky Knights	YM
VMR-1	Roadrunners	
Note: H&HS – Headquarters and Headquarters Squadron		

For over 30 years, the Sea King served as the premier antisubmarine warfare (ASW) helicopter in the navy until it was replaced by the SH-60 Seahawk. Based at NAS North Island, UH-3H 152137 is assigned to the Golden Gators of HC-85, while SH-3H 152112 serves in the SAR role at NAS Whidbey Island, Washington. *Paul Negri* (below), *Jim Dunn* (above)

UH-3H Sea King

The Sea King is best remembered as the rescue helicopter seen hovering over Apollo space capsules after splashdown. Today, flying with Marine Helicopter Squadron One (HMX-1), the helicopter is often seen departing the White House carrying the president of the United States. Development began in December 1957, and Sikorsky proposed a twin-turboshaft powered, five main rotor blade, amphibious helicopter with landing gear that retracted into sponsons. Originally designated the HSS-2, the prototype flew in March 1959, and the helicopter provided extensive service with the U.S. Navy and Marine Corps.

UH-3H Sea Kings in service today primarily fly search and rescue as well as logistical missions; its anti-submarine warfare duties having been taken over by the SH-60F Sea Hawk. In addition to the duties of HMX-1, the navy still operates a few Sea Kings as VIP transports.

UH-3H SEA KING

UNITS ASSIGNED

UNIT	NICKNAME	TAIL CODE
AOD		7A
AOD		7E
AOD		7G
AOD		7Q
AOD		7R
AOD	Barking Sands PMRF, HI	
HC-2	Fleet Angels	HU
HSL-51	Warlords	TA
HC-11	Gunbearers	VR
HC-85	Golden Gators	NW
HMX-1,	MCAF, Quantico,	VA
HX-21	Rotary Wing,	
	NAS Patuxent River, MD	
VC-8	Red Tails	GF

UH-3H SEA KING

Mission: Logistical support, search and rescue
Builder: Sikorsky Aircraft
Powerplant: Two General Electric T58-GE-402 engines
Length: 72 feet, 8 inches; 47 feet, 3 inches (rotor folded)
Height: 16 feet, 10 inches
Rotor Diameter: 62 feet
Speed: 138 miles per hour
MGTOW: 21,000 pounds
Range: 623 miles
Crew: Four (pilot, copilot, crew chief, mechanic)
Date Deployed: June 1961

CH-53D Sea Stallion • CH-53E Super Stallion

Sikorsky's CH-53D Sea Stallion is a twin-turboshaft-powered medium-lift helicopter used to transport troops, equipment, and supplies in all weather conditions. When the D model Sea Stallion arrived in Vietnam in 1970, it was employed by Special Operations groups that inserted Special Forces units and South Vietnamese

BELOW AND RIGHT: The heavy lifter for the marines is the CH-53E Super Stallion, with a maximum payload of 36,000 pounds or capacity for 55 fully equipped troops. *Rene J. Francillon*

troops for hit-and-run raids along the Ho Chi Minh Trail. The D model has been used in every conflict since, ranging from Panama and Grenada to Operation Desert Storm. Currently, the Marine Corps has concentrated its fleet of D-model Sea Stallions at MCAS Kaneohe Bay, Hawaii. The CH-53D will be phased out of service with the introduction of the MV-22 Osprey tilt-rotor in the coming years.

The CH-53E Super Stallion incorporated many of the lessons learned in Vietnam. The first Super Stallion was delivered to the Marine Corps on June 16, 1981. The three-engine Super Stallion is equipped with an in-flight refueling probe and the more powerful

General Electric T64-GE-416 engines rated at 4,750 shaft horse-power each. The helicopter can carry a crew of 3 plus 55 passengers or an external load of up to 36,000 pounds. Five Marine Heavy Helicopter Squadrons (HMH) flying Super Stallions participated in Operation Iraqi Freedom: HMH-361, HMH-461, HMH-462, HMH-464, and HMH-772.

CH-35E

Mission: Heavy-lift transport

Builder: Sikorsky Aircraft

Powerplant: Three General Electric T64-GE-413 turboshaft engines rated at 3,925 shaft horsepower each

Length: 67 feet, 6 inches

Height: 24 feet, 11 inches

Rotor Diameter: 72 feet, 3 inches

Speed: 184 miles per hour

MGTOW: 44,000 pounds

Range: 665 miles

Armament: Two .50-caliber machine guns

Crew: Three (two pilots and a load master)

Unit Cost: $26.1 million

Date Deployed: 1966

CH-35E

UNITS ASSIGNED		
UNIT	**NICKNAME**	**TAIL CODE**
HMT-301	Wind Walkers	SU
HMT-302	Phoenix	UT
HMH-361	Flying Tigers	YN
HMH-362	Ugly Angels	YL
HMH-363	Red Lions	YZ
HMH-461	Iron Horse	CJ
HMH-462	Heavy Haulers	YF
HMH-463	Pegasus	YH
HMH-464	Condors	EN
HMH-465	Warhorses	YJ
HMH-466	Wolfpack	YK
HMH-769	Road Hogs	MS
HMH-772	Flying Armadillos	MT
HMX-1		VA

Currently, two squadrons, the Vanguards of MH-14 based at Chambers Field in Norfolk, Virginia; and the Black Hawks of HM-15 at NAS Corpus Christi, Texas; are the only dedicated AMCM units in the navy. The MH-53E 162510 is assigned to HM-15. *Jim Dunn*

MH-53E Sea Dragon

The Sikorsky MH-53E Sea Dragon is the U.S. Navy's primary airborne mine countermeasures platform. The helicopter's enlarged sponsons hold additional fuel enabling Sea Dragons to tow either the Mk-103 mechanical minesweeping system, the Mk-105 minesweeping hydrofoil sled, or the AQS-14 side-scan sonar to detect mines under water. Mine countermeasures systems are lowered from the rear cargo ramp into the sea using the helicopter's 30,000-pound tension tow boom and winch. MH-53Es have a folding main rotor and tail

for storage onboard ship. Sea Dragons are also fitted with an air-to-air refueling probe.

In Operation Desert Storm, HM-14's MH-53Es were deployed on board the USS *Tripoli* (LPH-10), tasked with clearing the Northern Persian Gulf of mines. During Operation Iraqi Freedom, MH-53Es from Helicopter Mine Countermeasures Squadron 14 (HM-14), based on board the USS *Ponce* (LPD-15), were used to clear the Khawar Abd Allah River area and the port of Umm Qasr, Iraq, of underwater mines. Once these areas were clear, the port was used to bring in food and medicine for the local population and to support Coalition forces as they advanced into Iraq.

MH-53E SEA DRAGON

Mission: Airborne Mine Countermeasures
Builder: Sikorsky Aircraft
Powerplant: Three General Electric T64-GE-416 turboshaft engines rated at 4,380 shaft horsepower each
Length: 73 feet, 4 inches
Height: 28 feet, 4 inches
Rotor Diameter: 72 feet, 3 inches
Speed: 195 miles per hour
MGTOW: 73,500 pounds
Range: 1,289 miles
Armament: 50-caliber machine guns
Crew: Three to eight, depending upon mission
Date Deployed: 1983

MH-53E SEA DRAGON

UNITS ASSIGNED		
UNIT	**NICKNAME**	**TAIL CODE**
HC-4	Black Stallions	HC
HM-14	Vanguard	BJ
HM-15	Black Hawks	TB
HX-21	Rotary Wing, NAS Patuxent River, MD	

A Multi-Mission Helicopter Upgrade is now underway to create the SH-60R. Over a ten-year period that began in 2002, 243 SH-60B and F models are undergoing major airframe and avionics modifications. Besides adding a minimum of 10,000 hours of life to the airframe, a glass cockpit will be installed to allow the crew of the SH-60R to easily transition from one type of mission to another without any conversion time. *Jim Dunn*

SH-60B/F/R Seahawk, HH-60H Rescue Hawk, and CH-60S Knighthawk

The navy began searching for a new shipboard helicopter under the Light Airborne Multipurpose System III (LAMPS III) program. In response to the 1977 specification, Sikorsky developed the SH-60B Seahawk, a navalized version of the army's UH-60A, which featured a folding tail boom and main rotor powered by the General Electric T-700 engine. For antisubmarine warfare, the helicopter was fitted with AN/APS-124 search radar, an AN/ASQ-81 magnetic anomaly detector, and an AN/ARR-75 sonobuoy monitoring set. If a hostile submarine or surface ship was located, the helicopter could respond with Mk 46/50 torpedoes, AGM-114 Hellfire missiles, or AGM-119 Penguin antiship missiles.

The prototype SH-60B flew on December 12, 1979, and the helicopter was ordered into production in 1982. Helicopter

Antisubmarine Squadron (Light) 41 (HSL-41) became the first squadron to fly the SH-60B, accepting its first Seahawk on February 11, 1983. Two years later, the SH-60F was ordered to replace the SH-3 Sea Kings that were flying antisubmarine patrols from aircraft carriers. The F model, fielded in 1988, carries the AQS-13F dipping sonar, used by the helicopter to fly from one location to another, lower the sonar, search, and then retract the sonar, before moving to another location. In 1999, work began to remanufacture all existing SH-60Bs and a limited number of SH-60Fs into an SH-60R configuration with a glass cockpit with an updated flight control computer and satellite communications equipment, AN/APS-147 inverse synthetic aperture radar, and the AN/ALQ-210 electronic countermeasures suite.

Following the selection by the U.S. Army of the UH-60A Black Hawk, the navy placed an order with Sikorsky for a navalized version designated the UH-60B Seahawk. The UH-60B features the Light Airborne Multipurpose System III (LAMPS Mk III) that added search radar, magnetic anomaly detector, and sonobuoy launchers for the ASW mission. Seen here at Stead Field, Nevada, this SH-60B Seahawk is assigned to the Battle Cats of HSL-43 at NAS North Island. *Jim Dunn*

The navy's aircraft fleet plans call for phasing the CH-46 Sea Knight out of the vertical replenishment role and replacing it with the CH-60S Knighthawk. The CH-60S is an army UH-60L Blackhawk fuselage incorporating the SH-60B's shipboard features, such as the folding tail and main rotor. The cargo compartment will have an internal capacity of 4,800 pounds, and another 9,000 pounds can be slung beneath the helicopter. The CH-60S entered service in February 2002.

SH-60. HH-60H, CH-60s

UNITS ASSIGNED		
UNIT	**NICKNAME**	**TAIL CODE**
HC-3	Packrats	SA
HC-5	Providers	RB
HCS-4	Red Wolves	NW
HCS-5	Firehawks	NW
HS-2	Golden Falcons	NE
HS-3	Tridents	AJ
HS-4	Black Knights	NK
HS-5	Night Dippers	AG
HS-6	Chargers	HW
HS-7	Shamrocks	AC
HS-8	Eightballers	NG
HS-10	Warkawks	RA
HS-11	Dragonslayers	AB
HS-14	Chargers	NF
HS-15	Red Lyons	AA
HS-75	Emerald Knights	NW
HSL-37	Easyriders	TH
HSL-40	Airwolves	HK
HSL-41	Seahawks	TS
HSL-42	Proud Warriors	HN
HSL-43	Battle Cats	TT
HSL-44	Swamp Fox	HP
HSL-45	Wolfpack	TZ
HSL-46	Grandmasters	HQ
HSL-47	Saberhawks	TY
HSL-48	Vipers	HR
HSL-49	Scorpions	TX
HSL-51	Warlords	TA
HSL-60	Jaguars	NW
HX-21	Rotary Wings, NAS Pax River, MD—no tail code	
VX-1	Pioneers	JA
NSAWC		NAS, Fallon, NV
VH-60		
NMX-1		MCAF, Quantico, VA

The HH-60H Rescue Hawk was added to the inventory in 1990 for use in the combat search and rescue mission. Now deployed on carriers alongside the SH-60F, the Rescue Hawk on the right has a nose-mounted FLIR turret. *Jim Dunn*

SH-60. HH-60H, CH-60s

Mission: Medium lift or assault helicopter
Builder: Sikorsky
Powerplant: Two General Electric T700-GE-701C engines rated at 1,940 shaft horsepower
Length: 64 feet, 10 inches
Height: 12 feet, 5 inches
Rotor Diameter: 53 feet, 8 inches
Speed: 145 miles per hour
MGTOW: 21,884 pounds
Range: 380 nautical miles
Armament: Two window-mounted 7.62mm machine guns, Mk 46/50 torpedoes, AGM-114 Hellfire missiles, and AGM-119 Penguin antiship missiles
Crew: Four
Date Deployed: 1983

UH-1N, HH-1N Iroquois

HH-1Ns are the mainstay of the navy's light utility and shore-based search and rescue helicopter fleets. The Marine Corps uses its UH-1Ns for command and control of assault operations, forward air control, special operations tactical troop insertion and extraction, as well as aeromedical evacuation of wounded troops. All of the navy and Marine Corps N models, which were delivered beginning in January 1979, are now undergoing a fleet modernization to include a four-blade main rotor, new drive train, tail boom, and avionics to reduce maintenance costs and increase parts commonality between the UH-1 and the Marine Corps AH-1. Upgraded UH-1s will be designated UH-1Y, and they will replace older N models beginning in 2008. The last overhauled UH-1Y is slated for delivery to the Marine Corps in the year 2014.

UH-1N, HH-1N IROQUOIS

Mission: Utility and assault transport helicopter

Builder: Bell Helicopter Textron

Powerplant: Two Pratt & Whitney T400-CP-400 turboshaft engines rated at 1,250 shaft horsepower

Length: 57 feet

Height: 14 feet, 5 inches

Rotor Diameter: 48 feet

Speed: 126 miles per hour

MGTOW: 10,500 pounds

Range: 286 miles

Armament: 2.75-inch rocket pods, .50-caliber machine guns, 7.62mm minigun or door-mounted M240 7.62mm machine guns

Crew: Two pilots, crew chief, gunner, and up to eight fully equipped troops

Date Deployed: January 1971

PATROL AND ELECTRONIC WARFARE

E-2C Hawkeye

Known as "The Eyes of the Fleet," Grumman's E-2C Hawkeye is a carrier-based airborne early-warning aircraft. The Hawkeye ranges from the carrier battle group and monitors the airspace for hostile aircraft. If a threat is detected, controllers on board the Hawkeye can vector fighters to intercept the unidentified aircraft, or "Bogey." E-2Cs can also provide communications relay as well as command and control functions for the battle group. Typically, an aircraft carrier has five E-2Cs on board, with one in the air at all times.

Above the fuselage, the AN/APA-71 antenna in the 24-foot diameter radome rotates at 5 to 6 revolutions per minute. Each antenna sweep monitors 6 million cubic miles, from the surface of the ocean to nearly 50,000 feet. The AN/APA-71 antenna feeds the

UH-1N, HH-1N IROQUOIS

UNIT	NICKNAME	TAIL CODE
AOD		7F
AOD		7H
AOD		7S
AOD		8J
AOD		8F
AOD		7P
CSS Aviation Unit	Dragon Masters	Panama City, FL
H&HS	MCAS, Yuma, AZ	5Y
HX-21	Rotary Wing	NAS Pax River, MD
HMLA-167	Warriors	TV
HMLA-169	Vipers	SN
HMLA-267	Stingers	UV
HMLA-269	Gunrunners	HF
HMLA-367	Scarface	VT
HMLA-369	Gunfighters	SM
HMLA-773	Red Dog	MP
HMLA-773 DET A	Nomads	MM
HMLA-775	Coyotes	WR
HMLA-775 DET A	Coyotes	WG
HMT-303	Atlas	QT

Each Hawkeye squadron embarks four aircraft aboard carrier for a deployment. Assigned to the Bluetails of VAW-121, E-2C 163697 is based at Chambers Field, NAVSTA Norfolk, Virginia. *Jim Dunn*

The Hawkeye can simultaneously control 40 airborne intercepts at distances over 200 miles. *Rene J. Francillon*

AN/APS-145 search and tracking radar, capable of detecting up to 2,000 aircraft nearly 340 miles away from the Hawkeye. The AN/APS-145 radar can then direct interceptors to 40 different targets simultaneously.

In Operation Desert Storm, 29 E-2Cs flew 1,183 sorties monitoring Coalition aircraft during strikes over Iraq and Kuwait. Four Hawkeye squadrons flew during Operation Iraqi Freedom in 2003, including Airborne Early Warning Squadron 113 (VAW-113), VAW-115, VAW-116, and VAW-117.

The E-2C is the primary model in service with the U.S. Navy; however, the service is now taking delivery of newly built E-2C Hawkeye 2000s. The navy expects to attain an initial operating capability with the aircraft sometime in 2004 and will accept the last aircraft in 2006. After the last delivery, the service will begin

E-2C HAWKEYE

UNITS ASSIGNED		
UNIT	**NICKNAME**	**TAIL CODE**
VAW-77	Night Wolves	AF
VAW-78	Fighting Escargots	AF
VAW-112	Golden Hawks	NG
VAW-113	Black Hawks	NK
VAW-115	Liberty Bells	NF
VAW-116	Sun Kings	NE
VAW-117	Wallbangers	NH
VAW-120	Greyhawks	AD
VAW-121	Bluetails	AG
VAW-123	Screwtops	AB
VAW-124	Bear Aces	AJ
VAW-125	Tigertails	AA
VAW-126	Seahawks	AC
VX-20	Force	NAS Pax River, MD
NSAWC		NV

E-2C HAWKEYE

Mission: Airborne early warning, airspace command and control
Builder: Grumman
Powerplant: Two Allison T-56-A427 turboprop engines rated at 5,100 shaft horsepower each
Length: 57 feet, 6 inches
Height: 18 feet, 3 inches
Wingspan: 80 feet, 7 inches
Speed: 345 miles per hour
MGTOW: 53,000 pounds
Range: 930 miles
Crew: Five (two pilots, one combat information center officer, an air traffic controller, and radar operator)

remanufacturing its E-2C fleet with new radar slated for service in 2010. The Hawkeye 2000 upgrade includes a mission computer upgrade, satellite communications capabilities, and the ability to share its sensor information with a wider variety of aircraft.

Launching from catapult two, E-2C 164483 from VAW-113 will soon be on station ahead of the *Lincoln* battle group. *Jim Dunn*

The Grumman EA-6B Prowler is currently the primary tactical jamming aircraft in the U.S. inventory. Assigned to the Cougars of VAQ-139, EA-6B 161880 is based at NAS Whidbey Island, Washington. *Richard Vander Meulen*

EA-6B Prowler

The EA-6B is the electronic warfare modification of the A-6 Intruder. In July 1972, VAQ-132 aboard the USS *America* (CVA-66) first took the electronic warfare version of the Intruder into battle. The standard A-6 was lengthened with the addition of a 40-inch fuselage extension to accommodate two side-by-side seats behind the standard cockpit. The aircraft is crewed by a pilot and three electronic countermeasures officers (ECMOs). Sitting in the right seat is ECMO 1, who also has copilot, navigator, and radio-operator duties and is often the mission commander.

When flying combat, Prowlers escort air strikes to and from the target, providing airborne command and control, jamming enemy air defense radars, or monitoring radar emissions using its sensors as the strike flight passes by. Depending upon the threat level, the Prowler can electronically defeat the enemy radar or destroy it with an AGM-88 HARM missile. The

aircraft's electronic systems are built around the AN/ALQ-99 Tactical Jamming System, which has receivers and antennas mounted in a pod above the Prowler's tail. AN/ALQ-99 jammer pods, which look like fuel tanks with a large generator propeller on its nose, are carried on hardpoints under the wings.

Four aircraft are the normal complement of a Prowler squadron deployed with a carrier air wing. Three of the four Prowlers belonging to the Cougars of VAQ-139 are being readied for the next cycle of air operations aboard the *Lincoln*. *Jim Dunn*

Getting ready for a Red Flag sortie in September 2002 at Nellis AFB, EA-6B 162230 is configured with jamming pods on stations one, three, and four; a 400-gallon fuel tank on station two; and an AGM-88 HARM on station five. *Jim Dunn*

EA-6B PROWLER

UNITS ASSIGNED

UNIT	NICKNAME	TAIL CODE
VAQ-128	Fighting Phoenix	NL
VAQ-129	Vikings	NJ
VAQ-130	Zappers	AC
VAQ-131	Lancers	NE
VAQ-132	Scorpions	AA
VAQ-133	Warbirds	NL
VAQ-134	Garudas	NL
VAQ-135	Black Ravens	NH
VAQ-136	Gauntlets	NF
VAQ-137	Rooks	AB
VAQ-138	Yellowjackets	NG
VAQ-139	Cougars	NK
VAQ-140	Patriots	AG
VAQ-141	Shadowhawks	AJ
VAQ-142	Grey Wolves	NL
VAQ-209	Star Warriors	AF
VMAQ-1	Banshees	CB
VMAQ-2	Death Jesters	CY
VMAQ-3	Moon Dogs	MD
VMAQ-4	Seahawks	RM
VX-9	Vampires	XE
VX-23	Strike	SD

Marine Corps Prowlers can operate from forward land bases, and the aircraft are fitted with TERPES (Tactical Electronic Processing and Evaluation System). This system enables recordings of the mission's electronic sensors for post-mission review and monitoring of enemy radar signatures. The Marines currently operate 20 EA-6Bs.

During Operation Desert Storm, seven of the eight aircraft carriers participating in the conflict had EA-6Bs embarked, representing VAQ-136, VAQ-132, VAQ-131, VAQ-137, VAQ-130, VAQ-140, and VAQ-141. In addition, the U.S. Marines flew 12 EA-6Bs from Bahrain.

EA-6B PROWLER

Mission: Tactical electronic support
Builder: Grumman
Powerplant: Two Pratt & Whitney J52-P408 turbofan engines rated at 11,200 pounds thrust each
Length: 59 feet, 10 inches
Height: 16 feet, 3 inches
Wingspan: 53 feet
MGTOW: 61,500 pounds
Range: 977 miles (unrefueled)
Armament: AGM-88 High Speed Anti-Radiation Missile (HARM)
Crew: Four (one pilot, three electronic warfare sensor operators)
Unit Cost: $52 million
Date Deployed: July 1972

The Prowler was modified for the SEAD mission in the 1980s, and it became a shooter for the first time during the Gulf War in 1991. *Lou Drummond*

During Operation Iraqi Freedom, VAQ-136 EA-6Bs on board the USS *Kitty Hawk* flew 105 combat missions, launched six HARMs, and escorted dozens of air strikes into hostile territory. VAQ-136 Prowlers covered the landing of Special Operations Forces during the seizure of Iraq's southern oil fields on the Al Faw peninsula. VAQ-136 Prowlers were also airborne over Baghdad when the city fell to Coalition forces.

Grumman's EA-6B Prowler, operated by both the U.S. Navy and Marine Corps will serve through at least the year 2015, when plans call for the aircraft to be replaced by the electronic warfare version of the Super Hornet, the EF-18G Growler.

P-3 Orion

Lockheed's P-3 Orion began service with the navy in 1962 and kept watch over the Soviet submarine fleet for nearly 30 years. The service is now flying the P-3C Update III configuration, which standardizes the Orion's electronics suite, and will reduce crew training and maintenance costs over time. The patrol plane is also gaining a new, digital magnetic anomaly detector and periscope detection radar. The aircraft's data link capabilities are also being upgraded, which will enable the Orion to transmit target information from its sensors to attack aircraft in real time.

While the P-3's sea surveillance capabilities are being upgraded, its area of operation is slowly moving from the sea to the land. During Operation Desert Storm, 23 P-3s logged more than 12,000 hours in 1,200 combat surveillance sorties. P-3s participated in Operation Enduring Freedom over Afghanistan, working to identify ground targets and control the aerial situation using the plane's onboard sensors, including the AN/APS-137 inverse synthetic aperture radar (ISAR) and the AN/AAS-36 infrared detection system.

While the army and marines marched their way to Baghdad, P-3s of VP-1, the Screaming Eagles, supported Operation Iraqi Freedom with surveillance of the battlefield and developing targets. The aircraft's ability to loiter over a target and provide imagery to ground forces proved invaluable during the campaign. For attacking ground targets, Orions were fitted with AGM-65 Maverick missiles as well as the AGM-84E SLAM (Standoff Land Attack Missile).

Since 1962, the Lockheed P-3 Orion has been patrolling the skies above the world's oceans and keeping track of undersea threats. Only a few P-3Bs remain in the inventory, and the standard of the fleet is the P-3C Update III version. *Jim Dunn*

P-3 ORION

The Orion has taken on an increased role in the antiship mission and can now launch both the AGM-84 Harpoon and the AGM-65F Maverick antiship missiles. P-3C 157323 serves with the Tridents of VP-65. *Paul Negri*

In February 2003, the U.S. Navy awarded Boeing and Lockheed Martin each a $20.5 million contract for the second phase of the development of the Multi-mission Maritime Aircraft (MMA), the P-3 Orion's follow-on. Boeing's choice for the MMA is a modified C-40A Clipper, which is based on the commercial 737-700 jetliner, while Lockheed plans to propose a new version of the P-3, based on its P-7 patrol plane concept. The MMA will replace the P-3C and the signals-intelligence-gathering EP-3E. The service will award a contract for development of the P-3C's eventual replacement, the Multi-mission Maritime Aircraft (MMA) in 2004. However, the P-3 should be used in service through the year 2020.

UNITS ASSIGNED

UNIT	NICKNAME	TAIL CODE
VP-1	Screaming Eagles	YB
VP-4	Skinny Dragon	YD
VP-5	Mad Foxes	LA
VP-8	Tigers	LC
VP-9	Golden Eagles	PD
VP-10	Red Lancers	LD
VP-16	War Eagles	LF
VP-26	Tridents	LK
VP-30	Pro's Nest	LL
VP-40	Marlins	QE
VP-45	Pelicans	LN
VP-46	Grey Knights	RC
VP-47	Golden Swordmen	RD
VP-62	Broadarrows	LT
VP-64	Condors	LU
VP-65	Tridents	PG
VP-66	Liberty Bells	LV
VP-92	Minutemen	LY
VP-94	Crawfishers	PZ
VPU-1	Old Buzzards	OB
VPU-2	Wizards, MCAF Kaneohe Bay,	HI
VQ-1	World Watchers	PR
VQ-2	Batmen	JQ
VX-1	Pioneers	JA
VX-20	Force, NAS Patuxent River,	MD
VX-30	Bloodhounds	BH
NRL FSD		NAS, Pax River, MD
AOD/ETD		MCAF, Kaneohe Bay, HI

P-3 ORION

Mission: Antisubmarine and antisurface warfare
Builder: Lockheed
Powerplant: Four Rolls-Royce/Allison T56-A-14 turboprop engines rated at 4,910 shaft horsepower each
Length: 116 feet, 10 inches
Height: 33 feet, 8.5 inches
Wingspan: 99 feet, 8 inches
Speed: 345 miles per hour
MGTOW: 135,000 pounds
Range: 3,800 nautical miles
Armament: 20,000 pounds of internal and external ordnance
Crew: Nine (two pilots, flight engineer, navigator, tactical coordinator, plus four sensor operators)
Unit Cost: $36 million
Date Deployed: July 1962

P-3C 159321 serves with the Fighting Marlins of VP-40 at NAS Whidbey Island. *Jim Dunn*

EP-3A ARIES II

UNIT	NICKNAME	TAIL CODE
UNITS ASSIGNED		
VQ-1	World Watchers	PR
VQ-2	Batmen	JQ

EP-3E Aries II

The U.S. Navy flies the EP-3E ARIES II (Airborne Reconnaissance Integrated Electronic System II) in the signals intelligence (SIGINT) reconnaissance-gathering role. During Operation Desert Storm, EP-3s were based at Incirlik, Turkey.

The EP-3E Aries II caught the public's attention on April 1, 2001, when Bu. No. 156511 of VQ-1 was intercepted and bumped by a Chinese Shenyang F-8-II Finback fighter in international waters, approximately 70 miles from Hainan Island in the South China Sea. The impact severed the Chinese fighter's tail, causing it to lose control and crash into the sea, and the EP-3E went into an uncontrolled dive, which the pilots were able to recover from. The plane limped to Hainan, where it made an emergency landing and was subsequently interned. The crew returned to the United States after a dozen days as guests of the Chinese. After it was dismantled, the EP-3E was also returned to the United States. The EP-3E returned to service late in the spring of 2003 after an extensive overhaul.

EP-3Es serve with VQ-1's detachments at Naval Support Activity Bahrain International Airport, Bahrain, and Naval Air Field Misawa, Japan, as well as with VQ-2 at Naval Station Rota, Spain.

The mission of the Lockheed EP-3E is to gather electronic and signal intelligence. In the 1990s, 12 low-time P-3Cs were equipped with the airborne reconnaissance integrated electronic system (ARIES) that is identified by the OE-320 direction-finding antennas housed in the dorsal and ventral canoe fairings, and the OE-319 Big Look antenna in the ventral radome. *Jim Dunn*

E-6A Mercury and E-6B Looking Glass

Based on Boeing's commercial 707-320B, the E-6A Mercury replaced the EC-130 in the TACAMO (TAke Charge And Move Out) role. TACAMO E-6As use very low frequency radios to communicate with submarines under water. To do so, the E-6A is equipped with two trailing wire antennas; one is 4,000 feet long, and the other is 26,000 feet long. The antennas ride at a near 90-degree angle to the aircraft's flight path, as the plane intentionally circles over a point to allow the antenna to drop.

The E-6B Looking Glass serves in the command and control role, able to communicate with America's nuclear-equipped intercontinental ballistic missiles, bombers, and submarines. All E-6A aircraft are being converted to E-6B configuration, which is slated for completion at the end of 2003. The E-6 fleet is stationed at Tinker Air Force Base, Oklahoma.

The E-6 carries a crew of 14 for TACAMO missions or a crew of 22 for Looking Glass missions. All 16 aircraft will be converted to E-6Bs by the end of 2003. *Lou Drummond*

E-6A/E-6B

UNITS ASSIGNED		
UNIT	**NICKNAME**	**TAIL CODE**
VQ-3	Ironmen	Tinker AFB, OK
VQ-3 DET		Offutt AFB, NE
VQ-3 DET		Travis AFB, CA
VQ-4	Shadows	Tinker AFB, OK
VQ-4 DET		NAS Patuxent River, MD

E-6A/E-6B

Mission: E-6A and B: Ballistic missile submarine communications relay aircraft E-6B: Airborne command post
Builder: Boeing
Powerplant: Four CFM-56-2A-2 turbofan engines
Length: 150 feet, 4 inches
Height: 42 feet, 5 inches
Wingspan: 148 feet, 4 inches
Speed: 600 miles per hour
MGTOW: 342,000 pounds
Range: 7,590 miles
Crew: E-6A: 14; E-6B: 22
Unit Cost: $141.7 million
Date Deployed: October 1998

Both E-6 Mercury squadrons, the Ironmen of VQ-3 and the Shadows of VQ-4 are based at Tinker AFB, Oklahoma. Training is also conducted at Tinker AFB with two navy TC-18Fs being used for flight crew training. Here, E-6B 163919 returns to Travis AFB, California. *Jim Dunn*

S-3B Viking

Originally conceived during the Cold War as a carrier-based, antisubmarine warfare (ASW) platform, the versatile S-3 Viking has evolved into the main carrier-based aerial refueling platform. In 1999, the S-3B's antisubmarine warfare sensors were replaced, and the Viking was reconfigured for a new mission known as Sea Control. This mission focuses on antisurface warfare (ASUW) to protect carrier battle groups from over-the-horizon threats; the aircraft also performs in the armed reconnaissance and C^3 (command, control, and communications) roles. New and improved sensors were added to the S-3B including the APS-137 inverse synthetic aperture radar, GPS navigation, and the SW-33 Digital Flight Data Computer, as well as a next-generation FLIR (Forward Looking InfraRed).

S-3s of VS-32 flying from the USS *America* drew the first blood for the Vikings on February 20, 1991, when the aircraft destroyed an Iraqi gunboat during Operation Desert Storm. In Operation Desert Storm, the navy fielded 43 S-3s from five squadrons (VS-22,

Parked with wings folded on the deck of the USS *Abraham Lincoln* in May 2002, S-3B 160132, is one of the eight Vikings of CVW-14 Blue Wolves deployed with the carrier. Four of these Vikings serve in the sea-control mission, while the other four will serve as tankers and support aircraft. *Jim Dunn*

VS-24, VS-30, VS-32, and VS-38). Flying the sea control mission, Vikings reconnoitered the Red Sea and Persian Gulf sealanes, refueled returning strike aircraft, and served as command and control aircraft. Vikings flew 1,674 sorties during the operation.

Vikings were back in action on August 30, 1995, during the opening salvo of Operation Deliberate Force over Bosnia. On March 25, 2003, Operation Iraqi Freedom, an S-3B crew from VS-38 aboard the USS *Constellation* launched an AGM-65 Maverick missile at a target near Basra, Iraq, scoring a direct hit. This engagement marks the first time an S-3 has fired a Maverick missile at a hostile target.

When Operation Iraqi Freedom transitioned from shooting war to police action, the navy sent a number of its carriers home for a well-deserved rest. President George Bush decided to personally thank the participants of Iraqi Freedom and flew out to the USS *Abraham Lincoln* on May 1, 2003, while the ship was off the coast of San Diego, California. A VS-35 Blue Wolves S-3B wore the title *Navy One* to represent its famous passenger, the commander in chief. Although many presidents have sailed aboard U.S.

Navy ships, George W. Bush was the first president to make an arrested landing on a carrier.

The navy plans to keep the S-3 flying through at least the year 2015, through a series of service life extension programs (SLEPs). The service intends to field a new Common Support Aircraft (CSA), which will fulfill the Viking's sea control and aerial refueling missions.

Seen in the overhead break before landing at Nellis AFB, S-3B 159731 displays the externally loaded tubes that can carry up to 60 sonobuoys. This Viking is with the Dragonfires of VS-29 and CVW-11 of the USS *Nimitz. Jim Dunn*

Although the navy rejected a tanker version of the Viking to fill the void left by the retirement of the KA-6D, the S-3B is employed as a carrier-based buddy tanker. Equipped with a D-704 buddy pod under the left wing, and a 300-gallon fuel tank under the right wing, the S-3B acts as a single-point refueler to support air-wing operations. *Richard Vander Meulen*

RQ-2A Pioneer UAV

The RQ-2A is a small, unmanned aerial vehicle equipped with an electro-optical sensor (TV camera) and infrared sensors that provide over-the-horizon reconnaissance. A ground- or ship-based monitoring station controls up to five Pioneers, which can be launched conventionally from a runway or using RATO (Rocket Assisted Take Off) bottles for a zero-length launch. When a runway is not available, the RQ-2A is flown into a net for recovery. The U.S. Army also operates the Pioneer system.

During Operation Desert Storm, the RQ-2 was used for spotting and correcting the range of naval gunfire, reconnaissance, battle damage assessment, and ground target identification. The navy reports that the Iraqi occupiers of Faylaka Island, off the coast of Kuwait, surrendered to the RQ-2 from the USS *Wisconsin*.

S-3B VIKING

Mission: Air-to-surface warfare; aerial refueling
Builder: Lockheed
Powerplant: Two General Electric TF-34-GE-400B turbofans rated at 9,275 pounds of thrust each
Length: 53 feet, 4 inches
Height: 22 feet, 9 inches
Wingspan: 68 feet, 8 inches; 29 feet, 6 inches (folded)
Speed: 518 miles per hour
MGTOW: 52,539 pounds
Range: 2,645 miles
Armament: 3,960 pounds of missiles, torpedoes, or bombs including the AGM-84 Harpoon anti-ship missile, the AGM-65F Maverick infrared seeking air-to-surface missile, or the AGM-84 SLAM (Standoff Land Attack Missile—Expanded Response)
Crew: Three
Unit Cost: $27 million
Date Deployed: 1974

RQ-2A PIONEER UAV

Mission: Reconnaissance
Builder: AAI Corp. and Israeli Aircraft Industries Malav Division
Powerplant: One Sachs SF2-350 two-cycle engine rated at 26 horsepower
Length: 14 feet
Height: 3 feet, 3.5 inches
Wingspan: 16 feet, 10.75 inches
Speed: 110 miles per hour
MGTOW: 463 pounds
Range: 2,645 miles
Endurance: 6.5 hours loiter time up to 87 miles from base
Date Deployed: 1986

S-3B VIKING

UNITS ASSIGNED

UNIT	NICKNAME	TAIL CODE
VS-21	Redtails	NF
VS-22	Checkmater	AC
VS-24	Scouts	AJ
VS-29	Dragonfires	NH
VS-30	Diamondcutters	AA
VS-31	Topcats	AG
VS-32	Maulers	AB
VS-33	Screwbirds	NG
VS-35	Blue Wolves	NK
VS-38	Red Griffins	NE
VS-41	Shamrocks	NJ
VX-1	Pioneers	JA
VX-20	Force	NAS Pax River, MD

RQ-2A PIONEER UAV

UNITS ASSIGNED

UNIT	NICKNAME	TAIL CODE
VC-6	Firebees	FB
VMU-1	Watchdogs	FZ
VMU-2	Night Owls	FF

Apparently, when the RQ-2 flew low over the island, the Iraqis knew that a barrage of 16-inch naval gunfire would soon follow and elected to surrender to the UAV. Pioneers were also used to attract the attention of Iraqi radars, which were then destroyed by antiradiation missiles from nearby, low-flying Coalition aircraft. The RQ-2 system's success in Operation Desert Storm and Operation Enduring Freedom has ensured that the UAV will be used in service through the year 2010.

TRANSPORTS

C-2A Greyhound

Grumman's C-2A Greyhound is the mainstay of carrier aviation logistics. Known as COD, for Carrier On-board Delivery, the C-2A is the cargo version of the E-2 Hawkeye. Both aircraft share the same engines, folding wings, and tail surfaces. The C-2A's fuselage is wider than the E-2 and features a rear, fold-down cargo ramp. Cargo is strapped down or loaded into a cage, enabling the aircraft and its payload to be catapult-launched or to make an arrested landing. For operations to or from a carrier, Greyhounds can deliver 10,000 pounds of cargo including aircraft engines, 26 people, or 3 litter patients with 3 attendants. The aircraft's cargo ramp can also be opened in flight enabling aerial drops of special operations teams or supplies.

Beginning in 1964, Grumman built 19 Greyhounds for the U.S. Navy to replace the C-1A Trader. As the original 19 aircraft reached the limit of their service lives, the navy contracted for 39 new Greyhounds in 1984. All of the original-purchase C-2As were phased out of the fleet by 1987. Greyhounds from VRC-30, VRC-40, and VRC-50 operated at sea during Operations Desert Shield and Desert Storm.

Greyhounds are currently rated for 10,000 flight hours or 15,000 landings. The C-2A fleet is slated to undergo a "SLEP" or service life extension program, which will extend the type's service life to 15,000 hours and more than 35,000 landings. The SLEP should keep the C-2A in the navy's fleet until the year 2027.

C-2A GREYHOUND

Mission: Carrier-on-board delivery (COD)
Builder: Grumman
Powerplant: Two Allison T-56-A-425 turboprop engines rated at 4,600 shaft horsepower each
Length: 57 feet, 7 inches
Height: 17 feet
Wingspan: 80 feet, 7 inches; 29 feet, 4 inches (folded)
Speed: 296 miles per hour
MGTOW: 57,000 pounds
Range: 1,300 nautical miles
Crew: Four
Unit Cost: $38.9 million
Date Deployed: 1965

C-2A GREYHOUND

UNITS ASSIGNED		
UNIT	NICKNAME	TAIL CODE
VRC-20	Forces	NAS Patuxent River, MD
VRC-30	Providers	RW
VRC-40	Rawhider	Chambers Field Norfolk, VA

Just about to be catapulted from the USS *Abraham Lincoln*, C-2A 162150 is assigned to the Providers of VRC-30 at NAS North Island, California. *Jim Dunn*

The C-130T is the most numerous of the small but diverse navy inventory of Hercules and the largest transport aircraft in the navy. The Minutemen of VR-55 at Point Mugu, California, operate C-130T 165350. *Paul Negri*

C-130 Hercules and Variants
DC-130A/H • TC-130G • NC-130H • C-130T

More than 2,200 C-130s have been built since the aircraft's introduction in August 1954. The navy and Marine Corps operate a number of different C-130 configurations. The most visible is the navy's TC-130G, flown in support of the Blue Angels aerial demonstration team. This aircraft is affectionately known as *Fat Albert*.

Other interestingly configured Hercules are the DC-130A and H models, which are configured to launch and control BQM-34 subscale, subsonic target drones. The DC-130s support the Naval Air Warfare Center—Weapons Division at Point Mugu, California. On the East Coast, the Naval Air Warfare Center—Aircraft Division flies the NC-130H in support of various aircraft development programs. The C-130T is the navy's cargo-carrying version of the Hercules; 20 of the type are on strength.

C-130 HERCULES AND VARIANTS

Mission: Tactical and intra-theater airlift
Builder: Lockheed Martin Aeronautics Company
Powerplant: Four Allison T56-A-15 turboprops rated at 4,591 shaft horsepower each
Length: 97 feet, 9 inches
Height: 38 feet, 3 inches
Wingspan: 132 feet, 7 inches
Cargo Compartment: length, 40 feet; width, 119 inches; height, 9 feet; rear ramp: length, 123 inches; width, 119 inches
Speed: 366 miles per hour at 20,000 feet
MGTOW: 155,000 pounds
Maximum Allowable Payload: 43,550 pounds
Maximum Normal Payload: 35,220 pounds
Range at Maximum Normal Payload: 2,006 miles
Crew: Five (two pilots, navigator, flight engineer, and loadmaster)
Unit Cost: $30.1 million
Date Deployed: June 1974

C-130 HERCULES AND VARIANTS

UNITS ASSIGNED		
UNIT	**NICKNAME**	**TAIL CODE**
VR-53	Capital Express	AX
VR-54	Revelers	CW
VR-55	Minutemen	RU
VR-65	Nor' Easter	JW
VX-20	Force, NAS Patuxent River,	MD
VX-30	Bloodhounds	BH
VMGR-152	The Sumos	QD
VMGR-252	Otis	BH
VMGRT-253	Titans	GR
VMGR-352	Raiders	QH
VMGR-452	Yankees	NY

Another unusual Hercules in navy service, the single DC-130A, is used to launch and direct drones for the Bloodhounds of Naval Weapons Test Squadron Point Mugu. *Jim Dunn*

KC-130 HERCULES

Mission: Aerial refueling, tactical and intra-theater airlift

Builder: Lockheed Martin Aeronautics Company

Powerplant: Four Rolls-Royce/Allison AE 2100D3 turboprops; 4,637 horsepower

Length: 97 feet, 9 inches

Height: 38 feet, 3 inches

Wingspan: 132 feet, 7 inches

Cargo Compartment: length, 40 feet; width, 119 inches; height, 9 feet; rear ramp: length, 123 inches; width, 119 inches

Speed: 417 miles per hour at 22,000 feet

MGTOW: 155,000 pounds

Maximum Allowable Payload: 46,631 pounds

Maximum Normal Payload: 38,301 pounds

Range at Maximum Normal Payload: 2,729 miles

Crew: Two pilots and loadmaster; Aeromedical Evacuation Role: Flight crew plus one flight nurse and two medical technicians

Unit Cost: $48.5 million

Date Deployed: C-130J, February 1999

KC-130 HERCULES

UNITS ASSIGNED

UNIT	NICKNAME	TAIL CODE
VMGR-152	The Sumos	QD
VMGR-234	Rangers	QH
VMGR-252	Otis	BH
VMGRT-253	Titans	GR
VMGR-353	Raiders	QB
VMGR-452	Yankees	NY

KC-130F/J/R/T Hercules

The Marine Corps uses the Hercules in the tactical aerial refueling and cargo transportation role. The service began operating the cargo lifter in 1961 and outfitted it with under-wing refueling pods and plumbed a removable 3,600-gallon tank into the cargo compartment. The Corps' refueler Hercules was designated KC-130F. In 1976, the F was supplemented by the KC-130R, which is an H model set up to Marine Corps specifications. Similar to the KC-130R, the T model

was introduced in 1983 for use by the Marine Corps Reserve. KC-130Ts feature advanced avionics including AN/APS-133 color weather radar. A 15-foot fuselage plug was added to a pair of KC-130Ts during the fall of 1991. These aircraft were designated KC-130T-30H, but they did not enter full-scale production.

The new KC-130J is a more powerful, faster aircraft capable of off-loading a great amount of fuel to both rotary- and fixed-wing aircraft. The J model has a total off-load capacity of 8,455 gallons, and can transfer fuel at 300 gallons per minute using a computer-controlled aerial refueling system. KC-130Js are replacing the F model in the Corps' fleet.

Both the KC-130R and T models are based on the C-130H airframe. KC-130T 162311 is assigned to the Rangers of VMGR-234 at NAS Forth Worth JRB, Texas. *Jim Dunn*

C-40 Clipper

The U.S. Navy plans on replacing its aging C-9B fleet with new Boeing-built 737-700C convertible freighters. Known as the C-40 Clipper, the aircraft is based on Boeing's highly successful 737 commercial jetliner. The Clipper can seat 121 in an all-passenger configuration, 8 cargo pallets in an all-cargo configuration, or 3 pallets and 70 passengers in a combination load configuration. Cargo is loaded through a seven-foot-tall by eleven-foot-wide cargo door, which is positioned on the aircraft's port side behind the main cabin entry door.

The first of seven C-40As, based on the Boeing 737-700C, was delivered to the U.S. Naval Reserve in April 2001. The U.S. Air Force has also taken delivery of one aircraft as a replacement for a C-22.

C-40 CLIPPER

Mission: Logistics Support
Builder: Boeing
Powerplant: Two CFM56-7 turbofan engines rated at 24,000 pounds thrust each
Length: 110 feet, 4 inches
Height: 41 feet, 2 inches
Wingspan: 112 feet, 7 inches
Speed: 585 miles per hour
MGTOW: 171,000 pounds
Range: 3,400 nautical miles with 121 passengers or 40,000 pounds of cargo
Crew: Four
Date Deployed: 1974

C-40 CLIPPER

UNITS ASSIGNED		
UNIT	NICKNAME	TAIL CODE
VR-58	Sun Seekers	JV
VR-59	Lone Star Express	RY

AGGRESSORS

F-5E/F Tiger II

Developed from Northrop's T-38 Talon supersonic trainer, the nimble F-5 has been cast to simulate a Soviet fighter at both the navy and Marine Corps fighter tactics schools. The type first flew in 1959, and the advanced F-5E Tiger II flew on August 11, 1972.

In the United States, both the navy and Marine Corps fly F-5s as aggressor aircraft. Fighter Squadron Composite 13 (VFC-13) at NAS Fallon, Nevada, and Marine Fighter Training Squadron 401 (VMFT-401) based at MCAS Yuma, Arizona, fly the Tiger II in dissimilar air combat maneuver training. Air force, navy, Marine Corps, and Canadian pilots all fly against the F-5s in an effort to hone their air-to-air combat skills. In their role as aggressors, the Tiger IIs are painted in a wide variety of color schemes to represent the air forces of enemy nations. Aggressors also fly against navy and Marine Corps helicopter pilots to teach them proper evasive flying maneuvers should they ever encounter an enemy fighter.

Plans call for the F-5 fleet to receive new wings and additional avionics upgrades to extend their service lives beyond the year 2015.

F-5E/F TIGER II

Mission: Fighter aggressor
Builder: Northrop
Powerplant: Two General Electric J85-GE-21A turbojets rated at 5,000 pounds thrust each with afterburner
Length: 48 feet, 2 inches
Height: 13 feet, 4 inches
Wingspan: 26 feet, 8 inches
Speed: Mach .98 at 36,000 feet
MGTOW: 24,676 pounds
Range: 1,543 miles
Armament: Two M39A2 20mm cannon with 280 rounds each, plus two AIM-9 Sidewinder missiles
Crew: One
Date Deployed: 1974

F-5E/F TIGER II

UNITS ASSIGNED		
UNIT	NICKNAME	TAIL CODE
VFC-13	Saints	AF
VMFT-401	Snipers	MCAS Yuma, AZ

Currently operated by one Naval Reserve and one Marine Reserve squadron, the Northrop F-5 Tiger II has been a difficult aircraft to replace. The F-5 741558 is still serving with the Saints of VFC-13 at NAS Fallon. *Jim Dunn*

CODE	UNIT	LOCATION
(8A)	AOD	NAF Atsugi, Japan
(8C)	AOD	NAS Sigonella, Italy
(8D)	AOD	NAVSTA Rota, Spain
(8K)	FSD	NAF Bahrain IAP, Bahrain
(HL)	VQ-4	Tinker AFB, Oklahoma
(OB)	VPU-1	NAS Brunswick, Maine
(SP)	VPU-2	MCAF Kaneohe Bay, Hawaii
(TC)	VQ-3	Tinker AFB, Oklahoma
7A	AOD	NAS Patuxent River, Maryland
7B	AOD	NAS Atlanta, Georgia
7C	AOD	Chambers Field, Norfolk, Virginia
7D	AOD	NAS Fort Worth JRB, Texas
7E	AOD	NAS Jacksonville, Florida
7F	AOD	NAS Brunswick, Maine
7G/FW	AOD	NAS Whidbey Island, Washington
7H	AOD	NAS Fallon, Nevada
7M	AOD	NAS North Island, California
7N	AOD	NAF Washington, Maryland
7Q	AOD	NAS Key West, Florida
7R	AOD	NAS Oceana, Virginia
7S	AOD	NAS Lemoore, California
7W	AOD	NAS Willow Grove JRB, Pennsylvania
7X	AOD	NAS New Orleans JRB, Louisiana
8E	AOD	NAVSTA Roosevelt Roads, P.R.
8F	AOD	NAVSTA Guantanamo Bay, Cuba
8H	AOD	NAF Kadena, Okinawa, Japan
8J	AOD	Andersen AFB, Guam
8M	AOD	NAF Misawa, Japan
8N	AOD	NAF El Centro, California
A	(VT-7, VT-9)	NAS Meridian, Mississippi
AA	HS-15	NAS Jacksonville, Florida
AA	VAQ-132	NAS Whidbey Island, Washington
AA	VAW-125	Chambers Field, Norfolk, Virginia
AA	VF-103	NAS Oceana, Virginia
AA	(VFA-34, VFA-81, VFA-83)	NAS Oceana, Virginia
AA	VS-30	NAS Jacksonville, Florida
AB	HS-11	NAS Jacksonville, Florida
AB	VAQ-137	NAS Whidbey Island, Washington
AB	VAW-123	Chambers Field, Norfolk, Virginia
AB	VF-102	NAS Oceana, Virginia
AB	VFA-82	MCAS Beaufort, South Carolina
AB	VFA-86	MCAS Beaufort, South Carolina
AB	VS-32	NAS Jacksonville, Florida
AC	HS-7	NAS Jacksonville, Florida
AC	VAQ-130	NAS Whidbey Island, Washington
AC	VAW-126	Chambers Field, Norfolk, Virginia
AC	(VF-32, VFA-105, VFA-37)	NAS Oceana, Virginia
AC	VS-22	NAS Jacksonville, Florida
AD	VAW-120	Chambers Field, Norfolk, Virginia

CODE	UNIT	LOCATION
AC	(VF-32, VFA-105, VFA-37)	NAS Oceana, Virginia
AC	VS-22	NAS Jacksonville, Florida
AD	VAW-120	Chambers Field, Norfolk, Virginia
AD	VF-101	NAS Oceana, Virginia
AD	VFA-106	NAS Oceana, Virginia
AF	VAQ-209	NAF Washington, Maryland
AF	VAW-77	NAS Atlanta, Georgia
AF	VAW-78	Chambers Field, Norfolk, Virginia
AF	VFA-201	NAS Fort Worth JRB, Louisiana
AF	VFA-203	NAS Atlanta, Georgia
AF	VFA-204	NAS New Orleans JRB, Louisiana
AF	VFC-12	NAS Oceana, Virginia
AF	VFC-13	NAS Fallon, Nevada
AG	HS-5	NAS Jacksonville, Florida
AG	VAQ-140	NAS Whidbey Island, Washington
AG	VAW-121	Chambers Field, Norfolk, Virginia
AG	(VF-143, VFA-131, VFA-136)	NAS Oceana, Virginia
AG	VS-31	NAS Jacksonville, Florida
AG	VF-11	NAS Oceana, Virginia
AJ	HS-3	NAS Jacksonville, Florida
AJ	VAQ-141	NAS Whidbey Island, Washington
AJ	VAW-124	Chambers Field, Norfolk, Virginia
AJ	(VF-14, VF-41, VFA-15, VFA-87)	NAS Oceana, Virginia
AJ	VS-24	NAS Jacksonville, Florida
AX	VR-53	NAF Washington, Maryland
B	(VT-21, VT-22)	NAS Kingsville, Texas
BH	NWTS	NB Ventura County, California
BJ	HM-14	Chambers Field, Norfolk, Virginia
BR	HC-8	Chambers Field, Norfolk, Virginia
CW	VR-54	NAS New Orleans JRB, Louisiana
D	AOD	NAS Meridian, Mississippi
E	(HT-18, HT-8, VT-2, VT-3, VT-6)	NAS Whiting Field, Florida
F	(AOD, VT-10, VT-4, VT-86)	NAS Pensacola, Florida
FB	VC-6 Det.	NAS Patuxent River, Maryland
G	(AOD, VT-27, VT-28, VT-31, VT-35)	NAS Corpus Christi, Texas
GF	VC-8	NAVSTA Roosevelt Roads, P.R.
HC	HC-4	NAS Sigonella, Italy
HC	HC-4 Det.	Palese Macchie AP, Bari, Italy
HK	HSL-40	NAVSTA Mayport, Florida
HN	HSL-42	NAVSTA Mayport, Florida
HP	HSL-44	NAVSTA Mayport, Florida
HQ	HSL-46	NAVSTA Mayport, Florida
HR	HSL-48	NAVSTA Mayport, Florida
HU	HC-2	Chambers Field, Norfolk, Virginia
HW	HC-6	Chambers Field, Norfolk, Virginia
JA	VX-1	NAS Patuxent River, Maryland
JK	VR-1	NAF Washington, Maryland
JQ	VQ-2	NAVSTA Rota, Spain
JR	VR-48	NAF Washington, Maryland

CODE	UNIT	LOCATION
JS	VR-46	NAS Atlanta, Georgia
JT	VR-52	NAS Willow Grove JRB, Pennsylvania
JU	VR-56	Chambers Field, Norfolk, Virginia
JV	VR-58	NAS Jacksonville, Florida
JW	VR-62	NAS Brunswick, Maine
LA	VP-5	NAS Jacksonville, Florida
LC	VP-8	NAS Brunswick, Maine
LD	VP-10	NAS Brunswick, Maine
LF	VP-16	NAS Jacksonville, Florida
LK	VP-26	NAS Brunswick, Maine
LL	VP-30	NAS Jacksonville, Florida
LN	VP-45	NAS Jacksonville, Florida
LT	VP-62	NAS Jacksonville, Florida
LU	VP-64	NAS Willow Grove JRB, Pennsylvania
LV	VP-66	NAS Willow Grove JRB, Pennsylvania
LY	VP-92	NAS Brunswick, Maine
NE	HS-2	NAS North Island, California
NE	VAQ-131	NAS Whidbey Island, California
NE	VAW-116	NAS Point Mugu, California
NE	VF-2	NAS Oceana, Virginia
NE	(VFA-137, VFA-151)	NAS Lemoore, California
NE	VS-38	NAS North Island, California
NF	(HS-14, VAQ-136, VAW-115, VF-154, VFA-192, VFA-195, VFA-27, VS-21) NAF Atsugi, Japan	
NG	HS-8	NAS North Island, California
NG	VAQ-138	NAS Whidbey Island, California
NG	VAW-112	NAS Point Mugu, California
NG	VF-211	NAS Oceana, California
NG	(VFA-146, VFA-147)	NAS Lemoore, California
NG	VS-33	NAS North Island, California
NH	HS-6	NAS North Island, California
NH	VAQ-135	NAS Whidbey Island, Washington
NH	VAW-117	NAS Point Mugu, California
NH	VF-213	NAS Oceana, Virginia
NH	(VFA-22, VFA-94, VFA-97)	NAS Lemoore, California
NH	VS-29	NAS North Island, California
NJ	VAQ-129	NAS Whidbey Island, Washington
NJ	(VFA-122, VFA-125)	NAS Lemoore, California
NJ	VS-41	NAS North Island, California
NK	HS-4	NAS North Island, California
NK	VAQ-139	NAS Whidbey Island, Washington
NK	VAW-113	NAS Point Mugu, California
NK	VF-31	NAS Oceana, Virginia
NK	(VFA-113, VFA-115, VFA-25)	NAS Lemoore, California
NK	VS-35	NAS North Island, California
NL	(VAQ-128, VAQ-133, VAQ-134, VAQ-142) NAS Whidbey Island, Washington	
NW	HC-85	NAS North Island, California
NW	HCS-4	Chambers Field, Norfolk, Virginia

CODE	UNIT	LOCATION
NW	HCS-5	NB Ventura County, California
NW	HS-75	NAS Jacksonville, Florida
NW	HSL-60	NAVSTA Mayport, Florida
PD	VP-9	MCAF Kaneohe Bay, Hawaii
PG	VP-65	NB Ventura County, California
PJ	VP-69	NAS Whidbey Island, Washington
PR	VQ-1	NAS Whidbey Island, Washington
PR	VQ-1 Det.	NAF Bahrain IAP, Bahrain
PZ	VP-94	NAS New Orleans JRB, Louisiana
QE	VP-40	NAS Whidbey Island, Washington
RA	HS-10	NAS North Island, California
RB	HC-5	Andersen AFB, Guam
RC	VP-46	NAS Whidbey Island, Washington
RD	VP-47	MCAF Kaneohe Bay, Hawaii
RS	VR-61	NAS Whidbey Island, Washington
RU	VR-55	NB Ventura County, California
RW	VR-51	MCAF Kaneohe Bay, Hawaii
RW	VRC-30	NAS North Island, California
RX	VR-57	NAS North Island, California
RY	VR-59	NAS Fort Worth JRB, Texas
SA	HC-3	NAS North Island, California
SD	NSATS	NAS Patuxent River, Maryland
TA	HSL-51	NAF Atsugi, Japan
TB	HM-15	NAS Corpus Christi, Texas
TH	HSL-37	MCAF Kaneohe Bay, Hawaii
TS	HSL-41	NAS North Island, California
TT	HSL-43	NAS North Island, California
TX	HSL-49	NAS North Island, California
TY	HSL-47	NAS North Island, California
TZ	HSL-45	NAS North Island, California
VR	HC-11	NAS North Island, California
XE	VX-9	NAWS China Lake, California
XF	VX-9 Det.	NAS Point Mugu, California
YB	VP-1	NAS Whidbey Island, Washington
YD	VP-4	MCAF Kaneohe Bay, Hawaii

U.S. MARINE CORPS TAIL CODES

CODE	UNIT	LOCATION
5B	H&HS	MCAS Beaufort, South Carolina
(5C)	VMR-1	MCAS Cherry Point, North Carolina
5D	H&HS	MCAS New River, North Carolina
5F	H&HS	MCAS Futenma, Japan
5G	H&HS	MCAS Iwakuni, Japan
(5T)	H&HS	MCAS Miramar, California
5W	H&HS	MCAF Kaneohe Bay, Hawaii
5Y	H&HS	MCAS Yuma, Arizona
BH	VMGR-252	MCAS Cherry Point, North Carolina
CB	VMAQ-1	MCAS Cherry Point, North Carolina
CE	VMFA(AW)-225	MCAS Miramar, California
CF	VMA-211	MCAS Yuma, Arizona
CG	VMA-231	MCAS Cherry Point, North Carolina
CJ	HMH-461	MCAS New River, North Carolina
CY	VMAQ-2	MCAS Cherry Point, North Carolina
DC	VMFA-122	MCAS Beaufort, South Carolina
DR	VMFA-312	MCAS Beaufort, South Carolina
DT	VMFA(AW)-242	MCAS Miramar, California
DW	VMFA-251	MCAS Beaufort, South Carolina
EA	VMFA(AW)-332	MCAS Beaufort, South Carolina
ED	VMFA(AW)-533	MCAS Beaufort, South Carolina
EG	HMM-263	MCAS New River, North Carolina
EH	HMM-264	MCAS New River, North Carolina
EM	HMM-261	MCAS New River, North Carolina
EN	HMH-464	MCAS New River, North Carolina
EP	HMM-265	MCAS Futenma, Japan
ES	HMM-266	MCAS New River, North Carolina
ET	HMM-262	MCAS Futenma, Japan
EZ	MASD	NAS New Orleans JRB, Louisiana
FF	VMU-2	MCAS Cherry Point, North Carolina
FZ	VMU-1	MCAGCC Twentynine Palms, California
GR	VMGRT-253	MCAS Cherry Point, North Carolina
GX	VMMT-204	MCAS New River, North Carolina
HF	HMLA-269	MCAS New River, North Carolina
KD	VMAT-203	MCAS Cherry Point, North Carolina
MA	VMFA-112	NAS Fort Worth JRB, Texas
MB	VMFA-142	NAS Atlanta, Georgia
MD	VMAQ-3	MCAS Cherry Point, North Carolina
MF	VMFA-134	MCAS Miramar, California
MG	VMFA-321	NAF Washington, Maryland
ML	HMM-764	Edwards AFB, California
MM	HMLA-775 Det. A	NAS New Orleans JRB, Louisiana
MP	HMLA-773(-)	NAS Atlanta, Georgia
MQ	HMM-774	Chambers Field, Norfolk, Virginia
MS	HMH-769	Edwards AFB, California
MT	HMH-772	NAS Willow Grove JRB, Pennsylvania
(MX)	HMX-1	MCAF Quantico, Virginia

U.S. MARINE CORPS TAIL CODES CONTINUED

CODE	UNIT	LOCATION
NY	VMGR-452	Stewart ANGB, New York
PF	HMM-364	MCAS Camp Pendleton, California
QB	VMGR-352	MCAS Miramar, California
QD	VMGR-152	MCAS Futenma, Japan
QH	VMGR-234	NAS Fort Worth JRB, Texas
QT	HMT-303	MCAS Camp Pendleton, California
RM	VMAQ-4	MCAS Cherry Point, North Carolina
SH	VMFAT-101	MCAS Miramar, California
SM	HMLA-369	MCAS Camp Pendleton, California
SN	HMLA-169	MCAS Camp Pendleton, California
SU	HMT-301	MCAF Kaneohe Bay, Hawaii
TV	HMLA-167	MCAS New River, North Carolina
UT	HMT-302	MCAS New River, North Carolina
UV	HMLA-267	MCAS Camp Pendleton, California
VK	VMFA(AW)-121	MCAS Miramar, California
VE	VMFA-115	MCAS Beaufort, South Carolina
VM	MASD	NAF Washington, Maryland
VT	HMLA-367	MCAS Camp Pendleton, California
VW(NG)	VMFA-314	MCAS Miramar, California
(WB)	VMFT-401	MCAS Yuma, Arizona
WD	VMFA-212	MCAS Iwakuni, Japan
WE	VMA-214	MCAS Yuma, Arizona
WF	VMA-513	MCAS Yuma, Arizona
WG	HMLA-773 Det. A	NAS Willow Grove JRB, Pennsylvania
WH	VMA-542	MCAS Cherry Point, North Carolina
WK	VMFA(AW)-224	MCAS Beaufort, South Carolina
WL	VMA-311	MCAS Yuma, Arizona
WP	VMA-223	MCAS Cherry Point, North Carolina
WR	HMLA-775(-)	MCAS Camp Pendleton, California
WS	VMFA-323	MCAS Miramar, California
WT	VMFA-232	MCAS Miramar, California
YF	HMH-462	MCAS Miramar, California
YH	HMH-463	MCAF Kaneohe Bay, Hawaii
YJ	HMH-465	MCAS Miramar, California
YK	HMH-466	MCAS Miramar, California
YL	HMH-362	MCAF Kaneohe Bay, Hawaii
YM	HMM-365	MCAS New River, North Carolina
YN	HMH-361	MCAS Miramar, California
YP	HMM-163	MCAS Miramar, California
YQ	HMM-268	MCAS Camp Pendleton, California
YR	MMM-161	MCAS Miramar, California
YS	HMM-162	MCAS New River, North Carolina
YT	HMM(T)-164	MCAS Camp Pendleton, California
YW	HMM-165	MCAS Miramar, California
YX	HMM-166	MCAS Miramar, California
YZ	HMH-363	MCAF Kaneohe Bay, Hawaii

PART III

U.S. Army Aviation

The U.S. Army bases its offensive capabilities around five primary weapons systems. On the ground, the service relies on the Bradley fighting vehicle and the M-1 Abrams tank. In the air, the army flies the UH-60 Blackhawk, the AH-64 Apache, and AH-64D Apache Longbow. To protect its troops from tactical ballistic missiles, the service has fielded the Patriot missile system.

Like America's other military services, army aviation is in the process of phasing out many Vietnam War–era aircraft types that have served for more than a quarter-century. Gone from frontline service are the AH-1 Cobra gunship, OH-58 Kiowa scout helicopter, and the UH-1 Huey, each a legend of Vietnam army aviation. The army operates a robust force of AH-64A and AH-64D Apache Longbow helicopters in the scout and antiarmor roles. Both versions of the Apache decimated Iraqi Republican Guard troops and armor—not once, but twice. In the general-purpose helicopter category, the Sikorsky Blackhawk series of helicopters has replaced the UH-1 Huey in service.

As the army's force is now reduced to approximately 480,000 soldiers and civilian employees, the service is changing how it employs its aviation assets. The functions of moving soldiers, their equipment, and supplies, as well as the aeromedical role, are being moved from front line combat units to multi-functional battalions in the Army Reserve and National Guard. This shift enables the active force and its National Guard combat components to focus on the primary objective of defeating an enemy force, whether it is a formal army like Iraq's Republican Guards or the guerrilla fighters of the Taliban.

Army Aviation has been organized into twelve major commands, known as MACOMs, plus the Army National Guard and Army Reserve commands, which report to the chief of staff army. Offensive warfare is the primary domain of six of the MACOMs—U.S. Army Europe, U.S. Army Pacific, U.S. Army South, U.S. Army Forces Command, U.S. Army Special Operations Command, and the Eighth U.S. Army.

The army of the early twenty-first century is adapting to a new battlefield. Gone are the days when the U.S. Army planned for the former Soviet Union's anticipated wave of tanks advancing into NATO territory. Since the terrorist attacks of 2001, the service has shown it can adapt to fighting a variety of enemies in lower-intensity conflicts by employing its aviation assets to the fullest advantage.

Arizona ARNG UH-1H 70-16435 is viewed here on patrol over Fort Huachuca. *Rene J. Francillon*

The army's first dedicated attack helicopter is nearing the end of its long service career; the final variant remaining in army service is the AH-1F Cobra. Retired from active-duty service in 1999, final retirement for the Cobra is set for late 2004. *Rene J. Francillon*

AH-1F Cobra

When the Vietnam conflict evolved into a full-scale war in 1964, the U.S. Army requested proposals for its Advanced Aerial Fire Support System program. Bell proposed its model 209, which featured the engine, transmission, tail assembly, and other parts from the UH-1D mated to a new front fuselage. Known as the Huey Cobra, the first of these then-revolutionary helicopters came into service in May 1967 and reached units in Vietnam a year later.

The fuselage is 3 feet, 6 inches across at its widest point, presenting a small head-on target to enemy gunners on the ground. In the nose of the AH-1F is a three-barrel 20mm cannon loaded with 750 rounds. Although the gunner in the front of the two tandem cockpits can control the gun using a telescopic gunsight, both the gunner and the pilot wear the helmet-mounted sighting system that allows either crewmember to control the turret-mounted gun. The pilot is seated above and behind the gunner. A stub wing extends to each side of the fuselage, enabling the Cobra to carry a combination of 2.75-inch rockets and BGM-71 TOW (Tube Launched, Optically-Tracked, Wire Guided) antiarmor missiles. A wire-strike protection device is mounted on the fuselage above the cockpit, and the airborne laser tracker head is on the forward edge of the cowling. Most notable at the engine's exhaust point is the infrared signature suppressor that uses ambient air to cool the exhaust plume as well as the fuselage around it. Many AH-1Fs carry an infrared jammer above the engine cowling to defeat heat-seeking surface-to-air missiles.

U.S. ARMY MAJOR COMMANDS

U.S. Army Europe, Campbell Barracks, Heidelberg, Germany

U.S. Army Forces Command, Fort McPherson, Georgia

U.S. Army Intelligence & Security Command, Fort Belvoir, Virginia

U.S. Army Materiel Command, Alexandria, Virginia

U.S. Army Medical Command, Fort Sam Houston, Texas

U.S. Army Military District of Washington, Fort McNair, Washington, D.C.

U.S. Army National Guard, Arlington, Virginia

U.S. Army Pacific, Fort Shafter, Oahu, Hawaii

U.S. Army Reserve Command, Fort McPherson, Georgia

U.S. Army Space & Missile Defense Command, Arlington, Virginia

U.S. Army Special Operations Command, Fort Bragg, North Carolina

U.S. Army South, Fort Buchanan, Puerto Rico

U.S. Army Test & Evaluation Command, Alexandria, Virginia

8th U.S. Army, Yongsan Barracks, Seoul, Republic of Korea

U.S. ARMY DIRECT REPORTING UNITS

U.S. Military Academy, West Point, New York

U.S. Army Test & Evaluation Command, Alexandria, Virginia

U.S. Army Operational Test Command, Fort Hood, Texas

AH-1F COBRA

Mission: Ground Support

Builder: Bell Helicopter Textron

Powerplant: One Lycoming T53-L-703 turboshaft engine rated at 1,800 shaft horsepower

Length: 45 feet, 2 inches

Height: 13 feet, 6 inches

Main Rotor Diameter: 44 feet

MGTOW: 10,000 pounds

Speed: 171 miles per hour

Range: 310 nautical miles

Armament: One M197 three-barrel 20mm Gatling gun (750 rounds of ammunition), plus TOW and Hellfire missiles, and 2.75-inch rockets

Crew: Two

In Vietnam, this formidable, highly maneuverable gunship was appreciated by those who flew it, loved by the ground troops it supported, and was respected and feared by the enemy. However, from their introduction to combat and the cessation of hostilities, 173 Cobras were lost to enemy fire over the jungles of Vietnam.

Cobras have supported U.S. ground troops in nearly every major military operation since the Vietnam War. In Operation Desert Storm, the army sent 145 Cobras to fly armed reconnaissance and patrol missions in Kuwait and Iraq.

The AH-1F Cobra is now the primary helicopter gunship of the U.S. Army National Guard. The active force now operates the AH-64 Apache and 64D Apache Longbow. In theory, the AH-1F will continue in Air National Guard service through the year 2015.

OH-58A/C Kiowa, OH-58D Kiowa Warrior

Bell's OH-58 Kiowa looks very similar to the company's model 206 Jet Ranger family of business helicopters that are seen all over the world. The army bought Kiowas in May 1968 to serve in the light observation, transportation, medevac, and scout role. The helicopter served the army well, and after more than 30 years of service, it is in the process of being phased out. However, the army's Aviation Center at Fort Rucker, Alabama, will retain small numbers of the A and C models to train new helicopter pilots.

The OH-58D Kiowa Warrior is visibly different from its A- and C- model brothers and its executive helicopter cousins. The Kiowa Warrior's mast-mounted sight fitted with an electro-optical sight, laser range-finder, and infrared detection systems help to distinguish the helicopter. External fuselage racks can be fitted with any combination of 7.62mm machine gun pods, .50-caliber machine guns, 2.75-inch rockets, grenade launchers, Hellfire missiles, or AIM-9 air-to-air missiles. The army sent 130 Kiowa Warriors to Operation Desert Storm, where the helicopters scouted enemy positions and located Iraqi armour. The Kiowa Warrior's mast-mounted sight and its ability to carry a substantial amount of firepower make it a versatile scout helicopter that will be in service until replaced by the RAH-66 Comanche.

Scouts are the eyes of the Army, and one of the longest serving scouts is the OH-58 Kiowa. *Jim Dunn*

OH-58D KIOWA WARRIOR

Mission: Scout and Attack Helicopter

Builder: Bell Helicopter Textron

Powerplant: One Rolls-Royce/Allison 250-C30R turboshaft engine rate at 650 shaft horsepower

Length: 42 feet, 2 inches

Height: 12 feet, 9.5 inches

Main Rotor Diameter: 35 feet

MGTOW: 5,500 feet

Speed: 148 miles per hour

Range: 300 nautical miles

Armament: M296 .50-caliber machine guns, AGM-114 Hellfire missiles, 2.75-inch rockets, 7.62mm miniguns, 40mm grenade launchers

Crew: Two

Date Deployed: 1989

UH-1H/V HUEY

Mission: Support Helicopter

Builder: Bell Helicopter Textron

Powerplant: One Lycoming T53-L-13B turboshaft engine rated at 1,400 shaft horsepower

Length: 57 feet, 1 inch

Height: 14 feet, 7 inches

Main Rotor Diameter: 48 feet

MGTOW: 9,500 pounds

Speed: 145 miles per hour

Range: 300 nautical miles

Armament: Door-mounted 7.62 M60D machine guns

Crew: Three

Date Deployed: 1959

UH-1H/V Huey

The UH-1 was the army's first helicopter powered by a turboshaft engine. Bell Helicopter developed its Model 204 Iroquois in 1954 in response to an army request for a rotorcraft capable of deploying troops and carrying litter patients off the battlefield. More commonly called "Huey" (Hue-é), a word play on Helicopter Utility, the first HU-1, was accepted by the army in September 1958. Later redesignated the UH-1, Hueys have served the U.S. military for more than 40 years.

The Huey's ability to carry 12 passengers, 6 litter patients, or, with the seats removed, nearly 4,000 pounds of cargo, has made the UH-1 the definition of a utility helicopter. After years of service and numerous modifications, the UH-1H (transport) and UH-1V (medical evacuation) models still serve the U.S. Army today. They have been phased out of frontline service in favor of the UH-60 Blackhawk, and now Hueys primarily equip National Guard units. Plans had called for the Huey to be phased out of service by the end of 2004, but a recent decision to upgrade 160 aircraft will mean that the UH-1 should be in service through at least the year 2010.

The UH-1V serves as an air ambulance in Guard aeromed companies. This one, 69-15027, serves with the Nevada ARNG at Stead Field outside of Reno. *Jim Dunn*

CH-47D/F Chinook

When the army wants to move troops, supplies, and equipment, the service uses its fleet of more than 400 CH-47D Chinooks. In wartime, the helicopters also transport ammunition, trucks, and artillery pieces. In times of peace, Chinooks are fighting fires or delivering humanitarian aid. D-model Chinooks can move up to 25,000 pounds.

Introduced in 1962, A-, B-, and C-model Chinooks flew extensively in Vietnam. The daily routines of the Chinook crews included repositioning artillery from one fire base to another, bringing in supplies, and taking out the wounded. As the more powerful B and C models arrived in the country, Chinooks began salvaging downed aircraft and returning them for overhaul to fight again. During the war, 63 CH-47s were lost to enemy fire.

During Operation Desert Storm, 160 Chinooks were used in their primary role of cargo and equipment transport. In addition, the 101st Airborne Division used the CH-47 to rapidly advance across the desert, outflanking Iraqi troops.

The army currently operates more than 425 CH-47Ds, of which it plans to upgrade 300 to F-model configuration. The aircraft will be rebuilt, the cockpits modernized with digital avionics, and more powerful engines will be retrofitted. These modifications will keep the Chinook in service past the year 2030.

Kicking up clouds of dust during exercises at Camp Roberts, California, CH-47D 90-0195 is assigned to Co. G, 3-140th AVN, California ARNG at Stockton. *Rene J. Francillon*

Nose art can also sometimes be found on army helicopters, such as *Hell Raiser* on CH-47D 91-0269 of Det. 1 Co. G, 140th AVN, of the Nevada ARNG at Stead Field, Reno. *Jim Dunn*

CH-47D/E CHINOOK

Mission: Heavy-Lift Transport
Builder: Boeing
Powerplant: Two Textron Lycoming T55-L-712 turboshaft engines rated at 3,750 shaft horsepower each
Length: 52 feet, 2 inches
Height: 18 feet, 4 inches
Main Rotor Diameter: 99 feet total (overlapping), 60 feet each
MGTOW: 54,000 pounds
Speed: 161 miles per hour at MGTOW
Range: 230 nautical miles
Armament: Door- and ramp-mounted 7.62mm M60D machine guns
Crew: Three, plus 44 troops
Cargo Hook Capacity: Forward and aft hooks, 17,000 pounds each; center hook, 26,000 pounds

MH-47D/E Chinook

The MH-47D and E models have only one job: to insert Special Operations forces covertly up to 300 nautical miles behind enemy lines, in any weather. The army quickly gained this capability by converting 11 CH-47Ds to an MH-47D configuration. Boeing built the prototype and 25 new MH-47Es, the last of which was delivered in May 1995.

To accomplish its mission, the helicopter has been fitted with satellite navigation and communications systems, a FLIR, AN/APQ-174 terrain-following/terrain avoidance radar with moving map display for flying nap-of-the-Earth mission profiles, an in-flight refueling probe, and 2,068 gallons of internal fuel capacity. In addition, the MH-47E can carry up to three external 800-gallon fuel

tanks. To suppress the enemy, the crew can use three 7.62mm miniguns mounted on the rear ramp or in the main cabin doors. Defensive countermeasures include an APR-39A and AN/AAR-47 missile warning systems, ALQ-136 (V) and ALQ-162 jammers, a flare dispenser, and chaff to defeat missile and air defense radars. For pure power, the helicopter's twin 4,867 shaft horsepower engines can, at sea level, lift the MH-47E into the air a rate of 1,841 feet per minute.

Based at Fort Campbell, Kentucky, D-model Chinooks are flown by the 3rd Battalion, 160th Special Operations Aviation Regiment (Airborne), while E models are flown by the 2nd Battalion of the 160th, the Night Stalkers.

MH-47D/E CHINOOK

Mission: Heavy-Lift Special Operations Transport
Builder: Boeing
Powerplant: Two Textron Lycoming T55-L-714 turboshaft engines rated at 4,867 shaft horsepower each
Length: 52 feet, 2 inches
Height: 18 feet, 4 inches
Main Rotor Diameter: 99 feet total (overlapping), 60 feet each
MGTOW: 54,000 pounds
Speed: 161 miles per hour at MGTOW
Range: 613 nautical miles (internal fuel)
Armament: Door- and ramp-mounted 7.62mm M60D machine guns
Crew: Three
Cargo Hook Capacity: forward and aft hooks, 17,000 pounds each, center hook, 26,000 pounds
Date Deployed: January 1994

An earlier version of a modified CH-47D, the MH-47D has as its primary mission the setup of forward arming and refueling points (FARP), or Fat Cow missions. The MH-47Ds, including 10500 seen here at MCAS Yuma, are assigned to 3-160th AVN at Hunter AAF, Georgia. *Rene J. Francillon*

Better known as Little Birds, the remaining AH-6H/Js and MH-6H/Js are assigned to U.S. Army Special Operations Command for transporting small numbers of elite forces. *Rene J. Francillon*

AH-6J, MH-6C/J Little Bird

In 1960, the Department of Defense released a specification for a light observation helicopter (LOH) to transport personnel, carry wounded, and perform the escort, attack, and observations duties of a scout helicopter. Hughes Helicopters responded to the LOH requirement with its model 369, of which five prototypes were ordered in 1961. The army designated the Hughes model the OH-6A Cayuse; the first Cayuse flew on February 27, 1963. The OH-6 saw extensive service in Vietnam, where 654 were lost to enemy action. The Cayuse served the army until the type was retired in 1997.

As the OH-6 design evolved, so did its civil variant, the model 500. When McDonnell Douglas acquired Hughes Helicopters, the Hughes 500 became the MD-500. Improvements to the MD-500 were incorporated into the AH-6, including the five-blade main rotor and upgraded engine. Known as the Little Bird, the armed version is designated AH-6, while the assault transport aircraft is the MH-6 variant. The MH-6 has platforms rigged above the landing skids to enable up to six assault troops to ride outside the helicopter. Under the MELB (Mission-Enhanced Little Bird) improvement program, the aircraft are fitted with upgraded avionics, a six-blade main rotor, and a new engine and drive transmission. Little Birds are flown by the army's 1st Battalion, 160th Special Operations Aviation Regiment (Airborne), based at Fort Campbell, Kentucky.

AH-6J, MH-6C/J LITTLE BIRD

Mission: Special Operations Attack and Support
Builder: McDonnell Douglas Helicopter
Powerplant: One Rolls-Royce/Allison 250-C30 turboshaft engine rated at 650 shaft horsepower
Length: 24 feet, 7 inches
Height: 8 feet, 11 inches
Main Rotor Diameter: 26 feet, 5 inches
MGTOW: 3,950 pounds
Speed: 175 miles per hour
Range: 260 nautical miles
Armament: 7.62mm minigun pods or M296 .50-caliber machine guns, Mk 19 40mm grenade launcher pods, AGM-114 Hellfire missiles, 2.75-inch rockets
Crew: Two
Date Deployed: 1967

AH-64A, AH-64D Apache Longbow

Hughes Helicopters developed the prototype YAH-64 for the army's Advanced Attack Helicopter program in the mid-1970s. The AH-64 is the second generation of the army's purpose-built helicopter gunships, and it was designed to augment Bell's AH-1 Cobra with its superior firepower. The prototype Apache first flew on September 30, 1975, and the army received its initial production AH-64As in February 1984. Apaches are used primarily for close air support, destruction of enemy armor, and armed reconnaissance.

The AH-64A is configured with the pilot sitting in the rear of the tandem cockpits and the gunner/co-pilot seated in front. Every crew member wears a helmet-mounted sight; and wherever they look, the 30mm chain gun points. The gunner operates the AN/ASQ-170 target acquisition designation sight (TADS) that sights for the AGM-114 Hellfire missile.

The Panamanian Defense Force was the first to suffer at the hands of the army's Apache crews during Operation Just Cause in December 1989. Two years later, AH-64As opened Operation Desert Storm in the early morning of January 17, 1991, when formations totaling 10 Apaches destroyed two Iraqi air defense radar sites with Hellfire missiles. The attack opened a 25-mile-wide gap in the Iraqi radar network, enabling Coalition air forces to attack Baghdad. In all, 245 AH-64As participated in Operation Desert Storm.

Currently, 16 Army National Guard and 2 Army Reserve units are flying AH-64As. Immediate plans call for three Guard and two reserve units to transition into the Apache Longbow in the next two years.

The Apache carries a formidable punch with its Hughes M230A-1 30mm chain gun. Hung beneath the nose in an unfaired turret, this cannon can provide a rate of fire of 725 rounds per minute. *Rene J. Francillon*

It was an Apache using AGM-114As that fired the first shots of Operation Desert Storm on January 17, 1991, at Iraqi radar bunkers to open a corridor to Baghdad. At the end, the AH-64As had accounted for over 500 tanks, 120 APCs, 30 AAA sites, 10 helicopters, and 10 aircraft. *Jim Dunn*

This AH-64A is configured with the Aerial Rocket Delivery System pod of 19 2.75-inch rockets on each outboard station, and four AGM-114A Hellfire antitank missiles on each inboard station. *Jim Dunn*

RIGHT: The most significant feature of the AH-64D is the Longbow Fire Control Radar. Mounted above the rotor head, the Northrop Grumman millimeter-wave Longbow radar is unaffected by poor visibility and is highly resistant to countermeasures. In 30 seconds, an AH-64D can unmask its radar for a single scan and processors can then determine the location, speed, and direction of travel for up to 256 targets. *Richard Vander Meulen*

AH-64 Modernization: Apache Longbow

To expand the Apache's capabilities and take advantage of new weapons systems, the army began remanufacturing its existing AH-64 fleet. Modernized Apaches, designated AH-64Ds, receive an inertial navigation system, GPS, mission planning console, air-to-air missile capabilities, uprated GE T700-GE-701C engines, and the mast-mounted AN/APG-78 Longbow radar. New Hellfire missiles, designated AGM-114L, feature a new millimeter-wave radar seeker that locks onto its target before launch. The army is upgrading 748 A-model Apaches, and fitting the AN/APG-78 to 227 of those aircraft.

On February 25, 2003, the U.S. Army accepted its first upgraded Apache Longbow, incorporating Block II modifications featuring new avionics and battlefield situational awareness communications upgrades. By 2003, the army had eight combat-certified AH-64D battalions (24 helicopters each), and was in the process of training additional units.

Thirteen years after Iraq came to understand the AH-64A's capabilities, the AH-64D had its first engagement with the same enemy. During Operation Iraqi Freedom, Apaches from the 101st Airborne Division led the army's drive to Baghdad. During the fighting, on March 23, 2003, AH-64D serial number 99-5135 suffered a mechanical failure near the town of Karbala, Iraq. Both crew members were taken prisoner by the Iraqis but were subsequently freed.

During Operation Iraqi Freedom, modifications kits slated to be introduced on Block III Apaches were rushed into service. The kits enable the Apache's rotor blades and mast antenna to be folded, rather than dismantled, when transporting the helicopters by air. Reinstalling the rotor blades and antenna usually took 24 hours. With transportation kits installed, the Apaches could be battle-ready within two hours.

The manufacturer to date has delivered more than 1,000 Apache helicopters to the U.S. Army and a number of foreign armies. Another 1,000 are on order for delivery to the U.S. and foreign operators by the year 2010. Depending upon the army's future Apache Longbow modernization programs, the helicopter could see service past the year 2030.

AH-64 APACHE LONGBOW

Mission: Multi-mission combat helicopter
Builder: Boeing
Powerplant: Two General Electric T70-GE-701C turboshaft engines rated at 1,940 shaft horsepower each
Length: 49 feet, 5 inches
Height: 15 feet, 3 inches
Main Rotor Diameter: 48 feet
MGTOW: 16,027 pounds
Speed: 164 miles per hour
Endurance: 2.5 hours or 300 miles
Armament: 30mm M230 chain gun with up to 1,200 rounds, up to 76 2.75-inch rockets, up to 16 AGM-114 Hellfire antiarmor missiles, or AIM-9 Sidewinder air-to-air missiles
Crew: Two (pilot, co-pilot/gunner)
Date Deployed: AH-64 (1984), AH-64D (1998)

RC-7B Airborne Reconnaissance

The army has converted nine De Havilland (Canada) DHC-7 turbo-prop airliners to the intelligence-gathering role. Known as the RC-7B Airborne Reconnaissance Low-Multifunction (ARL-M), these aircraft collect communications intelligence, photographic and radar imagery, and can data-link this information to tactical commanders.

Northrop Grumman subsidiary California Microwave Systems has begun retrofitting the Wescam M-20 forward-looking infrared sensor with laser range finder and the Tactical Common Data Link (TCDL) system to send real-time synthetic-aperture radar images to ground forces. The aircraft is also equipped with a survivability equipment suite including threat radar warning detectors, flares to defeat infrared signature seeking missiles, and armor plate. RC-7s are used to patrol the demilitarized zone in Korea, and in support of the army's Kwajalein Atoll Missile Range.

RC-7B AIRBORNE RECONNAISSANCE

Mission: Communications Intelligence
Builder: De Havilland Canada
Powerplant: Four Pratt & Whitney (Canada) PT6A-50 turboprop engines rated at 1,120 shaft horsepower each
Length: 86 feet, 6 inches
Height: 26 feet, 2 inches
Wingspan: 93 feet
MGTOW: 44,000 pounds
Speed: 288 miles per hour
Range: 1,130 nautical miles
Crew: Six
Date Deployed: 1997

This civilian-registered DHC-7, seen landing at Nellis AFB, is similar to those operated by Raytheon under an army contract. Based at Dyess AAF, Kwajalein Atoll in the Republic of the Marshall Islands, these aircraft support the operations of the Kwajalein Missile Range. *Jim Dunn*

Built by Shorts in Belfast, Northern Ireland, the C-23 Sherpa is a light transport ordered by the army to replace the C-7 Caribou. C-23B 070113 is assigned to the 1106th AVCRAD in Fresno, California. *Jim Dunn*

C-23B/B+ Sherpa

The U.S. Army National Guard flies a number of C-23 Sherpa twin turboprops. The A (no longer in army service) and the B model were developed from the Shorts 330's fuselage and tail group and the Shorts 360's wing, engines, and nacelles. A versatile aircraft, the Sherpa can haul 15 litter patients, 30 troops, or 27 paratroops and 4 cargo pallets, and can air-drop both using the plane's rear ramp.

In 1993, the army contracted with Shorts for the conversion of another 28 aircraft, which were built-up from Shorts 330 airliners already in service. Fuselages of the Shorts 330 were lengthened by 36 inches, and the 330's single tail was replaced with the twin tail

of the 360. Bombardier in West Virginia converted these modified aircraft and designated them C-23B+.

In addition to Army National Guard units, the Army Aviation and Missile Command, Redstone Arsenal, Alabama, and the Army Communications-Electronics Command, Fort Monmouth, New Jersey. fly the C-23B and B+.

RC-12D/H/K/N/P/Q Guardrail

Army electronic intelligence collection is accomplished using the Beech RC-12 Guardrail aircraft. Six versions are currently operating, all based on the Super King Air executive transport. Guardrail aircraft typically cruise between 20,000 feet and 30,000 feet, where its sensors have a clear line of sight to detect an enemy's communication transmissions or its signal jammers. The RC-12s can remain on station for up to five hours and can data-link sensor information to ground stations up to 150 miles away from the aircraft.

Guardrail aircraft vary only in sensor and antenna configuration. There are currently six operational models of the Guardrail. The RC-12D Improved Guardrail V comprises 13 aircraft converted from C-12Ds already in inventory. Six RC-12H Guardrail Common Sensor (System 3 Minus) aircraft were built, all of which operate in South Korea. There are nine RC-12K Guardrail Common Sensor (System 4) examples. RC-12N Guardrail Common Sensor (System 1), of which 15 were built, has such upgrade as an AN/APR-39 radar warning receiver, AN/APR-44 radar warning system, and AN/ALQ-136, -156, and -162 countermeasure sets. The RC-12P Guardrail Common Sensor (System 2), of which nine were built, features such internal upgrades as fiber-optic-compatible electronics. Finally, three RC-12Q Direct Air Satellite Relay aircraft were built.

C-23B/B+ SHERPA

Mission: Utility Transport

Builder: Short Brothers

Powerplant: Two Pratt & Whitney (Canada) PT6A-65AR turboprop engines rated at 1,424 shaft horsepower each

Length: 58 feet

Height: 16 feet, 5 inches

Wingspan: 74 feet, 10 inches

MGTOW: 25,600 pounds

Speed: 276 miles per hour

Range: 1,030 nautical miles

Crew: Three plus 20 passengers, or 15 litter patients and 3 attendants

Date Deployed: 1985

Inventory:
Air National Guard – 42

The RC-12N 89-0273 is assigned to the 304th MIB (Training) at Libby AAF, Fort Huachuca, Arizona. The model has added a dual electronic flight instrumentation system and a number of defensive systems to increase aircraft survivability. *Jim Dunn*

RC-120 GUARDRAIL

Mission: Electronic Intelligence Collection
Builder: Beech (Raytheon)
Powerplant: Two Pratt & Whitney (Canada) PT6A-67 turboprop engines rated at 1,100 shaft horsepower each
Length: 43 feet, 9 inches
Height: 15 feet
Wingspan: 57 feet, 10 inches
MGTOW: 16,200 pounds
Speed: 288 miles per hour
Range: 1,200 nautical miles
Crew: Two, plus sensor operators

Delivered in 1999, the RC-12P features different mission equipment including datalink capability, fiber optic cabling, and smaller, lighter wingtip pods. Three RC-12Qs, including 93-0701, act as direct air satellite relays or mother ships for the RC-12Ps. These are the only RC-12s with a dorsal satcom antenna that allows the RC-12P to operate outside of direct satellite coverage. *Nicholas A. Veronico*

With two pilots and a crew chief, the Blackhawk can transport 11 fully armed troops up to 325 nautical miles. Blackhawks have provision for up to 10,000 pounds of stores fitted to the External Stores Suspension System (ESSS). *Rene J. Francillon*

UH-60A/L/Q • EH-60A/L • MH-60A/K/L

The development of Sikorsky's H-60 Blackhawk occurred shortly after the end of the Vietnam War, and it was intended as a replacement for the UH-1 Huey helicopter. The Blackhawk is more powerful, better armored, and has added construction features to improve a crewmember's chance of survival in a crash or from enemy ground fire. Blackhawks first saw service in Grenada and have participated in every armed conflict since. In addition, UH-60s have provided outstanding service in the humanitarian aid role, assisting in the myriad of natural disasters that strike the United States and its neighbors every year.

The U.S. Army operates more than 1,500 of the type in four major variants. The standard cargo/troop-carrying Blackhawks are the A and upgraded L models. The A model began operations in 1978, and production changed to the L in 1990. These helicopters move troops and supplies. They are also capable of lifting small howitzers and their ammunition or Humvees. The army is modernizing its fleet of A and older L models to M configuration through a remanufacturing process that will upgrade or replace most of the aircraft's life-limited systems, including the main rotor head and new, wider-chord main rotor blades.

The UH-60Q is the aeromedical version of the UH-60A and L models. When flying patient evacuation missions, the interior of the UH-60Q is configured with two stretcher racks, holding three litters each, which are accessible from either the port or starboard cargo doors. In addition to the three crew members, two medical attendants can be carried as well.

Configured for the electronic warfare command and control role is the EH-60A and L Quick Fix variant of the Blackhawk. The Quick Fix's sophisticated AN/ALQ-151 special purpose countermeasures set detects, locates, and jams enemy transmissions on VHF frequencies.

Special Operations Blackhawks include the MH-60A, K, and L models. These Blackhawks are used to deploy, supply, and recover Special Operations troops behind enemy lines and can be equipped with a variety of offensive armament.

UH-60, EH-60, MH-60

Mission: Light Transport Helicopter
Builder: Sikorsky
Powerplant: Two General Electric T700-GE-701C turboshaft engines rated at 1,890 shaft horsepower each
Length: 64 feet, 10 inches
Height: 12 feet, 4 inches
Main Rotor Diameter: 53 feet, 8 inches
MGTOW: 23,500 pounds with external load
Speed: 183 miles per hour
Range: 248 nautical miles, or 591 nautical miles with two 230 gallon external tanks
Armament: Hand-held 7.62mm M60D machine guns, or other armament depending upon mission
Crew: Three (two pilots, one load master/crew chief)

RQ-5A HUNTER UAV

Mission: Reconnaissance UAV
Builder: TRW-Israeli Aircraft Industries
Powerplant: Two 750cc Moto Guzzi engines rated at 60 horsepower each
Length: 22 feet, 6 inches
Height: 5 feet, 6 inches
Wingspan: 29 feet, 2 inches
MGTOW: 1,600 pounds
Speed: 80.5 miles per hour
Endurance: 10 hours

RQ-5A Hunter UAV

Developed by the Malat Division of Israeli Aircraft Industries (IAI) and TRW's Avionics and Surveillance Group (acquired by Northrop Grumman in 2002) for a 1989 U.S. Army, Navy, and Marine Corps specification for a tactical unmanned aerial vehicle, the RQ-5A is a small, fixed-wing, twin engine (push-pull configuration) reconnaissance aircraft. IAI and TRW delivered seven RQ-5A command and control systems to the U.S. Army, along with 75 UAV aircraft. Each system is composed of a mission-planning station, two ground control stations with two data terminals, and four remote video terminals, used to operate eight aircraft. RQ-5As can be launched conventionally from a runway, or where space is limited, such as from the deck of a ship, a zero-length launch can be accomplished using rocket-assisted take off (RATO) systems.

Hunters are capable of sending intelligence imagery to a tactical commander in real time, and this capability can be used for artillery spotting. The aircraft's sensors can also acquire and track targets on a battlefield and provide battle damage assessment images.

The RQ-5A system has been used to support U.S. forces in Kosovo and during Operation Allied Force. Hunters were used to support Operation Iraqi Freedom, as was the RQ-7A Shadow, also developed by IAI as a follow-on system to the RQ-5A. The army plans to field the Hunter system until 2007.

RAH-66A Comanche

The army intends to replace its AH-1 Cobras and OH-58 Kiowa Warriors with the RAH-66 Comanche manufactured by a team of companies led by Boeing and Sikorsky. Built primarily of composite materials and incorporating as much low-observable technology as possible for a helicopter, the RAH-66 will be employed by air cavalry and in support of light infantry divisions. To improve the helicopter's stealth characteristics, all armaments usually loaded on external pylons, such as Hellfire and Stinger missiles, are carried in internal bays, and the ship's multi-barrel Gatling gun is retractable.

The Comanche design benefits from many of the technological innovations of the 1990s; the helicopter is fitted with a five-blade, bearingless main rotor system, which makes it faster and more maneuverable. The helicopter also features a ducted tail rotor and

The Comanche was first flown in January 1996 and is being developed as the next generation reconnaissance/attack helicopter for the army. It is intended to replace the AH-1 and OH-58 and is the first combat helicopter to be designed using stealth technology. The RAH-66 is fitted with twin turboshaft engines, an all-composite, five-bladed main rotor system and eight-bladed fan-in-fin type tail rotor. The army hopes to have it operational by the end of 2006. *U.S. Army*

split-torque transmission system. Comanches feature a fly-by-wire control system, night-vision-compatible cockpit, FLIR, and low-light TV imaging system.

The success of the AH-64D and its increased life span has contributed to a reduction in the number of Comanches that will be acquired, down from 1,213 to 650. Full-scale production will begin in 2006, with production ultimately reaching 60 per year. The army's first combat-ready RAH-66 squadrons will be fielded in 2009.

RAH-66A COMANCHE

Mission: Armed Reconnaissance
Builder: Boeing/Sikorsky
Powerplant: Two LHTEC T800-LHT-801 turboshaft engines rated at 1,563 shaft horsepower each
Length: 46 feet, 10 inches
Height: 11 feet
Main Rotor Diameter: 39 feet, 3 inches
MGTOW: 10,600 pounds
Speed: 185 miles per hour
Range: 262 nautical miles on internal fuel
Armament: One 20mm Gatling gun, Hellfire and Stinger missiles, 2.75-inch rockets
Crew: Two (pilot, co-pilot/gunner)
Unit Cost: $32.2 million

ARMY AVIATION FACILITIES
WITHIN THE UNITED STATES (BY STATE)

Alabama: Fort Rucker; Redstone Arsenal
Alaska: Fort Richardson; Fort Wainwright
Arizona: Fort Huachuca
California: Fort Irwin
Colorado: Fort Carson
Georgia: Fort Benning; Fort Gordon; Fort Stewart; Hunter Army Air Field
Hawaii: Fort
Kansas: Fort Leavenworth; Fort Riley
Kentucky: Fort Campbell; Fort Knox
Louisiana: Fort Polk
Maryland: Aberdeen Proving Ground
New York: Fort Drum
North Carolina: Fort Bragg
Oklahoma: Fort Sill
Pennsylvania: Fort Indiantown Gap
Texas: Fort Bliss; Fort Hood; Fort Sam Houston
Virginia: Fort Belvoir; Fort Eustis; Fort Lee

PART IV

COAST
GUARD

U.S. Coast Guard Aviation

While various agencies patrol America's land borders, the country's 95,000 miles of shoreline, including the Great Lakes, the nation's inland waterways, and its 3.4-million-square-mile exclusive economic zone, are the U.S. Coast Guard's responsibility. The image most people have of the Coast Guard involves seeing an orange-and-white helicopter rescuing a boater in distress on the evening news. However, the Coast Guard does so much more than pluck swimmers from the water. Since the September 11, 2001, terrorist attacks, the Coast Guard has gained additional areas of responsibility, including homeland as well as port and waterway security. The Coast Guard's other responsibilities include national defense (in time of war the Coast Guard is part of the U.S. Navy), law enforcement, natural resources stewardship, and keeping sealanes and inland waterways open for commerce. In addition, from 1994 to 2000 the service saved more than 45,000 lives.

The Coast Guard is partnered with the U.S. Customs Service in the battle to stop illegal drugs from being smuggled into the United States. Tasked with patrolling the "Transit Zone," the drug highway from South America to the southern border of the United States, during fiscal year 2000, the Coast Guard seized cocaine, marijuana, and boats worth an estimated $4.4 billion.

The Coast Guard's motto is *Semper Paratus,* meaning "Always Ready." To maintain an "always-ready" state, the agency has a network of strategically situated shore bases and its cutter fleet (defined as any vessel greater than 65 feet in length). It also relies heavily on aviation assets. Air stations are located only a couple of minutes flying time from most major bodies of water, from the Atlantic Coast to the Great Lakes, across the Gulf of Mexico, and into the Pacific Ocean.

The service currently operates a mix of five different fixed- and rotary-wing aircraft. For long-range patrol and surveillance, the Coast Guard employs the long-range Lockheed HC-130 Hercules, the medium-range FalconJet HU-25A/B Guardian, and HU-25C Interceptor. From shore installations and cutters, the service flies the medium-range HH-60J Jayhawk, built by Sikorsky, and the short-range Aerospatiale HH-65 Dolphin. None of the Coast Guard's helicopters are amphibious; that capability was eliminated with the retirement of the service's Sikorsky HH-3F Pelican helicopters in 1994. In addition, the service leases eight Augusta A109E helicopters, designated MH-68 and flown fully armed, for drug interdiction use against fast-moving speedboats.

The service's aviation assets are organized under four commands, which report to the commandant of the Coast Guard. The Coast Guard Aviation Training Center (ATC) at Bates Field, Mobile, Alabama, provides initial and recurrent training for all aircraft except the HC-130s. The Aircraft Repair and Supply Center at Air Station Elizabeth City, North Carolina, handles logistics for the

The primary role of the Jayhawk is in medium-range SAR missions, but like all Coast Guard aircraft, it also has a role in marine environmental protection and drug interdiction. It is able to fly up to 300 miles offshore and remain on station for 45 minutes. It can hoist six people aboard before returning to base. *Nick Veronico*

Coast Guard's aviation fleet. Air stations operate under geographic districts, which in turn, are under the commander Atlantic Area or Pacific Area (see table *U.S. Coast Guard Air Stations*).

In the aftermath of the September 11, 2001, terrorist attacks, the U.S. government finally took action to modernize the Coast Guard. To improve the service's mission readiness, a modernization program known as the Integrated Deepwater System will upgrade all of the service's aircraft within the first five years. Beginning in 2005, the first of a dozen new CASA CN235 maritime patrol aircraft will arrive, followed the next year by the initial delivery of eight Bell Helicopter Textron HV-911 Eagle Eye VTOL unmanned aerial vehicles (UAV).

HU-25A/B Guardian, HU-25C Interceptor

In the mid-1970s, the Coast Guard chose the Dassault-Breguet Falcon 20 business jet to replace the Grumman HU-16 Albatross in the medium-range surveillance (MRS) role. The main components of the planes were built in France and assembled by Falcon Jet in Little Rock, Arkansas. Then, each aircraft was modified to Coast Guard standards by Grumman Aerospace and designated HU-25A Guardian.

All HU-25As were fitted with large observation windows ahead of the wing leading edge and APS-127 surface search radar built by Texas Instruments (now Raytheon). Initial deliveries began in February 1982, and all 41 HU-25As ordered were operational by December 1983.

To further expand the aircraft's mission, the service modified eight HU-25As to B-model configuration for pollution and environmental monitoring. HU-25Bs were fitted with AN/APS-131 side-looking airborne radar (SLAR) for oil slick monitoring, a KS-87B low-altitude reconnaissance camera, an RC-18C infrared/ultraviolet multi-spectral scanner, and a data-linked computer with moving map display to track and map oil spills. Coast Guard B-model Guardians also served with the International Ice Patrol

Beginning in 1988, the Coast Guard modified an additional nine HU-25As to HU-25C Interceptor configuration for combating drug smugglers. The AN/APS-127 radar was replaced by Westinghouse's AN/APG-66 pulse-doppler airborne search radar.

HU-25A/B/C

Mission: Medium-range surveillance

Builder: FalconJet

Powerplant: Two Garrett ATF3-6 turbofan engines rated at 5,440 pounds thrust each

Length: 56 feet

Height: 18 feet

Wingspan: 54 feet

MGTOW: 32,000 pounds

Speed: 402 to 471 miles per hour

Endurance: 5.5 hours

Crew: Five (two pilots, one surveillance systems operator, two visual search crew members)

Date Deployed: 1982

Inventory: Nine A models (25 in storage), three B models (7 in storage), eight C models (1 in storage)

HU-25A/B/C

UNITS ASSIGNED	
UNIT	**LOCATION**
CGAS	Borinquen, Puerto Rico
CGAS	Cape Cod, Massachusetts
CGAS	Corpus Christi, Texas
CGAS	Miami, Florida
CGAS	Mobile, Alabam

Mounted in the nose, the longer radome makes the C model easy to distinguish from its predecessors. In addition, the AN/APG-66 can be coupled to the HU-25C's belly-mounted WF-360 FLIR, enabling the aircraft to monitor aircraft suspected of hauling drugs while remaining undetected. HU-25Cs were used in Operation Desert Storm to monitor oil intentionally dumped into Gulf waters by Saddam Hussein's army.

The Coast Guard is planning for the type to be in service through the year 2010. At that point, a decision will have been made to either re-engine the HU-25 fleet or to phase out the type in favor of newer equipment.

HH-60J Jayhawk

Introduction of the Sikorsky HH-60J Jayhawk ended the Coast Guard's era of amphibious helicopters, because the Jayhawk's power and its ability to loiter eliminated the need for a helicopter that could land on water. Very similar in size and mission capabilities to the HH-3F Pelican that it replaced, the Jayhawk entered service in July 1991 at CGAS Elizabeth City, North Carolina. Altogether, the service acquired 42 Jayhawks for the medium-range recovery mission.

The helicopter is capable of carrying a 6,000-pound sling load. However, the Jayhawk is most famous for using its cargo hoist, capable of lifting 600 pounds, for rescuing stranded boaters and hikers.

HH-60J JAYHAWK

Mission: Medium-range search and rescue

Builder: Sikorsky

Powerplant: Two General Electric T700-401C engines rated at 1,662 shaft horsepower

Length: 65 feet

Height: 17 feet

Rotor Diameter: 54 feet

MGTOW: 21,884 pounds

Speed: 161 miles per hour

Endurance: 6 hours

Crew: Four (two pilots, two crew)

Date Deployed: 1991

Inventory: 35, plus 7 in maintenance/storage

HH-60J JAYHAWK

HH-60Js are equipped with an EFIS (electronic flight instrumentation system) and GPS navigation, as well as the Litton AN/APN-217 Doppler search and weather radar. The cockpits are night-vision-goggle compatible with an AN/AAQ-15 FLIR system for night-search operations.

When operating on an SAR mission, the Jayhawk can fly 300 miles from base at 175 miles per hour, perform the rescue of six people, and fly back with ample fuel reserves. Although it is primarily a shore-based asset, the Jayhawk can operate from the service's larger *Bear-* and *Hamilton*-class cutters or a multitude of U.S. Navy ships.

HH-65A Dolphin

For short-range search and rescue operations, the Coast Guard relies on the Aérospatiale HH-65A *Dauphin* or Dolphin helicopter. The helicopters were built in France but shipped to the United States for completion with Lycoming engines and U.S.-manufactured avionics. The Coast Guard acquired 96 HH-65As, and the type entered service in 1985. This was the first rotorcraft purchased by the service that had not been used previously with the U.S. Navy or Air Force.

The Dolphin's small size makes it the service's preferred cutter- and ice-breaker-based helicopter. The helicopter's ducted, 11-blade tail rotor, which gives off a unique whining sound when passing overhead, is another unique feature. But it is avionics that set the HH-65A apart from other smaller helicopters. Equipped with a full-authority digital electronic control system, the Dolphin can be automatically flown to a specific point, where it will enter a hover as low as 50 feet above the water. In addition, the flight crew can enter a search pattern into the flight control system, which the Dolphin will automatically fly, enabling the pilots to concentrate their focus outside the rotorcraft.

HH-65As are capable of flying 150 miles from base at 100 miles per hour, spending 30 minutes to rescue 3 survivors weighing 170 pounds each, and returning to base with a 20-minute fuel reserve. On an average day, Coast Guard helicopters fly more than 15 hours from cutters; these missions are primarily flown by HH-65s.

ABOVE AND BELOW: The most dramatic rescue involving the Jayhawk occurred on December 17, 2000, 225 nautical miles off the Virginia coast when the 600-foot cruise ship *Sea Breeze I* foundered. Two HH-60Js were scrambled from CGAS Elizabeth City, and in high seas with wind gusts of 50 miles per hour, the first Jayhawk hoisted 26 crewmen aboard, while the second rescued another 8 crewmen. All aboard the ship were rescued. *Nicholas A. Veronico*

A program begun in 2001 will see a number of Dolphins upgraded to either HH-65Bs or Cs. The HH-65B upgrade features a new cockpit with flight-management software that allows for flying a fully automatic search pattern or maintaining an automatic hover at 50 feet. The HH-65C upgrade includes the installation of full-authority digital engine control to increase reliability and safety. *Carol McKenzie*

HC-130H Hercules

Lockheed's C-130 Hercules forms the backbone of the Coast Guard's long-range search capability. In Coast Guard service, the H-model Hercules has been designated HC-130H. Primary missions for the HC-130H include fisheries patrol, drug interdiction, search and rescue, and support of the Coast Guard's International Ice Patrol missions.

Beginning in 1999, a number of Coast Guard HC-130Hs underwent a sensor upgrade to enhance the aircraft's capabilities. They were equipped with the Raytheon Pulse-Doppler AN/APS-137 Inverse Synthetic Aperture (ISAR) Radar, which can simultaneously

A unique design feature of the Dolphin is its 11-blade, shrouded tail rotor that helps to reduce noise levels. HH-65A 6572 is one of three Dolphins based at CGAS Los Angeles. *Jim Dunn*

HH-65 A DOLPHIN

Mission: Short-range search and rescue
Builder: Aérospatiale (Eurocopter)
Powerplant: Two Lycoming LTS-101-750B-2 turbine engines rated at 742 shaft horsepower each
Length: 44 feet, 5 inches
Height: 13 feet
Rotor Diameter: 39 feet, 2 inches
MGTOW: 9,200 pounds
Speed: 138 miles per hour
Endurance: 3.5 hours
Range: 400 miles
Date Deployed: 1985
Inventory: 80, plus 14 in storage

HH-65 A DOLPHIN

UNITS ASSIGNED

CGAS Atlantic City, New Jersey
CGAS Barbers Point, Hawaii
CGAS Borinquen, Puerto Rico
CGAS Corpus Christi, Texas
CGAS Detroit, Michigan
CGAS Houston, Texas
CGAS Humboldt Bay, California
CGAS Los Angeles, California
CGAS Miami, Florida
CGAS/ATC Mobile, Alabama
CGAS New Orleans, Louisiana
CGAS North Bend, Oregon
CGAS Port Angeles, Washington
CGAS San Francisco, California
CGAS Savannah, Georgia
CGAS Traverse City, Michigan

HC-130 HERCULES

Mission: Long-range surveillance
Builder: Lockheed
Powerplant: Four Allison T56-A-15 Turboprop engines rated at 4,910 shaft horsepower each
Length: 97 feet, 9 inches
Height: 38 feet, 3 inches
Wingspan: 132 feet, 7 inches
MGTOW: 175,000 pounds
Speed: 353 miles per hour
Range: 3,000 miles
Crew: Seven
Date Deployed: May 1968 (HC-130H)
Inventory: 22 active, 5 in storage

For over 40 years, the backbone of the Coast Guard long-range SAR mission has been the Lockheed C-130 Hercules. Currently 22 HC-130Hs, including 1703, are maintained in operational status, with five others in reserve. *Jim Dunn*

HC-130 HERCULES

UNITS ASSIGNED

CGAS Barbers Pt., Hawaii

CGAS Clearwater, Florida

CGAS Elizabeth City, North Carolina

CGAS Kodiak, Alaska

CGAS Sacramento, California

The latest weapon in the USCG drug enforcement war is the Agusta MH-68A Mako. Based on the civil A-109E Power, the Coast Guard plans to lease 10 MH-68As for up to five years beginning in 2002. As part of the airborne use of force (AUF) program, the MH-68 will be used to interdict Go-Fasts, the high-speed boats used by drug smugglers. *U.S. Coast Guard*

track 32 targets up to 50 miles away and a FLIR/electro-optical (TV) imaging system for use at night or in low-light conditions.

Aircraft flying ice patrol support missions have been fitted with the Motorola AN/APS-135 side-looking airborne surveillance

MH-68A SHARK

Mission: Airborne interdiction

Builder: Augusta

Powerplant: Two Pratt & Whitney 206C engines rated at 640 shaft horsepower each

Length: 42 feet, 9 inches

Height: 11 feet, 5 inches

Rotor Diameter: 36.09 feet (four blades)

MGTOW: 6,283 pounds

Max. Speed: 177 miles per hour

Max. Endurance: 5 hours, 4 minutes

Armament: One M240D 7.62mm machine gun and one .50-caliber Robar RC-50 sniper rifle

Crew: Four

Date Deployed: 2001

Inventory: Eight

radar. Typical ice patrol missions last up to seven hours and cover approximately 30,000 square miles of ocean.

The service's National Strike Force maintains oil spill management teams on the Atlantic, Gulf, and Pacific Coasts. Each team can draw upon HC-130H support to transport its oil containment equipment. In addition to containing oil spills, National Strike Force members have been deployed to minimize the environmental impact from a number of aviation incidents where an aircraft has struck the water.

A service life assessment program will review the future of the Hercules in Coast Guard service. However, it appears that the type will serve with the Coast Guard for the foreseeable future. When the H models eventually become worn out, they will probably be replaced by another C-130, the J model.

MH-68A SHARK

UNITS ASSIGNED

HITRON-10, Cecil Field, Jacksonville, Florida

MH-68A Shark

Deterring drug smugglers is a dangerous business. To improve the Coast Guard's odds at stopping drug-running speed boats, the service has new rules of engagement that enable it to stop vessels with force—from the air. After warning a speedboat to stop through the helicopter's loudspeaker, the Coast Guard is authorized to fire tracer rounds across a boat's bow, or to surgically destroy the boat's engine with gunfire. In order to combat increasingly well-armed foes, the Coast Guard needed a fast-moving helicopter that was also a stable gun platform. The service chose the Augusta A109E for the role, and designated the helicopter MH-68. Although the service has not given the helicopter an official name, Augusta calls the Coast Guard MH-68A the Mako, after the fierce man-eater, and its crews call them Sharks.

Flown by Helicopter Interdiction Tactical Squadron 10 (HITRON-10), based at Cecil Field, Jacksonville, Florida, eight of the fast MH-68As are now in the service's inventory. Capable of speeds in excess of 140 knots (161 miles per hour), the Sharks can overtake any boat with speed to spare. To detect boats at night, the helicopters are equipped with forward-looking infrared and are fitted with an M240D 7.62mm machine gun and a .50-caliber Robar RC-50 sniper rifle with laser sights for destroying a boat's engine.

HITRON-10 has sent detachments to the West Coast for operations in the Pacific, which were highly successful. The squadron is also developing new Airborne Use of Force tactics for the battle against terrorism.

U.S. COAST GUARD AIR STATIONS

EAST COAST
1st District
CGAS Cape Cod, Massachusetts
CGAS Brooklyn, New York

5th District
CGAS Atlantic City, New Jersey
CGAS Elizabeth City, North Carolina
CGAS Washington, D.C.

7th District
CGAS Borinquen, Puerto Rico
CGAS Clearwater, Florida
CGAS Miami, Florida
CGAS Savannah, Georgia

GULF COAST
8th District
CGAS Corpus Christi, Texas
CGAS Houston, Texas
CGAS Mobile, Alabama
CGAS New Orleans, Louisiana

GREAT LAKES
9th District
CGAS Detroit, Michigan
CGAS Traverse City, Michigan

PACIFIC
11th District
CGAS Humboldt Bay, California
CGAS Los Angeles, California
CGAS Sacramento, California
CGAS San Diego, California
CGAS San Francisco, California

13th District
CGAS Astoria, Oregon
CGAS North Bend, Oregon
CGAS Port Angeles, Washington

14th District
CGAS Barbers Point, Oahu, Hawaii

17th District
CGAS Kodiak, Alaska
CGAS Sitka, Alaska

PART V

DEMONSTRA
TEAMS

U.S. Navy Blue Angels

The U.S. military's first post–World War II aerial demonstration team was the U.S. Navy's Flight Demonstration Team, later dubbed the Blue Angels. Formed at Naval Air Station Jacksonville, Florida, in the spring of 1946, the team flew its first show on June 15, 1946, flying Grumman F6F Hellcats. Later that year, the Blue Angels transitioned into the F8F Bearcat. In 1949, the team acquired its first jet, the straight-wing F9F Panther, which the team flew until it volunteered to fly in the Korean War, forming the nucleus of VF-191 Satan's Kittens.

After the war, the team was reformed, flying the F9F-5, and in August 1953 it transitioned into the swept-wing F9F-8 Cougar. Supersonic flight came to the team in 1957 with the acquisition of Grumman's F11F-1 Tiger. The Tiger was the team's first aircraft to wear what has become its standard paint scheme, consisting of the team's name in italic letters with the logo moved behind the name, stripes down the shoulders of the aircraft, and an arrow on the belly pointing at the nose.

In 1969, the Blue Angels began flying the McDonnell Douglas F-4 Phantom II, but four years later, in the midst of an energy crisis, the team transitioned to the more fuel-efficient McDonnell Douglas A-4 Skyhawk. In 1985, the Blue Angels parked the A-4 in favor of the F/A-18 Hornet.

The Blue Angels team is composed of 16 officers and 110 enlisted personnel from both the navy and the Marine Corps. Blue Angel F/A-18 pilots must be carrier-qualified in tactical jets, have 1,250 hours of flight time, and serve a two-year tour. The team leader, known as Boss, is required to have 3,000 hours and have had command of a tactical jet squadron. Pilots for the team's Marine Corps C-130 support aircraft, known as *Fat Albert*, also fly a two-year tour, and must be pilot-in-command rated with 1,200 hours of flight time. Enlisted personnel serve on the team for three years, and must have achieved a minimum pay grade of E5. The team maintains six jets for demonstrations (aircraft numbers one through six), two aircraft for media flights (both wear the number seven), and three spare single-seat Hornets.

The team flies more than 40 practice shows at NAS Pensacola each spring before taking the show on the road. Each year, the team flies nearly 100 shows at more than 35 locations around the nation.

TION

The Navy Flight Demonstration Team, the Blue Angels, was formed in 1946 by order of then-Chief of Naval Operations Admiral Chester W. Nimitz. Since 1989, the team has flown the F/A-18 Hornet. *Jim Dunn*

The Blue Angels don't go anywhere without *Fat Albert Airlines*, the Marine TC-130G that is assigned to the squadron as a support aircraft. *Fat Albert* is a star performer in its own right when it takes to the air in spectacular fashion using JATO rockets at select shows. *Jim Dunn*

U.S. Air Force Thunderbirds

As the Korean War drew to a close, the U.S. Air Force recognized its need for an aerial demonstration team to showcase to the public the latest jet aircraft technology. The air force activated the 3600th Air Demonstration Team at Luke AFB, Arizona, on May 25, 1953, and 50 years later, crowds still marvel at the speed, power, and precision of air force jets flown in close formation.

The 3600th Air Demonstration Team's first aircraft type was the straight-wing Republic F-84G Thunderjet, which in 1955 was replaced with the swept-wing F-84F Thunderstreak. During its three-year service with the team, the F-84 was flown for more than nine million people throughout the Western Hemisphere.

In 1956, the Thunderbirds transitioned into the supersonic North American F-100C Super Sabre and moved to Nellis AFB, Nevada, where the team remains today. The F-100 enabled the Thunderbirds to truly become international ambassadors as the teams flew to different continents in the late 1950s and early 1960s. During a 40-day deployment to the Far East, the Thunderbirds flew 31 airshows in Japan, Korea, Okinawa, and the Philippines, which earned the team the Mackay Trophy for 1959.

In 1969, at the height of the Vietnam War, the Thunderbirds began flying the F-4E Phantom II, the air force's frontline air superiority fighter. Phantoms flew in more than 500 airshows before the energy crisis dictated that the Thunderbirds move to a more economical mount, the Northrop T-38A Talon, a supersonic fighter trainer. The Talon flew with the team for eight seasons and more than 600 demonstrations.

In 1983, the Thunderbirds transitioned into the air force's frontline fighter, the F-16A Fighting Falcon. The team's formation maneuvers showcase the flying abilities taught to all air force pilots, while the solo maneuvers demonstrate the performance capabilities of the

When the distance between shows is more than 800 miles, the Thunderbirds will often call on a buddy for help. Here, two Thunderbirds hold beneath their KC-10 buddy prior to performing at the 2002 USAF Academy graduation ceremony. *Lou Drummond*

To field a team such as the Thunderbirds, it takes a number of highly skilled people in a variety of career fields. Of the total of 12 officers, there are 8 pilots, and 6 of those, including the commanding officer, are the demonstration pilots. Another 130 enlisted members and 3 civilians staff the 25 career fields within the team. *Jim Dunn*

Both of the Golden Knights' C-31As, 85-1607 and 85-1608, are based at Simmons AAF at Forth Bragg, North Carolina. *Jim Dunn*

F-16 Fighting Falcon. In 1992, the team traded-in its A models for the more advanced F-16C, which they fly to this day.

The Thunderbirds estimate that more than 315 million people in the United States and 60 foreign nations have seen the team fly during more than 3,600 performances. This record has earned the team the nickname of the air force's Ambassadors in Blue.

U.S. Army Parachute Team: Golden Knights

The U.S. Army Parachute Team, known as the Golden Knights, traces its beginnings to 1959. At the time, teams from the Soviet Union and other Communist-bloc nations dominated sport parachuting competition. The army sent a team to the 1959 Adriatic Cup competition in Tivat, Yugoslavia, where they placed fourth overall. From the army's Adriatic Cup team, thirteen members were selected to form the Strategic Army Corps (STRAC) Sport Parachute Team.

The STRAC Team performed its first public demonstration for 20,000 spectators at Danville, Virginia, in 1959. In June 1961, the team was endorsed by the Department of Defense, renamed the U.S. Army Parachute Team, and its staffing was increased to 15 enlisted men and 4 officers. By the end of 1962, the team was renamed the Golden Knights for the army's colors and to reflect "the conquering symbol of warfare, the Knight."

The army has assigned the Golden Knights with the mission of "performing live aerial demonstrations for the public and to promote the army's public relations and recruitment efforts; to compete in national and international parachuting competitions; and to test and evaluate new parachuting equipment and techniques for improved operation and safety." To achieve these goals, the Golden Knights are divided into the Black and Gold Demonstration Teams, the Formation Skydiving Team, and the Style and Accuracy Team.

Supporting the 90 members of the Golden Knights, based at Fort Bragg, North Carolina, is an aviation section, responsible for the team's six aircraft and overseeing the team's safety, as well as a headquarters section that manages the team's administrative, maintenance, and supply requirements. The team's aircraft, two Fokker C-31A Friendships, two UV-18A Twin Otters, and a pair of Pilatus UV-20As, operate from Simmons Army Air Field.

Forty-four years after its formation, the Golden Knights have achieved an unparalleled record of success. According to the team, they have won "408 national championships, 65 world championships, as well as 14 national and 6 world team titles in formation skydiving." The Golden Knights are truly the army's Goodwill Ambassadors to the World.

The army operates two Fokker F-27-400M Friendships, designated C-31A Troopships, to support their Golden Knights Parachute Demonstration Team. *Jim Dunn*

APPENDIX I: BOMB TYPES (FREEFALL & GUIDED)

Bombs are generally made up of three sections—the bomb body, which contains the explosive charge; the fuse, installed either in the nose or tail of the bomb body; and the fins, which establish how the bomb travels through the air.

Bomb bodies come in three distinct types: general purpose; fragmentation, where the case bursts into shrapnel upon detonation (cluster bombs are included in this type); and penetration bodies, which have a hardened, thicker case with less explosive power for burrowing through thick layers of earth or concrete and subsequently exploding after penetration.

Fuses detonate the bomb, and the timing of the explosion is determined by how the fuse operates. Most common is the arming vane type, seen as a propeller that detonates the bomb after a preset number of revolutions. Inertia fuses detonate when the bomb stops moving. Electric fuses are battery-powered and activate at a pre-set time interval, which is useful if the bomb is intended to destroy a bunker or building because the bomb is then given time to penetrate floors or earthen berms.

Bomb fins can be used to steer the bomb, retard its flight through the use of high-drag devices, or be parachute-equipped to prevent the bomb's blast from damaging the aircraft that deployed it.

Selected bomb types used in the past 20 years include:

General Purpose
Mk-82: 500-pound, free-fall, general purpose, containing 192 pounds of explosives. Dropped by B-52s, F-16s, F/A-18s, and AV-8Bs.

Mk-83: 1,000-pound, free-fall, general purpose, containing 416 pounds of explosives. Dropped by F/A-18s and AV-8Bs.

Mk-84: 2,000-pound, free-fall, general purpose, containing 945 pounds of explosives. Primarily deployed by F-15Es, F-16s, and in Operation Desert Storm, F-111Fs.

M117: 750-pound, free-fall, general purpose, containing 386 pounds of explosives. Dropped primarily by B-52s.

BLU-109/B: 2,000-pound class (1,925 actual pounds), laser-guided, penetration, containing 550 pounds of explosives.

Cluster Types
CBU-52: 785-pound bomb loaded with 254 BLU-61B anti-personnel bomblets, each weighing 2.7 pounds and 3.5 inches in diameter.

CBU-58: 800-pound bomb loaded with 650 BLU-63A/B incendiary bomblets.

CBU-59 APAM: 750-pound anti-personnel, anti-materiel (APAM) weapon developed from the Rockeye cluster bomb dispenser (late-1960s vintage), and loaded with 717 BLU-77 bomblets.

CBU-71: 850-pound bomb loaded with 650 BLU-68B incendiary bomblets. The CBU-71 also has a fragmentation capability.

CBU-72: 550-pound fuel/air explosive (FAE) bomb loaded with three BLU-73B submunitions each weighing 100 pounds, of which 75 pounds is ethylene oxide. The BLU-73B submunitions burst 30 feet above the ground, creating a fuel/air mist 60 feet in diameter and 8 feet thick, which is then ignited. The resulting blast is extremely effective against troops and has been used to clear minefields.

CBU-78/B Gator: 500-pound bomb developed for the U.S. Navy based on the Rockeye dispenser, loaded with 45 BLU-91/B anti-tank and 15 BLU-92/B anti-personnel mines. BLU-91 and -92 submunitions can be pre-programmed to self-destruct after a predetermined period of time.

CBU-87 CEM: 1,000-pound combined effects munition (CEM) fitted with the SW-65 tactical munitions dispenser loaded with 202 BLU-97/B bomblets. The bomb case fragments into 300 pieces of shrapnel, and the bomblets cover a 600-foot-by-1,200-foot area.

CBU-89 Gator: 1,000-pound bomb using the SUU-64/B Tactical Munitions Dispenser, also based on the Rockeye dispenser, and loaded with 72 BLU-91/B anti-tank and 22 BLU-92/B anti-personnel mines.

CBU-94: 914-pound Black-Out Bomb used by F-117A Stealth Fighters to disrupt electrical service in an area. Fitted with BLU-114/B bomblets.

CBU-97 SFW: 914-pound bomb loaded with 10 BLU-108/B sensor-fused weapons (SFW) for destroying armor. CBU-97s can be dropped from as high as 20,000 feet and at speeds of up to 650 miles per hour.

CBU-105: Essentially a CBU-97 SFW fitted with a wind-corrected munitions dispenser (WCMD) tail kit.

Mk 20 Rockeye: 490-pound anti-armor bomb fitted with 247 Mk-118 armor-piercing, shaped-charge bomblets.

Laser-Guided Types
GBU-10 Paveway II: The Guided Bomb Unit (GBU) 10 is a Mk-84 2,000-pound bomb with a laser guidance head. An air- or ground-based laser illuminates the target, and the bomb corrects its path to the target. Paveway Is were delivered with fixed wings, while the Paveway II has folding wings and improved laser sensors. It is used primarily against bridges, bunkers, and other targets requiring precision delivery.

GBU-12: 500-pound bomb with Paveway I or II laser guidance assembly.

GBU-15: Mk-84 or BLU-109 2,000-pound glide bomb with TV or infrared guidance.

GBU-16: Mk-83 1,000-pound bomb with Paveway II laser guidance assembly.

GBU-24: Mk-84 or BLU-109 2,000-pound glide bomb with low-level laser guided bomb kit (LLLGB) for use in bad weather or minimum visibility. Can be launched up to 10 miles away from its target. Fitted with Paveway III laser guidance assembly.

GBU-27: GBU-24 (BLU-109 bomb) modified for exclusive use by the F-117A. The pilot illuminates the target with the aircraft's on-board laser to direct the bomb.

GBU-28 Bunker Buster: 5,000-pound bomb (BLU-113) designed for penetrating Iraqi underground command centers. Bomb case weighs 4,414 pounds and is loaded with 647 pounds of explosives and fitted with GBU-27 guidance kits.

GBU-31/32 Joint Direct Attack Munitions (JDAM): Tail guidance kit fitted to the 2,000-pound BLU-109/Mk-84 or the 1,000-pound BLU-110/Mk-83 bombs. Incorporates a global-positioning-satellite-enabled inertial navigation system.

Special Mission Types
GBU-15: Modular glide-bomb using the 2,000-pound Mk-84 bomb coupled with a TV (optical) or infrared guidance system. Flight path can be corrected during flight using a data-link to the deploying aircraft.

BLU-82: 15,000-pound, general-purpose, fuel/air bomb detonated above ground using a 38-inch fuse extension, containing 12,600 pounds of gelled slurry explosive (GSX), which produces a huge blast without digging a deep crater. The BLU-82 was used in Vietnam to clear vegetation for landing zones, tested in Operation Desert Storm to clear minefields, and dropped on Taliban caves in Afghanistan. The U.S. military determined that the BLU-82 had a tremendously negative psychological effect on troops of the Iraqi Republican Guards. The BLU-82 is so large that it is rolled out of the back of Special Operations Hercules transports.

GBU-28: 4,637-pound, laser-guided penetration bomb, containing 630 pounds of explosives. Designed specifically for penetrating Iraqi command bunkers.

Mk 77: 750-pound napalm canister.

M129 leaflet bomb: Modified Mk-20 Rockeye cluster bomb with paper leaflets replacing the bomblets. Weighs 225 pounds when loaded with 30,000 leaflets. The bomb's outer casing separates above the ground, scattering the rolled leaflets over the terrain.

APPENDIX II: MISSLE (AIR-TO-AIR & AIR-TO-GROUND)

Missiles are typically composed of five sections, from nose to tail: guidance system (radar, laser, infrared, or microwave/radiation seeker); explosive warhead; wing section; rocket motor; and tail fins (usually steerable). Missile motors determine the weapon's flight profile and time of flight; different types are all-boost, all-sustain, or boost-sustain types. All-boost provides rapid acceleration, but a short time of flight. All-sustain delivers slower missile acceleration away from the launcher, but provides greater range with a longer flight time. The all-sustain-type missiles can be used to down targets at higher altitudes. Boost-sustain maintains the missile's velocity once the boost phase has ended.

Air-to-Air

AIM-7M Sparrow: Radar-guided, capable of supersonic speeds. Firing aircraft must track the target aircraft by radar for the missile to "see" the target.

AIM-9 Sidewinder: Infrared emission seeking, capable of supersonic speeds using an all-boost motor. This is a "fire-and-forget" missile, enabling the launching pilot to aim, shoot, and take evasive action while the missile seeks the target using its own sensors. The Sidewinder can destroy its target through a direct hit or proximity fragmentation explosion.

AIM-54 Phoenix: Long-range missile for use with the F-14 Tomcat. Up to six can be carried by a navy fighter, and launched nearly simultaneously in any weather.

AIM-120A AMRAAM: The Advanced Medium-Range, Air-to-Air Missile is the follow-on to the AIM-7 Sparrow. Internal radar-guided missile with fire-and-forget capability and a proximity-fragmentation warhead.

Air-to-Surface

AGM-62B Walleye: TV-guided glide bomb for use against infrastructure targets such as bridges, fuel and ammunition storage, tunnels, and transportation facilities.

AGM-65 Maverick: Fire-and-forget-capable missile used against tactical targets such as armored vehicles, air defense sites, and storage facilities. A and B models are TV-guided, D is fitted with an infrared seeker, E model employs a laser-guidance seeker, F model is the naval version of the D model, and G model is a D model with improved infrared seeker.

AGM-84D Harpoon: All-weather, over-the-horizon, antiship missile currently used by B-52s and P-3s.

AGM-84E SLAM: The Standoff Land Attack Missile uses active radar guidance for targets on land or ships in port

AGM-86B/C CALCM: This conventional air-launched cruise missile (CALCM) was designed to enhance the B-52's offensive capabilities. The Boeing-built missile is powered by a Williams Research Corporation F-107-WR-10 turbofan engine developing 600 pounds of thrust, and it weighs 3,150 pounds. The missile has a range of 1,500 miles and flies at 550 miles per hour.

AGM-88 HARM: High-Speed Anti-radiation Missile (HARM) used to destroy enemy air defense radar. The HARM rides the enemy's radar beam and destroys the emitter.

AGM-114 Hellfire: Heliborne-Launched Fire and Forget, the standard antiarmor missile equipping the AH-64 Longbow Apache and A-10 Warthog.

AGM-123 Skipper: Antiship powered and guided Mk-83 bomb with Paveway II laser guidance and a rocket booster attached.

AGM-130: Rocket-powered version of the 2,000-pound GBU-15, capable of being launched 40 miles from its target, guided by a global positioning system, TV, or infrared seeker. Primarily deployed by F-15E Strike Eagles.

AGM-142 Have Nap: 3,000-pound missile with internal data link, TV, or infrared guidance. Explosive configurations include a 750-pound fragmentation or 770-pound penetrator warheads. Range 50 miles. Have Nap is the U.S. version of the Israeli Popeye missile and is built by Israeli Aircraft Industries.

AGM-154 JSOW: The Joint Standoff Weapon (JSOW) is a glide weapon capable of being launched 40 miles from target, using a global positioning system coupled to an inertial navigation system to navigate to the target. Built in the AGM-154A version for soft targets, -154B antiarmor version, and the-154C for destroying airfield or port infrastructure.

BGM-71 TOW: Tube Launched, Optically Tracked, Wire Guided antiarmor weapon, typically fired from army and Marine Corps AH-1 Cobra gunships.

APPENDIX III: AERIAL VICTORY CREDITS, 1981 TO PRESENT

U.S. NAVY, ENGAGEMENTS WITH LIBYAN AIRCRAFT, 1981 AND 1989

Date	Claim	Squadron	Type	Serial No.	Weapon	Ship	Pilot	Weapons System Officer
8/19/81	Su-22	VF-41	F-14A	160390	AIM-9L	CVN 68	CDR Hank Kleeman	LT Dave Venlet
8/19/81	Su-22	VF-41	F-14A	160403	AIM-9L	CVN 68	LT Larry Muczynski	LT Jim Anderson
1/4/89	MiG-23	VF-32	F-14A	159610	AIM-7	CV 67	LT Herman C. Cook III	LCDR Steven P. Collins
1/4/89	MiG-23	VF-32	F-14A	———	AIM-9	CV 67	CDR Joseph B. Connelly	CDR Leo F. Enwright Jr.
Gulf War								
1/17/91	MiG-21	VFA-81	F/A-18C	163508	AIM-9M	CV 60	LCDR Mark Fox	
1/17/91	MiG-21	VFA-81	F/A-18C	163502	AIM-9M	CV 60	LT Nick Mongillo	
2/6/91	Mi-8	VF-1	F-14A	162603	AIM-9M	CV 61	LT Stuart Broce	CDR Ron McElraft

Notes: VF–Fighter Squadron; VFA – Attack Fighter Squadron; CV-60 – *Saratoga*; CV-61 – *Ranger*; CV-67 – *John F. Kennedy*; CVN-68 – *Nimitz*.

U.S. AIR FORCE
GULF WAR • SOUTHWEST ASIA WAR

Date	Claim	Sqdrn	Type	S/N	Weapon	Pilot/Weapons System Officer Notes
1/17/91	F-1 Mirage (2)	33 TFW	F-15C	85-0105	AIM-7	Capt. Robert E. Graeter
1/17/91	MiG-29	33 TFW	F-15C	85-0125	AIM-7	Capt. Jon K. Kelk
1/17/91	MiG-29	33 TFW	F-15C	85-0119	AIM-7	Capt. Rhory R. Draeger
1/17/91	MiG-29	33 TFW	F-15C	85-0107	AIM-7	Capt. Charles Magill (USMC)
1/17/91	F-1 Mirage	1 TFW	F-15C	83-0017	AIM-7	Capt. Steven W. Tate
1/19/91	F-1 Mirage	36 TFW	F-15C	79-0069	AIM-7	Capt. David S. Prather
1/19/91	MiG-25	33 TFW	F-15C	85-0099	AIM-7	Capt. Lawrence E. Pitts
1/19/91	MiG-29	33 TFW	F-15C	85-0814	Ground*	Capt. Cesar A. Rodriguez
1/19/91	F-1 Mirage	36 TFW	F-15C	79-0021	AIM-7	Lt. David G. Sveden Jr.
1/19/91	MiG-25	33 TFW	F-15C	85-0101	AIM-7	Capt. Richard C. Tollini
1/19/91	MiG-29	33 TFW	F-15C	85-0122	AIM-7	Capt. Craig W. Underhill
1/26/91	MiG-23	33 TFW	F-15C	85-0108	AIM-7	Capt. Rhory R. Draeger
1/26/91	MiG-23	33 TFW	F-15C	85-0114	AIM-7	Capt. Cesar A. Rodriguez
1/26/91	MiG-23	33 TFW	F-15C	85-0104	AIM-7	Capt. Anthony E. Schiavi
1/27/91	MiG-23 (2)	36 TFW	F-15C	84-0025	AIM-9	Capt. Jay T. Denney
1/27/91	F-1 Mirage	36 TFW	F-15C	84-0027	AIM-7	Capt. Benjamin D. Powell
1/27/91	MiG-23	36 TFW	F-15C	84-0027	AIM-7	Capt. Benjamin D. Powell
1/28/91	MiG-23	32 TFS	F-15C	79-0021	AIM-7	Capt. Donald S. Watrous
1/29/91	MiG-23	33 TFW	F-15C	85-0102	AIM-7	Capt. David G. Rose
2/2/91	IL-76	36 TFW	F-15C	79-0064	AIM-7	Capt. Gregory P. Masters
2/6/91	MiG-21 (2)	36 TFW	F-15C	79-0078	AIM-9	Capt. Thomas N. Dietz
2/6/91	Su-25 (2)	36 TFW	F-15C	84-0023	AIM-9	Lt. Robert W. Hehemann
2/6/91	Bo-1059	26 TFG	A-10A	77-0205	GAU-8	Capt. Robert R. Swain Jr.
2/7/91	Helicopter	36 TFW	F-15C	80-003	AIM-7	Maj. Randy W. May
2/7/91	Su-22 (2)	33 TFW	F-15C	85-0102	AIM-7	Capt. Anthony R. Murphy
2/7/91	Su-7	33 TFW	F-15C	85-0124	AIM-7	Col. Rick N. Parsons
2/11/91	Mi-8 Hip	36 TFW	F-15C	80-0012	AIM-7	Capt. Steven S. Dingee (half credit with Capt. McKenzie)
2/11/91	Mi-8 Hip	36 TFW	F-15C	79-0048	AIM-7	Capt. Mark T. McKenzie (half credit with Capt. Dingee)
2/13/91	Mi-2	44 TFW	F-15E	89-0487	GBU-10	Capt. Richard T. Bennett/Capt. Daniel B. Bakke
2/15/91	Mi-8 Hip	10 TFW	A-10A	81-0964	GAU-8	Capt. Todd K. Sheehy
3/20/91	Su-22	36 TFW	F-15C	85-0014	AIM-9	Capt. John T. Doneski
3/22/91	Su-25	36 TFW	F-15C	84-0019	ground	Lt. Robert W. Hehemann
3/22/91	Su-22	36 TFW	F-15C	84-0010	AIM-9	Capt. Thomas N. Dietz
12/27/92	MiG-25	363 TFW	F-16D	90-0778	AIM-120	Lt. Col. Gary L. North
1/17/93	MiG-23	52 FW	F-16C	——–	——–	Lt. Craig D. Stevenson

BOSNIA • OPERATION DENY FLIGHT

Date	Claim	Sqdrn	Type	S/N	Weapon	Pilot/Weapons System Officer Notes
2/28/94	Jastreb-Galeb	526th FS	F-16C	89-2009	AIM-9	Capt. Stephen Allen
5/27/94	Jastreb-Galeb (3) AIM-9 (2)	526th FS	F-16C	89-2137	AIM-120	Capt. Robert Wright

KOSOVO • OPERATION ALLIED FORCE

Date	Claim	Sqdrn	Type	S/N	Weapon	Pilot/Weapons System Officer Notes
3/24/99	MiG-29	493 EFS	F-15C	——–	AIM-120	Lt. Col. Cesar Rodriguez
3/24/99	MiG-29	493 EFS	F-15C	——–	AIM-120	Capt. Michael Shower
3/26/99	MiG-29 (2)	493 EFS	F-15C	——–	AIM-120	Capt. Jeffery C.J. Hwang
4/05/99	MiG-29	493 EFS	F-16C	——–	AIM-120	Lt. Col. Michael Geczy

Notes: EFS – Expeditionary Fighter Squadron; FS – Fighter Squadron; TFG – Tactical Fighter Group; TFS – Tactical Fighter Squadron; TFW – Tactical Fighter Wing;

Source: Air Force Historical Research Agency; *Gulf War Air Power Survey: A Statistical Compendium and Chronology* (Government Reprints Press Edition, 2002).

INDEX